Why Do You Need this New Edition?

Good reasons why you should buy this *new* edition of *Good Reasons* . . .

1. In clear, accessible language, *Good Reasons* tells you why people take the time to write arguments—because they want to change attitudes and take action about issues they care about—and helps you find topics for your own writing.

2. Sample arguments in 6 student essays (four new) and 11 professional readings (eight new) show you how people write and support arguments on current issues. (See the inside back cover for a list of sample arguments.)

3. A brand new feature, *Finding Good Reasons* (in Parts 1 and 3), explores contemporary arguments—from banning cell phones while driving and surveillance cameras at traffic lights to a country's "right" to use natural resources—and invites you to join the conversation.

4. Over 75 illustrations show and analyze the pervasiveness and persuasiveness of photographs, charts, graphs, tables, and ads in arguments.

5. Brand new visual maps in Chapters 8–13 show at-a-glance how different kinds of argumentative papers are organized—definition, causal, evaluation, narrative, rebuttal, and proposal—the kinds you're likely to be assigned in college.

6. Step-by-step guides to writing arguments at the ends of Chapters 8–13 give you specific help with planning, organizing, and writing different kinds of argumentative projects.

7. Three new chapters give you more help with research writing, including using library databases, evaluating and using sources, avoiding plagiarism, and writing an argumentative research project.

8. New color-coded MLA and APA documentation examples help you understand the key elements of source citations.

Good Reasons

Good Reasons

Researching and Writing
Effective Arguments

FOURTH EDITION

Lester Faigley
University of Texas at Austin

Jack Selzer
The Pennsylvania State University

Longman

New York San Francisco Boston
London Toronto Sydney Tokyo Singapore Madrid
Mexico City Munich Paris Cape Town Hong Kong Montreal

Executive Editor: Lynn M. Huddon
Development Editor: Carol Hollar-Zwick
Senior Supplements Editor: Donna Campion
Senior Marketing Manager: Sandra McGuire
Production Manager: Eric Jorgensen
Project Coordination, Text Design, and Electronic Page Makeup: Pre-Press PMG
Cover Design Manager: Wendy Ann Fredericks
Cover Designer: Nancy Sacks
Cover Illustration/Photo: *topleft*: Photo courtesy of the U.S. Army; *topright*: Nicole Bengiveno-The New York Times; *bottom left-right*: Lester Faigley
Photo Researcher: Julie Tesser
Senior Manufacturing Buyer: Dennis J. Para
Printer and Binder: Quebecor World/Taunton
Cover Printer: Phoenix Color Corporation

For permission to use copyrighted material, grateful acknowledgment is made to the copyright holders listed below, which are hereby made part of this copyright page.

Text Credits: P.19:Excerpt from *Silent Spring* by Rachel Carson. Copyright © 1962 by Rachel L. Carson, renewed 1990 by Roger Christie. Reprinted by permission of Houghton Mifflin Company. All rights reserved. P.37: Yahoo! Screen shot, "Issues and Causes in the Yahoo! Directory." Reproduced with permission of Yahoo! Inc. Copyright © 2007 by Yahoo! Inc. YAHOO! and the YAHOO! logo are trademarks of Yahoo! Inc. P.84: Jordan, Barbara, "The Constitutional Basis for Impeachment" delivered to the House Judiciary Committee, July 24, 1974. P.121:Pages 2–9 from *Understanding Comics* by Scott McCloud. Copyright © 1993, 1994 by Scott McCloud. Reprinted by permission of HarperCollins Publishers. P.144: Annie Murphy Paul, "The Real Marriage Penalty," *The New York Times Magazine*, November 19, 2006. Copyright © 2006 by Annie Murphy Paul. Reprinted by permission. P.147:"Why Should I Be Nice to You? Coffee Shops and the Politics of Good Service," by Emily Raine, from *Bad Subjects*, issue 74, December 2005. Reprinted by permission of the author. P.162: From *Michael Eric Dyson Reader* by Michael Eric Dyson. Copyright © 2004 by Michael Eric Dyson. Reprinted by CIVITAS, a member of Perseus Books Group. P.119:Martin Luther King, Jr., from "Letter from Birmingham Jail." Copyright © 1963 by Martin Luther King, Jr., copyright renewed 1991 by Coretta Scott King. P.182:Leslie Marmon Silko, "The Border Patrol State." First published in *The Nation*, October 17, 1994. Copyright © 1994 by Leslie Marmon Silko, reprinted with permission of The Wylie Agency. P.187: Dagoberto Gilb, "My Landlady's Yard" from *Gritos*. Copyright © 2003 by Dagoberto Gilb. Used by permission of Grove/Atlantic, Inc. P.198: "Dulce et Decorum Est" by Wilfred Owen, 1921. P.200:"Crossing the Line" by Dan Stein, from the *Los Angeles Business Journal*, 2/26/07. Reprinted by permission of the author. P.202: Gregory Rodriguez, "Illegal Immigrants – They're Money," *Los Angeles Times*, March 4, 2007. Copyright © 2007 by *Los Angeles Times*. Reprinted with permission. P.216: Thomas Homer Dixon and S. Julio Friedman, "Coal is a Nice Shade of Green," *The New York Times*, March 25, 2005. Copyright © 2005 by The New York Times. Reprinted by permission.

Photo Credits: P. 10: Living Planet Report 2006—Published in October 2006 by WWF—World Wide Fund For Nature (formerly World Wildlife Fund), Gland, Switzerland. G Text and Graphics: 2006 WWF. All rights reserved.; 39: New York Times Graphics; 69: © The New Yorker Collection 1992 J.B. Handelsman from cartoonbank.com. All Rights Reserved.; 91B: Reproduced from the Collections of the Library of Congress; 94: New York Times Graphics; 95: New York Times Graphics; 97: Hofstra University advertisement. Copyright © by Hofstra University and Joseph Berger Photography. Reprinted by permission of Hofstra University and Joseph Berger Photography 109: Tony Cenicola/The New York Times; 118: Reproduced from the collections of the Library of Congress.; 117: Adbusters; 137: Stuart Isett/The New York Times; 140: Ruby Washington/The New York Times; 161: Richard Perry/The New York Times; 159: Charles Pertwee/The New York Times; 180: Vincent Laforet/The New York Times; 192: Steve Ruark/The New York Times; 195: Universal Press Syndicate; Unless otherwise credited, all photos © Lester Faigley Photos

Library of Congress Cataloging-in-Publication Data

Faigley, Lester, 1947-
 Good reasons : researching and writing effective arguments / Lester Faigley, Jack Selzer. — 4th ed.
  p. cm.
 Includes index.
 ISBN 0-205-74335-8
 1. English language—Rhetoric. 2. Persuasion (Rhetoric) 3. Report writing.
 I. Selzer, Jack. II. Title.
PE1431.F35 2008
808'.042—dc22
                                                                    2007045652

This book includes 2009 MLA guidelines.

Longman
is an imprint of

ISBN-13: 978-0-205-74335-3
ISBN-10: 0-205-74335-8

Visit us at **www.pearsonhighered.com**   12345678910—QWT—12 11 10 09

In memory of our teacher and friend, James L. Kinneavy (1920–1999)

Detailed Contents

PART 2   Analyzing Arguments

PART 3

Writing Arguments

PART 4
Designing and Presenting Arguments

PART 5
Researching Arguments

Chapter 21: Documenting Sources in APA Style   304

Preface

We've enjoyed teaching with *Good Reasons*, now in its fourth edition, for many semesters and have benefited from the experiences of many instructors and students across the country. The increasing number of users for each edition further convinces us that a course focusing on argument is an essential part of a college education. College courses frequently require students to analyze the structure of arguments, to identify competing claims, to weigh the evidence offered, to recognize assumptions, to locate contradictions, and to anticipate opposing views. Just as important, students need to be able to read arguments critically and write arguments skillfully to succeed in the workplace and to participate in public life after college. The long-term issues that affect life after college—education, the environment, social justice, and quality of life, to name a few—have many diverse stakeholders and long, complex histories. They cannot be reduced to slogans and sound bites.

A Straightforward Approach to Argument

Good Reasons begins by considering why people take the time to write arguments in the first place. People write arguments because they want to change attitudes and beliefs about particular issues, and they want things done about problems they identify. We start out by examining exactly why people write arguments and how written arguments can lead to extended discussion and long-term results. We then provide the practical means to find good reasons that support arguments convincingly. *Good Reasons* presents steps for analyzing written and visual arguments and for writing definition, causal, evaluation, narrative, rebuttal, and proposal arguments.

A Rhetorical Approach to Finding Good Reasons

You won't find a lot of complicated terminology in *Good Reasons*. The only technical terms in this book are the classical concepts of *pathos*, *ethos*, and *logos*—sources of good reasons that emerge from the audience's most passionately held values, from the speaker's expertise and credibility, or from reasonable, commonsense thinking. The crux of teaching argument, in our view, is to appreciate its rhetorical nature. A reason becomes a *good reason* when the audience accepts the writer or speaker as credible and accepts the assumptions and evidence on which the argument is based.

The Oral and Visual Aspects of Argument

Good Reasons is also distinctive in its attention to the delivery and presentation of arguments—to oral and visual aspects of argument in addition to the written word. We encourage students to formulate arguments in different genres and different media. Commonly used word-processing programs and Web-page editors now allow writers to include pictures, icons, charts, and graphs; these make design an important part of an argument. While the heart of an argument course should be the critical reading and critical writing of prose, we also believe that students should understand and use visual persuasion when appropriate.

New to This Edition

■ **A new chapter on reading arguments and eight new professional readings provide ample instruction and practice in critical reading.**

Chapter 2, "Reading Arguments," helps students to become critical readers, to read actively, to recognize fallacies, and to respond to readings as a writer.

Eight engaging new readings have been added throughout Parts 2 and 3 to exemplify how people write and support arguments about current issues such as rap music, the income gap, the service economy, immigration, and clean energy.

■ **Much new material has been added on using sources to form and support arguments and on incorporating sources into arguments.**

A new section in Chapter 3 encourages students to find arguments to write about in what they read, see, and hear and guides them in formulating a thesis in relation to the positions of others.

A new chapter on finding sources, Chapter 17, includes valuable advice on using library databases.

A new chapter on evaluating and keeping track of sources, Chapter 18, offers instruction on how to evaluate print, database, and Web sources and what information you need to record to document each source.

A new chapter on writing a research paper, Chapter 19, helps students think through how to synthesize ideas from outside sources with their own and add to an ongoing argument, and it describes how to quote and summarize sources without plagiarizing.

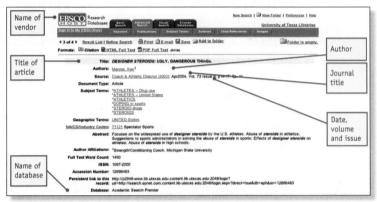

Citing a database article from Academic Search Premier.

Evaluate Web Sources

All electronic search tools share a common problem: They often give you too many sources. Web search engines pull up thousands of hits, and these hits may vary dramatically in quality. No one regulates or checks most information put on the Web, and it's no surprise that much of what is on the Web is highly opinionated or false.

Misleading Web sites

Some Web sites are put up as jokes. Other Web sites are deliberately misleading. Many prominent Web sites draw imitators who want to cash in on the commercial visibility. The Web site for the Campaign for Tobacco-Free Kids (www.tobaccofreekids.org), for example, has an imitator (www.smokefreekids.com) that sells software for antismoking education. The *.com* URL is often a tip-off that a site's main motive is profit.

Biased Web sites

Always approach Web sites with an eye toward evaluating their content. For example, Web sites with *.com* URLs that offer medical information often contain strong biases in addition to the motive to make money. The creators of the Web site Thinktwice.com, sponsored by the Global Vaccine Institute, oppose the vaccination

- The importance of visuals in argument is emphasized throughout with a new full-color design and many new visuals.

  Chapter 6, "Analyzing Visual Arguments," includes a new analysis of an ad that explains many of the nuances of visual persuasion.

  New diagrams in each chapter of Part 3, "Writing Arguments," provide visual maps of the structure of each kind of argument.

  More visuals—larger, and in color—such as cartoons, advertisements, charts and graphs, and photographs demonstrate and analyze the pervasiveness and persuasiveness of images in arguments.

Understand How Proposal Arguments Work

Proposal arguments call for some action to be taken (or not to be taken). The challenge for writers is to convince readers that they should take action, which usually involves their commitment of effort or money. It's always easier to do nothing and wait for someone else to act. Thus, the key is using good reasons to convince readers that good things will result if some action is taken and bad things can be avoided. If readers are convinced that the proposal serves their interests, they will take action. Proposal arguments take this form:

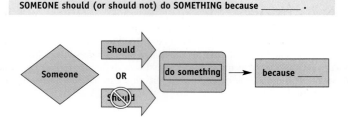

- A new full-page feature in Parts 1 and 3, "Finding Good Reasons," gets students thinking and writing about the arguments that surround contemporary issues.

  Each "Finding Good Reasons" feature introduces a contemporary issue, such as the use of natural resources, surveillance technologies and policies, health and obesity, diversity, and community activism, and highlights key points in the arguments surrounding the issue.

  A half-page illustration, such as a cartoon, photograph, or advertisement provides another angle on the issue.

  Writing prompts encourage students to explore and enter the conversation about the issue.

Finding Good Reasons
WHO SHOULD MAKE DECISIONS ABOUT ECONOMIC DEVELOPMENT?

Northcross Mall in Austin, Texas, is a declining neighborhood shopping center with several empty stores. In 2006, Wal-Mart proposed taking over the site and building a Supercenter. Surrounding neighborhood associations rallied together and formed Responsible Growth for Norcross. They agreed that Northcross Mall should be re-developed, but they objected to Wal-Mart because of the traffic the Supercenter would generate and because the sprawling structure and large parking lot would not comply with the city's guidelines for redevelopment. Their opposition raises an important question: should surrounding neighborhoods have the right to decide on the kinds of businesses that are appropriate for their neighborhood on commercially zoned property?

Write about it

1. If you were the spokesperson for Wal-Mart, what reasons would you give to the Austin City Council to persuade them to allow Wal-Mart to build a Supercenter on the site?

2. If you were the spokesperson for Responsible Growth for Norcross, what good reasons would you give to convince the city council to deny Wal-Mart permission to build a Supercenter?

■ **MLA and APA documentation guidelines are updated and redesigned for clarity.**

MLA and APA guidelines and examples reflect the most recent guidelines.

Color-coded sample entries help students recognize and organize key elements such as the author, title, publication information, and so on.

Works-cited entries for periodicals

Entries for periodicals (scholarly journals, newspapers, magazines) have three main elements.

> MacDonald, Susan Peck. "The Erasure of Language." *College Composition and Communication* 58 (2007): 585-625. Print.

1. Author's name.
■ List the author's name with the last name first, followed by a period.

2. "Title of article."
■ Place the title of the article inside quotation marks.
■ Insert a period before the closing quotation mark.

3. Publication information.
■ Italicize the title of the journal.
■ Give the volume number.
■ List the date of publication, in parentheses, followed by a colon.
■ List the page numbers, followed by a period.
■ Give the medium of publication (Print), followed by a period.

Works-cited entries for library database sources

Basic entries for library database sources have four main elements. See pages 266–267 for where to find this information.

■ **A greater emphasis on student work encourages students to understand themselves as writers.**

Six student essays, four new to this edition, provide examples of the kinds of papers students are often asked to write—rhetorical analysis, visual analysis, definition, evaluation, proposal, and a research paper documented in MLA style—and demonstrate how to develop extended written arguments.

Supplements

The **Instructor's Manual** that accompanies this text was revised by John Jones and is designed to be useful for new and experienced instructors alike. The Instructor's Manual briefly discusses the ins and outs of teaching the material in each chapter. Also provided are in-class exercises, homework assignments, discussion questions for each reading selection, and model paper assignments and syllabi. This revised Instructor's Manual will make your work as a teacher a bit easier. Teaching argumentation and composition becomes a process that has genuine—and often surprising—rewards.

　　MyCompLab is a Web application that offers comprehensive and integrated resources for every writer. With MyCompLab, students can learn from interactive tutorials and instruction; practice and develop their skills with grammar, writing, and research exercises; share their writing and collaborate with peers; and receive comments on their writing from instructors and tutors. Go to www.mycomplab. com (www.mycomplab.com) to register for these premier resources and much more.

Acknowledgments

We are much indebted to the work of many outstanding scholars of argument and to our colleagues who teach argument at Texas and at Penn State. In particular, we thank the following reviewers for sharing their expertise: Angie Berdahl, Portland Community College; Dan Ferguson, Amarillo College; Christy Friend, University of South Carolina; Jay L. Gordon, Youngstown State University; Glenn Harris, Mott Community College; Kimberly Harrison, Florida International University; Crystal McCage, Central Oregon Community College; Michael Rovasio, California State University, East Bay; and Kyle Torke, United States Air Force Academy. We would also like to acknowledge the work of Gerald Graff and Cathey Birkenstein on strategies for developing arguments in response to sources.

　　We are grateful also to the faculty and students at New Mexico State University, in particular to Stuart C. Brown, who reviewed the third edition and, with Kathryn Valentine, helped us gather feedback from teachers and students who used *Good Reasons* in their writing classes. We thank those teachers who sent feedback on their classroom experiences: Skye Anicca, Elizabeth Brasher, Justin Chrestman, Kara Dorris, Blase Drexler, Jeff Frawley, Becki Graham, Joe Killiany, Ryan Lang, Lisa Ramirez, D. H. Retzinger, Yeruwelle de Rouen-Barth, Michaela Spampinato, Melanie D. Viramontes, Nick Voges, Stephen Webber; and we also thank the students who commented honestly on our book: Adam Burnett, Jeremy Calder, Jessica Dunlap, Norma Escobedo, Kelly Harrington, Kevin Hill, Valery

Candice Lopez, Emily Mechenbier, Alex Mertz, Kasey Moore, Veronica Salazar, Victoria Schuetze, Manoly Souraphol, and Toan Tran.

We are also grateful to the many students we've taught in our own classes, who have given us opportunities to test these materials in class and who have taught us a great deal about the nature of argument.

We have greatly benefited from working with three of the best editors in publishing: Lynn Huddon, executive editor; Joseph Opiela, editor-in-chief; and Carol Hollar-Zwick, development editor. Lynn and Joe have given us excellent advice and continuing support throughout. We've worked with Carol closely, and she has been a delight from the beginning, encouraging us to rethink the book, making the process of writing new and interesting, and shaping and refining our ideas throughout. Victoria Davis also worked with us in the revision and made many fine contributions. Special thanks go to John Jones for an outstanding revision of the Instructor's Manual. Katy Bastille and Nikki Bruno Clapper at Pre-Press PMG and Eric Jorgensen at Pearson Longman did splendid work in preparing our book for publication. Finally, we thank our families, who make it all possible.

LESTER FAIGLEY
JACK SELZER

Persuading with Good Reasons

What Do We Mean by *Argument?*

For over thirty years, the debate over legal abortion has raged in the United States. The following scene is a familiar one: Outside an abortion clinic, a crowd of pro-life activists has gathered to try to stop women from entering the clinic. They carry signs that read ABORTION = MURDER and A BABY'S LIFE IS A HUMAN LIFE. Pro-choice organizers have staged a counterdemonstration. Their signs read KEEP YOUR LAWS OFF MY BODY and WOMEN HAVE THE RIGHT TO CONTROL THEIR BODIES. Police keep the two sides apart, but they do not stop the shouts of "Murderer!" from the pro-life side and "If you're anti-abortion, don't have one!" from the pro-choice side.

When you imagine an argument, you might think of two people engaged in a heated exchange, or two groups of people with different views, shouting back and forth at each other like the pro-choice and pro-life demonstrators. Or you might think of district attorneys and defense lawyers debating strenuously in the courthouse. Like oral arguments, written arguments can resemble these oral arguments in being heated and one sided.

Bumper stickers, for example, usually consist of unilateral statements such as "Be Green," "Save the Whales," or "Share the Road." They provide no supporting evidence or reasons for why anyone should do what they say. Many other kinds of writing lack reasoned argument. Writers of instruction manuals do not try to persuade their readers. Authors assume readers want to do whatever the manual tells them to do; otherwise they would not be consulting the manual. Likewise, an article written by a person committed to a particular cause or belief often assumes that everyone should think the same way. These writers can count on certain words and phrases to produce predictable responses.

In college courses, in public life, and in professional careers, however, written arguments cannot be reduced to signs or slogans. Writers of effective arguments do not assume that everyone thinks the same way or holds the same beliefs. They attempt to change people's minds by convincing them of the validity of new ideas or the superiority of a particular course of action. Writers of such arguments not only offer evidence and reasons to support their position but also examine the assumptions on which an argument is based, address opposing arguments, and anticipate their readers' objections.

Extended written arguments make more demands on their readers than most other kinds of writing. Like bumper stickers, these arguments often appeal to our emotions. But they typically do much more. They expand our knowledge with the depth of their analysis. They lead us through a complex set of claims by providing networks of logical relationships and appropriate evidence. They build on what has been written previously by providing trails of sources. Finally, they cause us to reflect on what we read, in a process that we will shortly describe as critical reading.

What Does Argument Mean for College Writers?

Writing in college varies considerably from course to course. A lab report for a biology course looks quite different from a paper in your English class, just as a classroom observation in an education course differs from a case study report in an accounting class.

Nevertheless, much of the writing you will do in college will consist of arguments. Some common expectations about arguments in college writing extend across disciplines. For example, you could be assigned to write a proposal for a downtown light-rail system in a number of different classes—civil engineering, urban planning, government, or management. The emphasis of such a proposal would change depending on the course. In all cases, however, the proposal would require a complex argument in which you describe the problem that the light-rail system would improve, make a specific proposal that addresses the problem, explain the benefits of the system, estimate the cost, identify funding sources, assess alternatives to your plan, and anticipate possible opposition. It's a lot to think about, but you will find that arguments place many demands on writers.

Even though the formats may differ across college courses, setting out a specific proposal or claim supported by reasons and evidence is at the heart of most college writing. Some expectations of arguments—such as making a claim in a thesis statement—may be familiar to you, but others—such as the emphasis on finding alternative ways of thinking about a subject and finding facts that might run counter to your conclusions—may be unfamiliar. The table opposite lists the major expectations of arguments in college and what writers do to fulfill them.

WRITTEN ARGUMENTS . . .	WRITERS ARE EXPECTED TO . . .
State explicit claims	Make a claim that isn't obvious. The main claim is often called a **thesis.**
Support claims with reasons	Express reasons in a because clause after the claim (We should do something *because* _____).
Base reasons on evidence	Provide evidence for reasons in the form of facts, statistics, testimony from reliable sources, and direct observations.
Consider opposing positions	Help readers understand why there are disagreements about issues by accurately representing differing views.
Analyze with insight	Provide in-depth analysis what they read and view.
Investigate complexity	Explore the complexity of a subject by asking "Have you thought about this?" or "What if you discard the usual way of thinking about a subject and take the opposite point of view?"
Organize information clearly	Make the major parts evident to readers and to indicate which parts are subordinate to others.
Signal relationships of parts	Indicate logical relationships clearly so that readers can follow an argument without getting lost.
Document sources carefully	Provide the sources of information so that readers can consult the same sources the writer used.

How Can You Argue Responsibly?

In Washington, D.C., it is common to see cars with diplomatic license plates parked illegally. Their drivers know they will not be towed or ticketed. People who abuse the diplomatic privilege are announcing, "I'm not playing by the rules."

When you begin an argument by saying "in my opinion," you are making a similar announcement. First, the phrase is redundant. A reader assumes that if you make a claim in writing, you believe that claim. More important, a claim is rarely *only* your opinion. Most beliefs and assumptions are shared by many people. If a claim truly is only your opinion, it can be easily dismissed. If your position is likely to be held by at least a few other people, however, then a responsible reader must consider your position seriously.

You argue responsibly when you set out the reasons for making a claim and offer facts to support those reasons. You argue responsibly when you allow readers to examine your evidence by documenting the sources you have consulted. Finally, you argue responsibly when you acknowledge that other people may have positions different from yours.

How Can You Argue Respectfully?

Our culture is competitive, and our goal often is to win. Professional athletes, top trial lawyers, or candidates for president of the United States either win big or lose. But most of us live in a world in which our opponents don't go away when the game is over.

Most of us have to deal with people who disagree with us at times but continue to work and live in our communities. The idea of winning in such situations can only be temporary. Soon enough, we will need the support of those who were on the other side of the most recent issue. You can probably think of times when a friendly argument resulted in a better understanding of all peoples' views. And probably you can think of a time when an argument created hard feelings that lasted for years.

Usually, listeners and readers are more willing to consider your argument seriously if you cast yourself as a respectful partner rather than as a competitor. Put forth your arguments in the spirit of mutual support and negotiation—in the interest of finding the *best* way, not "my way." How can you be the person that your reader will want to join rather than resist? Here are a few suggestions for both your written arguments and for discussing controversial issues.

- **Try to think of yourself as engaged not so much in winning over your audience as in courting your audience's cooperation.** Argue vigorously, but not so vigorously that opposing views are vanquished or silenced. Remember that your goal is to invite a response that creates a dialogue.

- **Show that you understand and genuinely respect your listener's or reader's position even if you think the position is ultimately wrong.** Remember to argue against opponents' positions, not against the opponents themselves. Arguing respectfully often means representing an opponent's position in terms that he or she would accept. Look for ground that you already share with your opponent, and search for even more. See yourself as a mediator. Consider that neither you nor the other person has arrived at a best solution. Then carry on in the hope that dialogue will lead to an even better course of action than the one you now recommend. Expect and assume the best of your listener or reader, and deliver your best.

■ **Cultivate a sense of humor and a distinctive voice.** Many textbooks about argument emphasize using a reasonable voice. But a reasonable voice doesn't have to be a dull one. Humor is a legitimate tool of argument. Although playing an issue strictly for laughs risks not being taken seriously, nothing creates a sense of goodwill quite as much as tasteful humor. A sense of humor can be especially welcome when the stakes are high, the sides have been chosen, and tempers are flaring.

Consider your argument as just one move in a larger process that might end up helping you. Most times we argue because we think we have something to offer. In the process of developing and presenting your views, however, realize that you might learn something in the course of your research or discussion. You might even change your mind. Holding on to that attitude will keep you from becoming too overbearing and dogmatic.

Reading and Discovering Arguments

PART 1   Reading and Discovering Arguments

Why Argue?

Brown pelicans are common along the coasts of the South and California, but they were headed toward extinction by 1970 because the pesticide DDT caused their eggs to be too thin to support developing chicks to maturity. Although DDT was banned in the United States, many countries continue to use it for agricultural spraying and malaria control even though insects and mosquitoes have developed resistance to it. Should there be an international ban on DDT?

In 1958, Rachel Carson received a copy of a letter that her friend Olga Huckens had sent to the *Boston Herald*. The letter described what had happened the previous summer when Duxbury, Massachusetts, a small town just north of Huckens's home in Cape Cod, had been sprayed several times with the pesticide DDT to kill mosquitoes. Despite the spraying, the mosquitoes had come back as hungry as ever, but the songbirds, bees, and other insects had vanished except for a few dead birds that Huckens had found in her yard. Huckens asked Carson if she knew anyone in Washington, D.C. who could help stop the spraying.

Why Do People Write Arguments?

The letter from Olga Huckens struck a nerve with Rachel Carson. Carson was a marine biologist who had worked for the U.S. Fish and Wildlife Service and had written three highly acclaimed books about the sea and wetlands. In 1945 the editors at *Reader's Digest* had asked Carson if she could write something else for them. Carson replied that she wanted to write about experiments using DDT, which was being hyped as the solution for controlling insect pests. As early as 1945, Carson knew that widespread spraying of DDT would harm fish, waterfowl, and other animals. Eventually people could die too. *Reader's Digest* was not interested in Carson's proposed article, so she dropped the idea and went on to write about other things.

Huckens's 1958 letter brought Carson back to the subject of chemical spraying. In the late 1940s and 1950s, pesticides—especially the chlorinated hydrocarbons DDT, aldrin, and dieldrin—were sprayed on a massive scale throughout the

Finding Good Reasons
WHO'S USING UP EARTH'S RESOURCES?

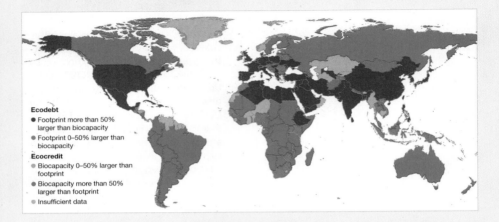

Ecodebt
- Footprint more than 50% larger than biocapacity
- Footprint 0–50% larger than biocapacity

Ecocredit
- Biocapacity 0–50% larger than footprint
- Biocapacity more than 50% larger than footprint
- Insufficient data

In the *Living Planet Report* for 2005, the World Wildlife Federation calculated the ecological footprint for each country on earth. The ecological footprint of a country is determined by its population, the amount of food, timber, and other resources consumed by its average citizen, the area required to produce food, fishing grounds, and the area required to absorb CO_2 emissions minus the amount absorbed by oceans.

Countries fall into four categories: ecological debtor nations (which consume more resources than they can produce), ecological creditor nations (which produce more than they consume), and two categories of ecologically balanced nations, where production and consumption are relatively balanced. In this map you can see that the United States, Mexico, Western Europe, China, India, Pakistan, Japan, and the nations of the Middle East are ecological debtors with footprints more than 50 percent of their biocapacity—what they are able to produce. Nations such as Canada, Russia, Australia, New Zealand, and most nations in South America are ecological creditors, with footprints less than 50 percent of their biocapacity. In its entirety, the *Living Planet Report* makes the argument that nations should live in balance with what their land, rivers, lakes, and seas can support.

Write about it

1. What might be some of the causes of the differences among the ecological footprints of nations?
2. What is likely to happen in the future when some nations have enough resources (such as clean water and food) and others lack them?
3. Does the map succeed as an argument on its own? Does it contain any of the features of written arguments listed on page 3?

United States. Politicians hailed them as a cure for world hunger. In 1957 much of the greater New York City area, including Long Island, was sprayed with DDT to kill gypsy moths. But there were noticeable side effects. Many people complained about the deaths of not only birds, fish, and useful insects but also their own plants, shrubs, and pets. Scientists had written about the dangers of widespread spraying of pesticides, but they had not convinced the public of the hazards or of the urgency for change.

Carson decided that she needed to write a magazine article about the facts of DDT. But when she contacted *Reader's Digest* and other magazines, she found that they still would not consider publishing anything about the subject. Carson then concluded that she should write a short book. She knew that her job was not going to be easy because people in the United States still trusted scientists to solve all problems. Scientists had brought the "green revolution," which greatly increased crop yields through the use of fertilizers and pesticides.

Carson's subject matter was also technical and difficult to communicate to the general public. At that time the public did not think much about air and water pollution, and most people were unaware that pesticides could poison humans as well as insects. Furthermore, Carson was sure to face opposition from the pesticide industry, which had become a multimillion-dollar business. She knew the pesticide industry would do everything it could to stop her from publishing or to discredit her if she did. Still, she wanted to inform people of the dangers of pesticides and argue for limiting their use. Like other writers of arguments, Carson had a **purpose** for writing the book that would become *Silent Spring*.

Silent Spring indeed sounded the alarm about the dangers of pesticides, and the controversy it raised still has not ended. No book has had a greater impact on our thinking about the environment. *Silent Spring* was first published in installments in *The New Yorker* in the summer of 1962, and it created an immediate furor. Chemical companies threatened to sue Carson, and the trade associations that the companies sponsored launched full-scale attacks against the book in pamphlets and magazine articles. The chemical companies treated *Silent Spring* as a public-relations problem. They hired scientists whose only job was to ridicule the book and to dismiss Carson as a "hysterical woman." Some scientists even accused *Silent Spring* of being part of a communist plot to ruin U.S. agriculture.

The public controversy over *Silent Spring* had another effect. It helped to make the book a success shortly after it was published in September 1962. A half-million hardcover copies of *Silent Spring* were sold, and the book stayed on the best-seller list for thirty-one weeks. President John F. Kennedy read *Silent Spring* and met with Carson and other scientists to discuss the pesticide problem. Kennedy requested that the President's Scientific Advisory Committee study the effects of pesticides and write a report. This report found evidence of high levels of pesticides around the world, both in the environment and in the tissues of humans. The report confirmed what Carson had described in *Silent Spring*.

In the words of a news commentator at the time, *Silent Spring* "lit a fire" under the government. Congress held several hearings on the effects of pesticides and other pollutants on the environment. In 1967 the Environmental Defense Fund was formed. It developed the guidelines under which DDT was eventually banned. Three years later, President Richard Nixon became convinced that only an independent agency within the executive branch could operate with enough independence to enforce environmental regulations. Nixon created the Environmental Protection Agency (EPA) in December 1970.

The United States was not the only country to respond to *Silent Spring*. Widely translated, the book inspired legislation on the environment in nearly all industrialized nations. Moreover, it changed the way we think about the environment. Carson pointed out that the nerve gases that were developed for use on America's enemies in World War II were being used as pesticides after the war. She criticized the view that the environment is a battlefield where people make war on natural forces that they believe impede their progress. Instead, she advocated living in coexistence with the environment because people are part of it. She was not totally opposed to pesticides. Her larger goal was to make people more aware that changing one part would affect other parts of the whole. Her message was to try to live in balance with nature. The fact that we still talk so much about the environment is testimony to the lasting power of *Silent Spring*.

Why Do Some Arguments Succeed?

A book titled *Our Synthetic Environment*, which covered much of the same ground as *Silent Spring*, had been published six months earlier. The author, Murray Bookchin, writing under the pen name Lewis Herber, wrote about the pollution of the natural world and its effects on people. Bookchin was as committed to warning people about the hazards of pesticides as Carson, but only a small community of scientists read *Our Synthetic Environment*. Why, then, did Carson succeed in reaching a larger audience?

Carson had far more impact than Bookchin not simply because she was a more talented writer or because she was a scientist while Bookchin was not. Like other writers of successful arguments, she not only knew her purpose for writing *Silent Spring*, but she also thought a great deal about who she was writing for—her audience. If she was going to stop the widespread spraying of dangerous pesticides, she knew she would have to connect with the values of a wide audience, an audience that included a large segment of the public as well as other scientists.

The opening chapter of *Silent Spring* begins not by announcing Carson's thesis or listing facts and statistics. Instead, the book starts with a short fable about a small town located amid prosperous farmland, where wildflowers bloom much of the year, trout swim in the streams, and wildlife is abundant. Suddenly, a

TACTICS OF *SILENT SPRING*

Chapter 1 of *Silent Spring* tells a parable of a rural town where the birds, fish, flowers, and plants die and people become sick after a white powder is sprayed on the town. At the beginning of Chapter 2, Rachel Carson begins her argument against the mass aerial spraying of pesticides. Most of her readers were not aware of the dangers of pesticides, but they were well aware of the harmful effects of radiation. Let's look at her tactics:

> The interrelationship of people and the environment provides the basis for Carson's argument.

The history of life on earth has been a history of interaction between living things and their surroundings. To a large extent, the physical form and the habits of earth's vegetation and its animal life have been molded by the environment. Considering the whole span of earthly time, the opposite effect, in which life actually modifies its surroundings, has been relatively slight. Only within the moment of time represented by the present century has one species—man—acquired significant power to alter the nature of his world.

> Carson shifts her language to a metaphor of war against the environment rather than interaction with the natural world.

During the past quarter century this power has not only increased to one of disturbing magnitude but it has changed in character. The most alarming of all man's assaults upon the environment is the contamination of air, earth, rivers, and sea with dangerous and even lethal materials. This pollution is for the most part irrecoverable; the chain of life it initiates not only in the world that must support life but in living tissues is for the most part irreversible. In this now universal contamination of the environment, chemicals are the sinister and little-recognized partners of radiation in changing the very nature of the world—the very nature of its life.

> In 1963 the United States and the Soviet Union signed the first treaty that banned the testing of nuclear weapons above ground, under water, and in space.

> The key move: Carson associates the dangers of chemical pesticides with those of radiation.

Strontium 90, released through nuclear explosions into the air, comes to earth in rain or drifts down as fallout, lodges in the soil, enters into the grass or corn or wheat grown there, and in time takes its abode in the bones of a human being, there to remain until his death. Similarly, chemicals sprayed on croplands or forests or gardens lie long in soil, entering into living organisms, passing from one to another in a chain of poisoning and death. Or they pass mysteriously by underground streams until they emerge and, through the alchemy of air and sunlight, combine into new forms that kill vegetation, sicken cattle, and work unknown harm on those who drink from once-pure wells. As Albert Schweitzer has said, "Man can hardly even recognize the devils of his own creation."

> Albert Schweitzer (1875–1965) was a concert musician, philosopher, and doctor who spent most of his life as a medical missionary in Africa.

strange blight comes on the town, as if an evil spell has been cast upon it. The chickens, sheep, and cattle on the farms grow sick and die. The families of the townspeople and farmers alike develop mysterious illnesses. Most of the birds disappear, and the few that remain can neither sing nor fly. The apple trees bloom, but there are no bees to pollinate the trees, and so they bear no fruit. The wildflowers wither as if they have been burned. Fishermen quit going to the streams because the fish have all died.

But it isn't witchcraft that causes everything to grow sick and die. Carson writes that "the people had done it to themselves." She continues, "I know of no community that has experienced all the misfortunes I describe. Yet every one of these disasters has actually happened somewhere, and many real communities have already suffered a substantial number of them. A grim specter has crept upon us almost unnoticed, and this imagined tragedy may easily become a stark reality." Carson's fable did come true several times after *Silent Spring* was published. In July 1976, a chemical reaction went out of control at a plant near Seveso, Italy, and a cloud of powdery white crystals of almost pure dioxin fell on the town. Children ran out to play in the powder because it looked like snow. Within four days, plants, birds, and animals began dying, and shortly people started getting sick. Most of the people had to go to the hospital, and everyone had to move out of the town. An even worse disaster happened in December 1984, when a storage tank in a pesticide plant exploded near Bhopal, India, showering the town. Two thousand people died quickly, and another 50,000 became sick for the rest of their lives.

If Carson were alive today and writing a book about the dangers of pesticides, she might begin differently. But remember that at the time she was writing, people trusted pesticides and believed that DDT was a miracle solution for all sorts of insect pests. She first had to make people aware that DDT could be harmful to them. In the second chapter of *Silent Spring* (reprinted at the end of this chapter), Carson continued appealing to the emotions of her audience. In 1962 people knew about the dangers of radiation even if they were ignorant about pesticides. They knew that the atomic bombs that had been dropped on Hiroshima and Nagasaki at the end of World War II were still killing Japanese people through the effects of radiation many years later. They feared the fallout from nuclear bombs that were still being tested and stockpiled in the United States and the Soviet Union.

Getting people's attention by exposing the threat of pesticides wasn't enough. There are always people writing about various kinds of threats, and most aren't taken seriously except by those who already believe that the threats exist. Carson wanted to reach people who didn't think that pesticides were a threat but might be persuaded to take this view. To convince these people, she had to explain why pesticides are potentially dangerous, and she had to make readers believe that she could be trusted.

Carson was an expert marine biologist. To write *Silent Spring*, she had to read widely in sciences that she had not studied. She read research about insects, toxic chemicals, cell physiology, biochemistry, plant and soil science, and public health. Then she had to explain complex scientific processes to people who had very little or no background in science. Throughout the book, Carson succeeds in translating scientific facts into language that, to use her words, "most of us" can understand. She establishes her credibility as a scientist by correctly using technical terms such as *necrosis*. At the same time, however she identifies with people who are not scientists and gains their trust by taking their point of view.

Carson's legacy is our awareness of our environment. She reminds us that we share this planet with other creatures and that "we are dealing with life—with living populations and all their pressures and counterpressures, their surges and recessions." She warns us not to dismiss the balance of nature:

> The balance of nature is not the same today as in Pleistocene times, but it is still there: a complex, precise, and highly integrated system of relationships between living things which cannot safely be ignored any more than the law of gravity can be defied with impunity by a man perched on the edge of a cliff. The balance of nature is not a *status quo;* it is fluid, ever shifting, in a constant state of adjustment.

Scientists predict that as many as half the species on Earth will disappear over the next 100 years. Yet other species, including squirrels, rats, coyotes, raccoons, and white-tailed deer, thrive in suburban environments. Should we be concerned about loss of species when there are plenty of animals living nearby?

Since the publication of *Silent Spring*, people around the world have grown much more conscious of the large-scale effects of global warming, acid rain, and the depleted ozone layer in addition to the local effects of pesticides described in Carson's book. The long-term influence of *Silent Spring* helped inspire the nations of today as they attempt to control air and water pollution, to encourage more efficient use of energy and natural resources, and to promote sustainable patterns of consumption.

What Are the Goals of Arguments?

When writing *Silent Spring*, Rachel Carson had two purposes. In the book, she first makes an effective position argument against the massive use of synthetic pesticides. This argument alone, however, does not solve the problem of what to do about harmful insects that destroy crops and spread disease. As her second purpose, Carson tackles the more difficult job of offering solutions. In her final chapter, "The Other Road," Carson makes a proposal argument for alternatives to the massive use of pesticides.

Carson's two kinds of arguments represent a basic distinction. Some arguments get us to understand something better or to believe something. Others urge us to do something. Most arguments can be characterized as either position arguments or proposal arguments, depending on their purpose.

Position Arguments

In a **position argument,** the writer makes a claim about a controversial issue.

- **The writer first has to define the issue.** Before she could begin arguing against pesticides, Carson had to explain what synthetic pesticides are and how they work. She also had to provide a history of their increasing use after World War II.

- **The writer should take a clear position.** Carson wasted no time setting out her position by describing the threat that high levels of pesticides pose to people worldwide.

- **The writer should make a convincing argument and acknowledge opposing views.** In support of her position, Carson used a variety of strategies, including research studies, quotations from authorities, and her own analyses and observations. She took into account opposing views by acknowledging that harmful insects needed to be controlled and conceded that selective spraying is necessary and desirable.

Proposal Arguments

In a **proposal argument,** the writer proposes a course of action in response to a recognizable problem. The proposal outlines what can be done to improve the situation or to change it altogether.

- **The writer first has to define the problem.** The problem that Carson had to define was complex. The overuse of pesticides was killing helpful insects, plants, and animals and threatening people. In addition, the harmful insects that the pesticides were intended to eliminate were becoming increasingly resistant to the chemicals. More spraying and more frequent spraying produced pesticide-resistant "superbugs." Mass spraying resulted in helping bad bugs such as fire ants by killing off their competition.

- **The writer has to propose a solution or solutions.** Carson does not provide a particular approach to controlling insects, but she does advocate biological solutions. She proposes alternatives to pesticides, such as sterilizing and releasing large numbers of male insects and introducing predators of pest insects. Above all, she urges that we work with nature rather than being at war with it.

- **The solution or solutions must work, and they must be feasible.** Writers should identify the projected consequences of their proposed solution. They should argue that good things will happen, bad things will be avoided, or both. Carson discusses research studies that indicate her solutions would work, and she argues that her alternatives would be less expensive than massive spraying.

Today, we can look at Carson's book with the benefit of hindsight. Not everything that Carson proposed ended up working, but her primary solution—learn to live with nature—has been a powerful one. Mass spraying of pesticides has stopped in the United States, and species that were threatened by the excessive use of pesticides, including falcons, eagles, and brown pelicans, have made remarkable comebacks.

What are Rhetorical Appeals?

When the modern concept of democracy was developed in Greece in the fifth century BCE, the study of rhetoric also began. It's not a coincidence that the teaching of rhetoric was closely tied to the rise of democracy. In the Greek city-states, all citizens had the right to speak and to vote at the popular assembly and in the committees of the assembly that functioned as the criminal courts. Citizens took turns serving as the officials of government. Because the citizens of Athens and other city-states took their responsibilities quite seriously, they highly valued the ability to speak effectively in public. Teachers of rhetoric were held in great esteem.

In the following century, the most important teacher of rhetoric in ancient Greece, Aristotle (384–323 BCE), made the study of rhetoric systematic. He defined **rhetoric** as the art of finding the best available means of persuasion in any situation. Aristotle set out three primary tactics of argument: appeals to the emotions and the deepest-held values of the audience (***pathos***), appeals based on the trustworthiness of the speaker (***ethos***), and appeals to reason (***logos***). Rachel Carson makes these appeals with great skill in *Silent Spring*.

Appeals to Pathos: the Values of the Audience

Appeals to pathos are often associated with emotional appeals, but the term has a broader meaning. Pathos in arguments means connecting with the underlying values, beliefs, and attitudes of readers. Carson appeals to pathos by making us care about nature as well as raising concerns about our own safety. She uses the fate of robins to symbolize her crusade. Robins were the main victims when people sprayed pesticides to battle Dutch elm disease. Robins feed on earthworms, which in turn process fallen elm leaves. The earthworms act as magnifiers of the pesticide, which either kills the robins outright or renders them sterile. Thus, when no robins sang, it was indeed a silent spring.

Appeals to Ethos: the Trustworthiness of the Speaker or Writer

Ethos refers to the credibility of a speaker or writer. We tend to believe people we respect. We also believe people who have our best interests in mind. Readers believe Rachel Carson not just because she is an expert. She convinces us first by establishing that she has people's well-being at heart. She anticipates possible objections and demonstrates that she has thought about opposing positions. She takes time to explain concepts that most people do not understand fully, and she discusses how everyone can benefit if we take a different attitude toward nature. She shows that she has done her homework on the topic. By creating a credible ethos, Carson makes an effective moral argument that humans as a species have a responsibility not to destroy the world they live in.

Appeals to Logos: the Good Reasons or Logic Used to Support an Argument

Logos means persuading by using reasons. It is sometimes referred to as "the argument itself." Logos is the method preferred by Aristotle, scientists, and academic writers in general. Carson offers good reasons to support her main claims. She describes webs of relationships among the earth, plants, animals, and humans, and she explains how changing one part will affect the others. Her point is not that we should never disturb these relationships but that we should be aware of the consequences.

Rachel Carson

The Obligation to Endure

Rachel Carson (1907–1964) was born and raised in Springdale, Pennsylvania, 18 miles up the Allegheny River from Pittsburgh. As she wandered on the family farm, Carson developed the love of nature that she maintained throughout her life. At age 22 she began her career as a marine biologist at Woods Hole, Massachusetts, and she later went to graduate school at Johns Hopkins University in Baltimore. In 1936 she began working in the agency that later became the U.S. Fish and Wildlife Service. Soon she was recognized as a talented writer as well as a meticulous scientist. Carson wrote three highly praised books about the sea and wetlands: Under the Sea Wind *(1941),* The Sea Around Us *(1951), and* The Edge of the Sea *(1954).*

Carson's decision to write Silent Spring *marked a great change in her life. For the first time, she became an environmental activist in addition to being an enthusiastic writer about nature. She had written about the interconnectedness of life in her previous three books, but with* Silent Spring *she had to convince people that hazards lay in what had seemed familiar and harmless. Carson was the first scientist to make a comprehensive argument that links cancer to environmental causes. Earlier in this chapter, we saw how Carson compares pesticides with the dangers of radiation from nuclear weapons. Notice another way that she gets her readers to think differently about pesticides in this selection, which begins Chapter 2 of* Silent Spring.

The history of life on earth has been a history of interaction between living things and their surroundings. To a large extent, the physical form and the habits of the earth's vegetation and its animal life have been molded by the environment. Considering the whole span of earthly time, the opposite effect, in which life actually modifies its surroundings, has been relatively slight. Only within the moment of time represented by the present century has one species—man—acquired significant power to alter the nature of his world.

2   During the past quarter century this power has not only increased to one of disturbing magnitude but it has changed in character. The most alarming of all man's assaults upon the environment is the contamination of air, earth, rivers, and sea with dangerous and even lethal materials. This pollution is for the most part irrecoverable; the chain of evil it initiates not only in the world that must support life but in living tissues is for the most part irreversible. In this now universal contamination of the environment, chemicals are the sinister and little recognized partners of radiation in changing the very nature of the world—the very nature of its life. Strontium 90, released through nuclear explosions into the air, comes to earth in rain or drifts down as fallout, lodges in soil, enters into the grass or corn or wheat grown there, and in time takes up its abode in the bones of a human being, there to remain until his death. Similarly, chemicals sprayed on croplands or forests or gardens lie long in soil,

entering into living organisms, passing from one to another in a chain of poisoning and death. Or they pass mysteriously by underground streams until they emerge and, through the alchemy of air and sunlight, combine into new forms that kill vegetation, sicken cattle, and work unknown harm on those who drink from once-pure wells. As Albert Schweitzer has said, "Man can hardly even recognize the devils of his own creation."

3   It took hundreds of millions of years to produce the life that now inhabits the earth—eons of time in which that developing and evolving and diversifying life reached a state of adjustment and balance with its surroundings. The environment, rigorously shaping and directing the life it supported, contained elements that were hostile as well as supporting. Certain rocks gave out dangerous radiation; even within the light of the sun, from which all life draws its energy, there were short-wave radiations with power to injure. Given time—time not in years but in millennia—life adjusts, and a balance has been reached. For time is the essential ingredient; but in the modern world there is no time.

4   The rapidity of change and the speed with which new situations are created follow the impetuous and heedless pace of man rather than the deliberate pace of nature. Radiation is no longer merely the background radiation of rocks, the bombardment of cosmic rays, the ultraviolet of the sun that have existed before there was any life on earth; radiation is now the unnatural creation of man's tampering with the atom. The chemicals to which life is asked to make its adjustment are no longer merely the calcium and silica and copper and all the rest of the minerals washed out of the rocks and carried in rivers to the sea; they are the synthetic creations of man's inventive mind, brewed in his laboratories, and having no counterparts in nature.

5   To adjust to these chemicals would require time on the scale that is nature's; it would require not merely the years of a man's life but the life of generations. And even this, were it by some miracle possible, would be futile, for the new chemicals come from our laboratories in an endless stream; almost five hundred annually find their way into actual use in the United States alone. The figure is staggering and its implications are not easily grasped—500 new chemicals to which the bodies of men and animals are required somehow to adapt each year, chemicals totally outside the limits of biologic experience.

6   Among them are many that are used in man's war against nature. Since the mid-1940s over 200 basic chemicals have been created for use in killing insects, weeds, rodents, and other organisms described in the modern vernacular as "pests"; and they are sold under several thousand different brand names.

7   These sprays, dusts, and aerosols are now applied almost universally to farms, gardens, forests, and homes—nonselective chemicals that have the power to kill every insect, the "good" and the "bad," to still the song of birds and the leaping of fish in the streams, to coat the leaves with a deadly film, and to linger on in soil—all this though the intended target may be only a few

weeds or insects. Can anyone believe it is possible to lay down such a barrage of poisons on the surface of the earth without making it unfit for all life? They should not be called "insecticides," but "biocides."

8   The whole process of spraying seems caught up in an endless spiral. Since DDT was released for civilian use, a process of escalation has been going on in which ever more toxic materials must be found. This has happened because insects, in a triumphant vindication of Darwin's principle of the survival of the fittest, have evolved super races immune to the particular insecticide used, hence a deadlier one has always to be developed—and then a deadlier one than that. It has happened also because, for reasons to be described later, destructive insects often undergo a "flareback," or resurgence, after spraying, in numbers greater than before. Thus the chemical war is never won, and all life is caught in its violent crossfire.

9   Along with the possibility of the extinction of mankind by nuclear war, the central problem of our age has therefore become the contamination of man's total environment with such substances of incredible potential for harm—substances that accumulate in the tissues of plants and animals and even penetrate the germ cells to shatter or alter the very material of heredity upon which the shape of the future depends.

10   Some would-be architects of our future look toward a time when it will be possible to alter the human germ plasm by design. But we may easily be doing so now by inadvertence, for many chemicals, like radiation, bring about gene mutations. It is ironic to think that man might determine his own future by something so seemingly trivial as the choice of an insect spray.

11   All this has been risked—for what? Future historians may well be amazed by our distorted sense of proportion. How could intelligent beings seek to control a few unwanted species by a method that contaminated the entire environment and brought the threat of disease and death even to their own kind? Yet this is precisely what we have done. We have done it, moreover, for reasons that collapse the moment we examine them. We are told that the enormous and expanding use of pesticides is necessary to maintain farm production. Yet is our real problem not one of *overproduction*? Our farms, despite measures to remove acreages from production and to pay farmers *not* to produce, have yielded such a staggering excess of crops that the American taxpayer in 1962 is paying out more than one billion dollars a year as the total carrying cost of the surplus-food storage program. And is the situation helped when one branch of the Agriculture Department tries to reduce production while another states, as it did in 1958, "It is believed generally that reduction of crop acreages under provisions of the Soil Bank will stimulate interest in use of chemicals to obtain maximum production on the land retained in crops."

12   All this is not to say there is no insect problem and no need of control. I am saying, rather, that control must be geared to realities, not to mythical situations, and that the methods employed must be such that they do not destroy us along with the insects.

2

Reading Arguments

We constantly "read" what is going on around us. But can we tell what these people might be thinking?

Along with learning to write well, thinking critically is one of the most important abilities you will develop in college. You will be asked to think in depth about what you read, as well as what you see in movies, television shows, print advertisements, paintings, photographs, or Web sites. Becoming a better thinker will help you to become a better writer because you will understand subjects in greater complexity and you will be better able to evaluate and to revise what you write.

Critical thinking begins with critical reading. Reading arguments requires you to read critically because you need know more than the writer's main points. Arguments don't fall out of the sky but instead are part of a larger conversation about ideas. Reading one turn in a conversation is not enough to understand why a subject is being discussed at a particular time or to gain a sense of the major points of view. To become aware of how a particular argument fits into the larger conversation, you must explore beyond the text itself.

Read Critically

Critical reading is the four-part process described in the box on the facing page, and you will often need to read an assignment more than once to cover all of the points in the process. First, ask where a piece of writing came from and why it was written. Second, read the text carefully to find the author's central claim or thesis and the major points. Third, decide if you can trust the author. Fourth, read the text again to understand how it works.

Read Actively

If you own what you are reading, read with a pencil in hand. (Avoid pens and highlighters—they don't erase, and often you won't remember why you highlighted a particular sentence.)

QUESTIONS FOR READING ARGUMENTS CRITICALLY

1. Where did the argument come from?

- Who wrote this argument? What do you know about the author?
- Where did the argument first appear? Was it published in a book, newspaper, magazine, or electronic source?
- What else has been written about the topic or issue? Is the topic new, or has it been written about for many years?
- What do you expect after reading the title?

2. What does the argument say?

- What is the topic or issue?
- What is the writer's thesis or overall point?
- What reasons or evidence does the writer offer?
- Who are the intended readers? What does the writer assume the readers know and believe?

3. Can you trust the writer?

- Does the writer have the necessary knowledge and experience to write about this subject? You may need to do some research to find out more about the author.
- Do you detect a bias in the writer's position? Does the writer seem to favor one side or another?
- Are the facts relevant to the writer's claims? Are the facts correct? Where did the facts come from?
- Does the writer refer to expert opinions or research about this subject? Are these sources reliable?
- Does the writer acknowledge alternative views and unfavorable evidence? Does the writer deal fairly with the views of others?

4. How does the argument work?

- How is the piece of writing organized? How are the major points arranged?
- How does the writer conclude his or her argument? Does the conclusion follow logically from the evidence the writer offers? What impression does the reader take away?
- How would you characterize the writing style? Describe the language that the writer uses.
- How does the writer represent herself or himself?
- Is the page design attractive and correctly formatted? Are photos, tables, and graphics well integrated into the text and clearly labeled?

Finding Good Reasons

HAS THE INTERNET MADE EVERYONE WRITERS?

Before the Internet was invented, readers had to make some effort to respond to writers by writing to them directly, sending a letter to the editor, or even scribbling or spray-painting a response. The Internet has changed the interaction between writers and readers by allowing readers to respond easily to writers and, in turn, turning readers into writers. Look, for example, at Amazon.com. An incredible amount of writing surrounds any best-selling book—often an author's Web site and blog, newspaper reviews, and over a hundred readers' reviews. Or read a political, sports, culture, fashion, or parenting blog and the comments by readers of those blogs. Think about how the Internet has changed the relationship between readers and writers.

To find a blog that interests you, use a blog search engine such as Bloglines (www. bloglines. com), Google Blog Search (blogsearch.google.com), IceRocket (blogs.icerocket.com), or Technorati (www. technorati. com).

Write about it

1. Using a blog search engine or an online newspaper, find a blog by an author, politician, or news columnist. Answer as many of the questions for critical reading on page 23 as you can.

2. Write a summary of the blog entry.

3. What kinds of reasons do blog writers give for their responses to what they read?

4. How are blogs and online book reviews like or unlike traditional book reviews in print?

Annotating what you read

Using annotating strategies will make the effort you put into reading more rewarding.

- **Mark major points and key concepts.** Sometimes major points are indicated by headings, but often you will need to locate them.
- **Connect with your experience.** Think about your own experiences and how they match up or don't match up with what you are reading.
- **Connect passages.** Notice how ideas connect to each other. Draw lines and arrows. If an idea connects to something from a few pages earlier, write a note in the margin with the page number.
- **Ask questions.** Note anything that puzzles you, including words you don't know and need to look up.

The passage below is from Nell Irvin Painter's *Creating Black Americans: African-American History and Its Meanings, 1619 to the Present* (2006). Painter argues that while history and culture connect African Americans to Africa, the identity of African Americans is a New World identity. Painter uses the term *African Diaspora* to refer to the dispersion of African people from their native lands in Africa.

Definition: African Americans are a new people born in the Western Hemisphere

language as indicator

The three centuries separating African Americans from their immigrant ancestors profoundly influenced their identity. A strong case can be made for seeing African Americans as a new, Creole people, that is, as a people born and forged in the Western Hemisphere. Language provides the most obvious indicator: people of African descent in the Diaspora do not speak *Look up* languages of Africa as their mother tongue. For the most part, they speak Portuguese, Spanish, English, and French as a mother tongue, although millions speak Creole languages (such as Haitian Creole and South Carolinian Gullah) that combine African grammars and English vocabulary. As the potent engine of culture, language influences thought, psychology, and education. Language boundaries now divide descendants whose African ancestors may have been family and close neighbors speaking the same language. One descendant in Nashville, Tennessee, may not understand the Portuguese of her distant cousin now living in Bahia, Brazil. Today, with immigrants from Africa forming an increasing proportion of people calling themselves African American, the woman in *example—differen languages divide Af Ams from African ancestor* Nashville might herself be an African immigrant and speak an African language that neither her black neighbors in Tennessee nor her distant cousin in Brazil can understand. Religion, another crucial aspect of *religion another indicator* culture, distinguishes the different peoples of the African Diaspora. Millions of Africans are Muslims, for instance, while most African

example–Af Ams would not agree to be judged by Muslim law

Americans see themselves as Christian. They would hardly agree to place themselves under the Sharia, the legal system inspired by the Koran, which prevails in Northern Nigeria.

Mapping

Drawing a map of a text can help you to identify key points and to understand the relationships among concepts. Below is a map of the passage by Nell Irvin Painter.

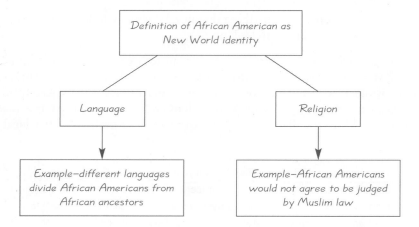

Recognize Fallacies

Just as important as understanding the structure of an argument is recognizing where it goes off track. To be convincing, good reasons rely on evidence that readers will accept as valid. Often this evidence is missing or distorted.

Recognizing where good reasons go off track is one of the most important aspects of critical reading. What passes as political discourse is often filled with claims that lack evidence or substitute emotions for evidence. Such faulty reasoning often contains one or more **logical fallacies**. For example, politicians know that the public is outraged when the price of gasoline goes up, and they try to score political points by accusing oil companies of price gouging. It sounds good to angry voters—and it may well be true—but unless the politician defines what *price gouging* means and provides evidence that oil companies are guilty, the argument has no more validity than children calling each other bad names on the playground.

Following are some of the more common fallacies.

Fallacies of logic

- **Begging the question** *Politicians are inherently dishonest because no honest person would run for public office.* The fallacy of begging the question occurs when the claim is restated and passed off as evidence.

- **Either-or** *Either we eliminate the regulation of businesses or else profits will suffer.* The either-or fallacy suggests that there are only two choices in a complex situation. Rarely, if ever, is this the case. Consider, for example, the case of Enron, which was unregulated but went bankrupt.

- **False analogies** *Japan quit fighting in 1945 when we dropped nuclear bombs on them. We should use nuclear weapons against other countries.* Analogies always depend on the degree of resemblance of one situation to another. In this case, the analogy fails to recognize that circumstances today are very different from those in 1945. Many countries now possess nuclear weapons, and we know their use could harm the entire world.

- **Hasty generalization** *We have been in a drought for three years; that's a sure sign of climate change.* A hasty generalization is a broad claim made on the basis of a few occurrences. Climate cycles occur regularly over spans of a few years. Climate trends, however, must be observed over centuries.

- **Non sequitur** *A university that can raise a billion dollars from alumni should not have to raise tuition.* A non sequitur (a Latin term meaning "it does not follow") ties together two unrelated ideas. In this case, the argument fails to recognize that the money for capital campaigns is often donated for special purposes such as athletic facilities and is not part of a university's general revenue.

- **Oversimplification** *No one would run stop signs if we had a mandatory death penalty for doing it.* This claim may be true, but the argument would be unacceptable to most citizens. More complex, if less definitive, solutions are called for.

- ***Post hoc* fallacy** *The stock market goes down when the AFC wins the Super Bowl in even years.* The *post hoc* fallacy (from the Latin *post hoc, ergo propter hoc,* which means "after this, therefore because of this") assumes that events that follow in time have a causal relationship.

- **Rationalization** *I could have finished my paper on time if my printer had been working.* People frequently come up with excuses and weak explanations for their own and others' behavior. These excuses often avoid actual causes.

- **Slippery slope** *We shouldn't grant citizenship to illegal immigrants now living in the United States because no one will want to obey our laws.* The slippery slope fallacy maintains that one thing inevitably will cause something else to happen.

Fallacies of emotion and language

- **Bandwagon appeals** *It doesn't matter if I copy a paper off the Web because everyone else does.* This argument suggests that everyone is doing it, so why shouldn't you? But on close examination, it may be that everyone really isn't doing it—and in any case, it may not be the right thing to do.
- **Name calling** Name calling is frequent in politics and among competing groups. People level accusations using names such as *radical, tax-and-spend liberal, racist, fascist, right-wing ideologue.* Unless these terms are carefully defined, they are meaningless.
- **Polarization** *Feminists are all man haters.* Like name calling, polarization exaggerates positions and groups by representing them as extreme and divisive.
- **Straw man** *Environmentalists won't be satisfied until not a single human being is allowed to enter a national park.* A straw man argument is a diversionary tactic that sets up another's position in a way that can be easily rejected. In fact, only a small percentage of environmentalists would make an argument even close to this one.

Respond as a Writer

Engage in a dialogue with what you read. Talk back to the author. If you are having trouble understanding a difficult section, read it aloud and listen to the author's voice. Hearing something read will sometimes help you to imagine being in a conversation with the author.

Making notes

As you read, write down your thoughts. Something you read may remind you of something else. Jot that down.

- Imagine that the author is with you. Which of the writer's points would you respond to in person?
- What questions would you like to ask the author? You may need to look up the answers to these questions.
- What ideas might you develop or interpret differently?

Writing a summary

A useful way to distill information from a reading is to summarize it. When you summarize, you state the major ideas of an entire source or part of a source in your own words. Most summaries are much shorter than the original because they include just the main points, not most of the examples and supporting material. The keys to writing a good summary are identifying the main points and then putting those points into your own words. Note that if you use the exact words from a source in your summary, you must enclose those words in quotation marks.

Example summary

Nell Irvin Painter argues that while African Americans draw much of their heritage from Africa, the concept of an African American identity was forged in the New World. She points out that among the many differences between Africans and their descendants outside Africa, the differences of language and religion are crucial to African American identity.

Building on what you read

A reading journal can help you both as a reader and as a writer. In a reading journal, you'll have a record of your thoughts that you can return to later, a space where you can connect ideas from different readings, and a place to test ideas that you can later develop for a writing assignment.

Example reading journal

Painter writes, "Hip-hop's preoccupation with authentic blackness reflects the difficulty of characterizing African Americans as a whole" (343). I agree because there is much more than hip-hop in the larger African American community and hip-hop has become a world youth culture well established in Britain, France, the Caribbean, Africa, Latin America, Asia—indeed, just about everywhere.

But hip-hop culture also helps to confirm her main point that African American identity has been created in the New World. Think about breakdancing, which is a major part of hip-hop culture that developed on sidewalks, playgrounds, and basketball courts. Like jazz and the blues, breakdancing grew up in African American communities in the United States and spread around the world rather than coming from somewhere else.

3

Finding Arguments

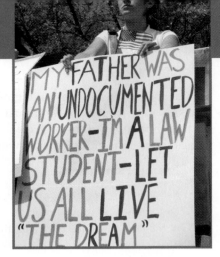

Slogans and bumper stickers are meant to persuade, but technically they are not arguments because they lack reasons. Nevertheless, you can often supply a reason for a claim made on a sign or bumper sticker. What reason might the demonstrator give to support her claim LET US ALL LIVE "THE DREAM"?

Many people think of the term *argument* as a synonym for *debate*. College courses and professional careers, however, require a different kind of argument—one that, most of the time, is cooler in emotion and more elaborate in detail than oral debate. At first glance an argument in writing doesn't seem to have much in common with debate. But the basic elements and ways of reasoning used in written arguments are similar to those we use in everyday conversations.

Find Arguments in Everyday Conversations

Let's look at an example of a conversation. When the pain in his abdomen didn't go away, Jeff knew he had torn something while carrying his friend's heavy speakers up a flight of stairs. He went to the student health center and called his friend Maria when he returned home.

JEFF: I have good news and bad news. The pain is a minor hernia that can be repaired with day surgery. The bad news is that the fee we pay for the health center doesn't cover hospital visits. We should have health coverage.

MARIA: Jeff, you didn't buy the extra insurance. Why should you get it for nothing?

JEFF: Because health coverage is a right.

MARIA: No it's not. Everyone doesn't have health insurance.

JEFF: Well, in some other countries like Canada, Germany, and Britain, they do.

MARIA: Yes, and people who live in those countries pay a bundle in taxes for the government-provided insurance.

JEFF: It's not fair in this country because some people have health insurance and others don't.

MARIA: Jeff, face the facts. You could have bought the extra insurance. Instead you chose to buy a new car.

JEFF: It would be better if the university provided health insurance because students could graduate in four years. I'm going to have to get a second job and drop out for a semester to pay for the surgery.

MARIA: Neat idea, but who's going to pay for it?

JEFF: OK, all students should be required to pay for health insurance as part of their general fee. Most students are healthy, and it wouldn't cost that much more.

In this discussion, Jeff starts out by making a **claim** that students should have health coverage. Maria immediately asks him why students should not have to pay for health insurance. She wants a **reason** to accept his claim.

Distinguishing arguments from other kinds of persuasion

Scholars who study argument maintain that an argument must have a claim and one or more reasons to support that claim. Something less might be persuasive, but it isn't an argument.

A bumper sticker that says NO TOLL ROADS is a claim, but it is not an argument because the statement lacks a reason. Many reasons support an argument against building toll roads.

- We don't need new roads but should build light-rail instead.
- We should raise the gas tax to pay for new roads.
- We should use gas tax revenue only for roads rather than using it for other purposes.

When a claim has a reason attached, then it becomes an argument.

The basics of arguments

A reason is typically offered in a **because clause,** a statement that begins with the word *because* and that provides a supporting reason for the claim. Jeff's first attempt is to argue that students should have health insurance *because* health insurance is a right.

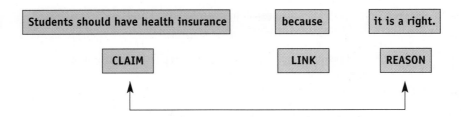

The word *because* signals a link between the reason and the claim. Every argument that is more than a shouting match or a simple assertion has to have one or more reasons. Just having a reason for a claim, however, doesn't mean that the audience will be convinced. When Jeff tells Maria that students have a right to health insurance, Maria replies that students don't have that right. Maria will accept Jeff's claim only if she accepts that his reason supports his claim. Maria challenges Jeff's links and keeps asking "So what?" For her, Jeff's reasons are not good reasons.

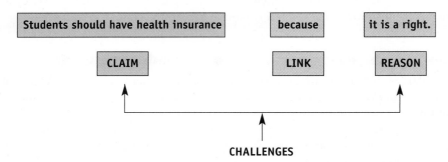

By the end of this short discussion, Jeff has begun to build an argument. He has had to come up with another claim to support his main claim: All students should be required to pay for health insurance as part of their general fee. If he is to convince Maria, he will probably have to provide a series of claims that she will accept as linked to his primary claim. He will also need to find evidence to support these claims.

Benjamin Franklin observed, "So convenient a thing it is to be a rational creature, since it enables us to find or make a reason for every thing one has a mind to do." It is not hard to think of reasons. What *is* difficult is to convince your audience that your reasons are good reasons. In a conversation, you get immediate feedback that tells you whether your listener agrees or disagrees. When you are writing, you usually don't have someone you can question immediately. Consequently, you have to (1) be more specific about what you are claiming, (2) connect with the values you hold in common with your readers, and (3) anticipate what questions and objections your readers might have, if you are going to convince someone who doesn't agree with you or know what you know already.

When you write an argument, imagine a reader like Maria who is going to listen carefully to what you have to say but who is not going to agree with you automatically. Readers like Maria will expect the following.

- A **claim** that is interesting and makes them want to find out more about what you have to say
- At least one **good reason** that makes your claim worth taking seriously
- Some **evidence** that the good reason or reasons are valid
- Some acknowledgment of the **opposing views** and **limitations** of the claim

The remainder of this chapter will guide you through the process of finding a topic, making a claim, finding good reasons and evidence, and anticipating objections to your claim.

Find a Topic That Interests You

When your instructor gives you a writing assignment, look closely at what you are asked to do. Assignments typically contain a great deal of information, and you have to sort through that information. First, circle all the instructions about the length, the due date, the format, the grading criteria, and anything else about the production and conventions of the assignment. This information is important to you, but it doesn't tell you what the paper is supposed to be about.

Reading your assignment

Often your assignment will contain key words such as *analyze, define, evaluate,* or *propose* that will assist you in determining what direction to take. *Analyze* can mean several things. Your instructor might want you to analyze a piece of writing (see Chapter 5), an image (see Chapter 6), or the causes of something (see Chapter 9). *Define* usually means writing a **definition argument,** in which you argue for a definition based on the criteria you set out (see Chapter 8). *Evaluate* indicates an **evaluation argument,** in which you argue that something is good, bad, the best, or the worst in its class according to criteria that you set out (see Chapter 10). An assignment that contains the instructions *Write about an issue using your personal experience* indicates a **narrative argument** (see Chapter 11), while one that says *Take a position in regard to a reading* might lead you to write a **rebuttal argument**

WHAT IS NOT ARGUABLE

Statements of fact. Most facts can be verified by doing research. But even simple facts can sometimes be argued. For example, Mount Everest is usually acknowledged to be the highest mountain in the world at 29,028 feet above sea level. But if the total height of a mountain from base to summit is the measure, then the volcano Mauna Loa in Hawaii is the highest mountain in the world. Although the top of Mauna Loa is 13,667 feet above sea level, the summit is 31,784 above the ocean floor. Thus the "fact" that Mount Everest is the highest mountain on the earth depends on a definition of *highest*. You could argue for this definition.

Claims of personal taste. Your favorite food and your favorite color are examples of personal taste. If you hate fresh tomatoes, no one can convince you that you actually like them. But many claims of personal taste turn out to be value judgments using arguable criteria. For example, if you think that *Alien* is the best science-fiction movie ever made, you can argue that claim using evaluative criteria that other people can consider as good reasons (see Chapter 8). Indeed, you might not even like science fiction and still argue that *Alien* is the best science-fiction movie ever.

Statements of belief or faith. If someone accepts a claim as a matter of religious belief, then for that person, the claim is true and cannot be refuted. Of course, people still make arguments about the existence of God and which religion reflects the will of God. Whenever an audience will not consider an idea, it's possible but very difficult to construct an argument. Many people claim to have evidence that UFOs exist, but most people refuse to acknowledge that evidence as even being possibly factual.

(see Chapter 12). *Propose* means that you should identify a particular problem and explain why your solution is the best one (see Chapter 13).

If you remain unclear about the purpose of the assignment after reading it carefully, talk with your instructor.

Thinking about what interests you

Your assignment may specify the topic you are to write about. If your assignment gives you a wide range of options and you don't know what to write about, look first at the materials for your course: the readings, your lecture notes, and discussion boards. Think about what subjects came up in class discussion.

If you need to look outside class for a topic, think about what interests you. Subjects we argue about often find us. There are enough of them in daily life. We're late for work or class because the traffic is heavy or the bus doesn't run on time. We can't find a place to park when we get to school or work. We have to negotiate through various bureaucracies for almost anything we do—making an appointment to see a doctor, getting a course added or dropped, or correcting a mistake on a bill. Most of the time we grumble and let it go at that. But sometimes we stick with a subject. Neighborhood groups in cities and towns have been especially effective in getting something done by writing about it—for example, stopping a new road from being built, getting better police and fire protection, and getting a vacant lot turned into a park.

Listing and analyzing issues

A good way to get started is to list possible issues to write about. Make a list of questions that can be answered "YES, because . . ." or "NO, because. . . ." (Following are some lists to get you started.) You'll find out that often before you can make a claim, you first have to analyze exactly what is meant by a phrase like *censorship of the Internet*. Does it mean censorship of the World Wide Web or of everything that is transmitted on the Internet, including private email? To be convincing, you'll have to argue that one thing causes another, for good or bad.

Think about issues that affect your campus, your community, the nation, and the world. Which issues interest you? About which issues could you make a contribution to the larger discussion?

Campus

- Should students be required to pay fees for access to computers on campus?
- Should smoking be banned on campus?
- Should varsity athletes get paid for playing sports that bring in revenue?
- Should admissions decisions be based exclusively on academic achievement?
- Should knowledge of a foreign language be required for all degree plans?
- Should your college or university have a computer literacy requirement?
- Should fraternities be banned from campuses if they are caught encouraging alcohol abuse?

Community

- Should people who ride bicycles and motorcycles be required to wear helmets?
- Should high schools be allowed to search students for drugs at any time?

- Should high schools distribute condoms?
- Should bilingual education programs be eliminated?
- Should the public schools be privatized?
- Should bike lanes be built throughout your community to encourage more people to ride bicycles?
- Should more tax dollars be shifted from building highways to funding public transportation?

Nation/World

- Should driving while talking on a cell phone be banned?
- Should capital punishment be abolished?
- Should the Internet be censored?
- Should the government be allowed to monitor all phone calls and all email to combat terrorism?
- Should handguns be outlawed?
- Should beef and poultry be free of growth hormones?
- Should a law be passed requiring that the parents of teenagers who have abortions be informed?
- Should people who are terminally ill be allowed to end their lives?
- Should the United States punish nations with poor human rights records?

Narrowing a list

1. Put a check beside the issues that look most interesting to write about or the ones that mean the most to you.
2. Put a question mark beside the issues that you don't know very much about. If you choose one of these issues, you will probably have to do in-depth research—by talking to people, by using the Internet, or by going to the library.
3. Select the two or three issues that look most promising. For each issue, make another list:
   - Who is most interested in this issue?
   - Whom or what does this issue affect?
   - What are the pros and cons of this issue? Make two columns. At the top of the left one, write "YES, because." At the top of the right one, write "NO, because."
   - What has been written about this issue? How can you find out what has been written?

Finding a topic on the Web

Online subject directories can help you identify the subtopics of a large, general topic. Try the subject index of your library's online catalog. You'll likely find subtopics listed under large topics. Online encyclopedias, such as Britannica.com, also can be helpful in identifying subtopics.

One of the best Web subject directories for finding arguments is Yahoo's Issues and Causes directory. This directory provides subtopics for major issues and provides links to the Web sites of organizations interested in particular issues.

Yahoo! Issues and Causes directory
(dir.yahoo.com/Society_and_Culture/Issues_and_Causes/)

Find a Claim by Exploring

Once you have identified a general topic, the next step is to explore that topic to find a possible claim. You don't have to decide exactly what to write about at this stage. Your goal is to find out how much you already know and what you need to learn more about. Experienced writers use several strategies for exploring a topic.

Freewriting

The goal of **freewriting** is to write as quickly as you can without stopping for a set time—usually five or ten minutes. Set a timer and then write as fast as you can, even if you wander off the topic. Don't stop to correct mistakes. Write the same sentence again if you get stuck momentarily. The constant flow of words will generate ideas, some useful and some not. After you've finished, read what you have written and single out any key ideas.

> *Freewrite on privacy*
>
> I get so much junk email and junk mail. How did so many people get my email and mail addresses? How is it collected? How does it get passed around? How do I find this out? Friend told me about a question in an interview—they had asked him about personal data but it wasn't about him. A lot of people have the same names. Easy to mix up people. Scary. How could you fix it? Amazon account tracks what I buy. Do they sell that information? What are the laws? Data is sold to the highest bidder. And there are breaches in security where credit card numbers are stolen but people aren't informed.
>
> Ideas to Use
> 1. The sharing of personal information and mistakes that can result.
> 2. The misuse of personal information by corporations.
> 3. Breaches in security without people being notified.

You may want to take one of the ideas you have identified to start another freewrite. After two or three rounds of freewriting, you should begin to identify a claim such as the following.

- There should be federal laws that give people access to the personal information that businesses collect and the opportunity to correct mistakes.
- There should be federal laws that protect the personal data of individuals from being sold to the highest bidder.
- There should be federal laws that make it a crime to conceal breaches of security that expose the personal data of individuals.

Brainstorming

Another method of discovery is to brainstorm. The end result of **brainstorming** is usually a list—sometimes of questions, sometimes of statements. These questions and statements give you ways to develop your topic. A list of questions on secondhand smoke is on page 40.

Finding Good Reasons

ARE TRAFFIC CAMERAS INVADING YOUR PRIVACY?

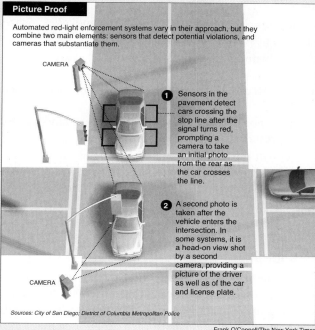

Picture Proof

Automated red-light enforcement systems vary in their approach, but they combine two main elements: sensors that detect potential violations, and cameras that substantiate them.

CAMERA

1 Sensors in the pavement detect cars crossing the stop line after the signal turns red, prompting a camera to take an initial photo from the rear as the car crosses the line.

2 A second photo is taken after the vehicle enters the intersection. In some systems, it is a head-on view shot by a second camera, providing a picture of the driver as well as of the car and license plate.

CAMERA

Sources: City of San Diego; District of Columbia Metropolitan Police

Frank O'Connell/The New York Times

Cameras that photograph the license plates and drivers of vehicles who run red lights are currently in use in 22 U.S. states. Cameras aimed at catching speeders, already common in Europe, are beginning to be installed in U.S. cities as well. Traffic cameras have become money machines for some communities, but they also have provoked intense public opposition and even vandalism—people have spray painted and shot cameras in attempts to disable them.

Write about it

1. How do you feel about using cameras to catch red-light runners? Speeders? People who don't pay parking tickets? Make a list of as many possible topics as you can think of about the use of cameras to scan license plates.

2. Select one of the possible topics. Write it at the top of a sheet of paper, and then write nonstop for five minutes. Don't worry about correctness. If you get stuck, write the same sentence again.

3. When you finish, read what you have written and circle key ideas.

4. Put each key idea on a sticky note. If you think of other ideas, write them on separate sticky notes. Then look at your sticky notes. Put a star on the central idea. Put the ideas that are related next to each other. You now have the beginning of an idea map.

- How much of a risk is secondhand smoke?
- What are the effects of secondhand smoke on children?
- How do the risks of secondhand smoke compare to other kinds of pollution?
- Which states ban all exposure to secondhand smoke? exposure in restaurants? exposure in the workplace?
- Who opposes banning exposure to secondhand smoke?

Answering such questions can lead you to potential claims such as these.

- Smoking should be prohibited in all workplaces, including restaurants and bars, to prevent health risks to nonsmokers.
- Because over half the children under five years of age in the United States live in households with at least one adult smoker, a massive education campaign should target these adults about the harm they are inflicting on their children.

Making an idea map

When you have an ample amount of information about a topic, you need to begin making connections among the facts, data, and ideas you have collected. One method of assembling ideas is an **idea map**, which describes visually how the many aspects of a particular issue relate to each other. Idea maps are useful because you can see everything at once and make connections among the different aspects of an issue—definitions, causes, proposed solutions, and opposing points of view.

A good way to get started is to write down ideas on sticky notes. Then you can move the sticky notes around until you figure out which ideas fit together. Constructing an idea map will help you identify claims and begin to think about reasons that can support those claims.

Find a Claim by Reading

Much college writing draws on and responds to sources—books, articles, reports, and other material written by other people. Every significant issue discussed in today's world has an extensive history of discussion involving many people and various points of view. Before you formulate a claim about a significant issue, you need to become familiar with the conversation that's already happening by reading about it.

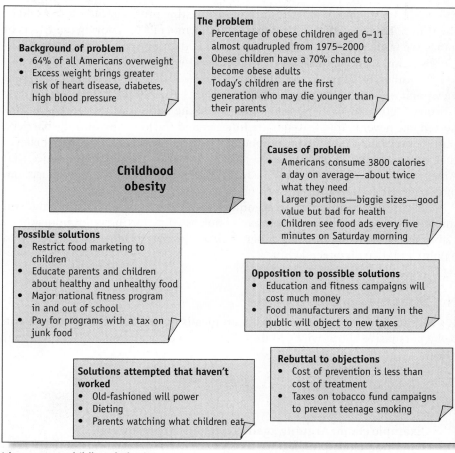

The problem
- Percentage of obese children aged 6–11 almost quadrupled from 1975–2000
- Obese children have a 70% chance to become obese adults
- Today's children are the first generation who may die younger than their parents

Background of problem
- 64% of all Americans overweight
- Excess weight brings greater risk of heart disease, diabetes, high blood pressure

Childhood obesity

Causes of problem
- Americans consume 3800 calories a day on average—about twice what they need
- Larger portions—biggie sizes—good value but bad for health
- Children see food ads every five minutes on Saturday morning

Possible solutions
- Restrict food marketing to children
- Educate parents and children about healthy and unhealthy food
- Major national fitness program in and out of school
- Pay for programs with a tax on junk food

Opposition to possible solutions
- Education and fitness campaigns will cost much money
- Food manufacturers and many in the public will object to new taxes

Solutions attempted that haven't worked
- Old-fashioned will power
- Dieting
- Parents watching what children eat

Rebuttal to objections
- Cost of prevention is less than cost of treatment
- Taxes on tobacco fund campaigns to prevent teenage smoking

Idea map on childhood obesity

One of the most controversial and talked-about subjects in recent years is the outsourcing of white-collar and manufacturing jobs to low-wage nations. Since 2000 an estimated 400,000 to 500,000 American jobs each year have gone to cheap overseas labor markets. The Internet has made this migration of jobs possible, allowing companies to outsource highly skilled jobs in fields such as software development, data storage, and even examining X-rays and MRI scans along with low-skilled jobs.

You may have read about this or another complex and controversial topic in one of your courses. Just as in a conversation with several people who hold different views, you may agree with some people, disagree with some, and with others agree with some of their ideas up to a point but then disagree.

CNN commentator Lou Dobbs has been sharply critical of outsourcing. In *Exporting America: Why Corporate Greed Is Shipping American Jobs Overseas*

(2006), Dobbs blames large corporations for putting profits ahead of the good of the nation. He accuses both Republicans and Democrats of ignoring the effects of a massive trade deficit and the largest national debt in American history, which Dobbs claims will eventually destroy the American way of life.

Thomas Friedman, columnist for *The New York Times*, takes a different viewpoint on outsourcing in *The World Is Flat: A Brief History of the Twenty-first Century* (2006). By *flat*, Friedman means that the nations of the world are connected like never before through the Internet and the lowering of trade barriers, putting every nation in direct competition with all the others. Friedman believes that outsourcing is not only unstoppable, but also desirable. He argues that Americans need to adapt to the new reality and rethink our system of education, or else we will be left hopelessly behind.

If you decide to write an argument about the issue of outsourcing, you might use either Dobbs's or Friedman's book as your starting point in making a claim. You could begin by using either book to disagree, to agree, or to agree up to a point and then disagree.

No: Disagreeing with a source

It's easy to disagree by simply saying an idea is dumb, but readers expect you to be persuasive about why you disagree and to offer reasons to support your views.

> X claims that _____, but this view is mistaken because _____.

Example claim: Arguing against outsourcing resulting from free-trade policies

> Thomas Friedman claims that the world is "flat," giving a sense of a level playing field for all, but it is absurd to think that the millions of starving children in the world have opportunities similar to those in affluent countries who pay $100 for basketball shoes made by the starving children.

Example claim: Arguing in favor of outsourcing resulting from free-trade policies

> Lou Dobbs is a patriotic American who recognizes the suffering of manufacturing workers in industries like steel and automobiles, but he neglects that the major cause of the loss of manufacturing jobs in the United States and China alike is increased productivity—the 40 hours of labor necessary to produce a car just a few years ago has now been reduced to 15.

Yes: Agreeing with a source with an additional point

Sources should not make your argument for you. With sources that support your position, indicate exactly how they fit into your argument with an additional point.

> I agree with _____ and will make the additional point that _____.

Example claim: Arguing against outsourcing resulting from free trade policies

> Lou Dobbs's outcry against the outsourcing of American jobs also has a related argument: We are dependent not only on foreign oil, but also on foreign clothing, foreign electronics, foreign tools, foreign toys, foreign cars and trucks—indeed, just about everything—which is quickly eroding the world leadership of the United States.

Example claim: Arguing in favor of outsourcing resulting from free trade policies

> Thomas Friedman's claim that the Internet enables everyone to become an entrepreneur is demonstrated by thousands of Americans, including my aunt, who could retire early because she developed an income stream by buying jeans and children's clothes at garage sales and selling them to people around the world on eBay.

Yes, but: Agreeing and disagreeing simultaneously with a source

Incorporating sources is not a matter of simply agreeing or disagreeing with them. Often you will agree with a source up to a point, but you will come to a different conclusion. Or you may agree with the conclusions, but not agree with the reasons put forth.

> I agree with _____ up to a point, but I disagree with the conclusion _____ because _____.

Example claim: Qualifying the argument against outsourcing resulting from free-trade policies

> Lou Dobbs accurately blames our government for giving multinational corporations tax breaks for exporting jobs rather than regulating the loss of

> millions of jobs, but the real problem lies in the enormous appetite of Americans for inexpensive consumer products like HD televisions that is supported by borrowing money from overseas to the point that our dollar has plummeted in value.

Example claim: Qualifying the argument in favor of outsourcing resulting from free-trade policies

> Thomas Friedman's central claim that the world is being "flattened" by globalization and there is not much we can do to stop it is essentially correct, but he neglects the social costs of globalization around the world, where the banner of free trade has been the justification for devastating the environment, destroying workers' rights and the rights of indigenous peoples, and ignoring laws passed by representative governments.

Find Good Reasons

A good reason works because it includes a valid link to your claim. Your readers are almost like a jury that passes judgment on your good reasons. If they accept them and cannot think of other, more compelling good reasons that oppose your position, you will convince them.

Most good reasons derive from mulling things over "reasonably" or, to use the technical term, from logos. *Logos* refers to the logic of what you communicate; in fact, logos is the root of our modern word *logic*. Good reasons are thus commonly associated with logical appeals. Over the years, rhetoricians have devised questions to help speakers and writers find good reasons to support their arguments.

Use the questions in the box on the next two pages to guide you in thinking about the good reasons you can use to develop your argument. Get in the habit of asking these questions every time you are asked to write an argument. If one question does not seem to work for you at first, try it again on your next assignment. If you ask the questions systematically, you will probably have more good reasons than you need for your arguments.

Can you argue by definition?

Probably the most powerful kind of good reason is an **argument from definition.** You can think of a definition as a simple statement: _____ *is a* _____. You use these statements all the time. When you need a course to fulfill your social-science requirement, you look at the list of courses that are defined as social-science courses. You find out that the anthropology class you want to take is one of them. It's just as

QUESTIONS FOR FINDING GOOD REASONS

Can you argue by definition—from "the nature of the thing"?

- Can you argue that while many (most) people think X is a Y, X is better thought of as a Z?

  Most people do not think of humans as an endangered species, but small farmers have been successful in comparing their way of life to an endangered species and thus have extended the definition of an endangered species to include themselves.

- Can you argue that while X is a Y, X differs from other Ys and might be thought of as a Z?

  Colleges and universities are similar to public schools in having education as their primary mission, but unlike public schools, colleges and universities receive only part of their operating costs from tax revenues and therefore, like a business, must generate much of their own revenue.

Can you argue from value?

- Can you grade a few examples of the kind of thing you are evaluating as good, better, and best (or bad and worse)?

  There have been lots of great actors in detective films, but none compare to Humphrey Bogart.

- Can you list the features you use to determine whether something is good or bad and then show why one is most important?

  Coach Powers taught me a great deal about the skills and strategy of playing tennis, but most of all, she taught me that the game is fun.

Can you compare or contrast?

- Can you think of items, events, or situations that are similar or dissimilar to the one you are writing about?

  We should require a foreign language for all students at our college because our main competitor does not have such a requirement.

- Can you distinguish why your subject is different from one usually thought of as similar?

(continued)

QUESTIONS FOR FINDING GOOD REASONS *(continued)*

While poor people are often lumped in with the unemployed and those on welfare, the majority of poor people do work in low-paying jobs.

Can you argue from consequence?

- Can you argue that good things will happen or that bad things will be avoided if a certain course of action is followed?

Eliminating all income tax deductions would save every taxpayer many hours and would create a system of taxation that does not reward people for cheating.

- Can you argue that while there were obvious causes of Y, Y would not have occurred had it not been for X?

A 17-year-old driver is killed when her car skids across the grass median of an interstate highway and collides with oncoming traffic. Even though a slick road and excessive speed were the immediate causes, the driver would be alive today if the median had had a concrete barrier.

- Can you argue for an alternative cause rather than the one many people assume?

Politicians take credit for reducing the violent crime rate because of "get-tough" police policies, but in fact, the rate of violent crime is decreasing because more people are working.

Can you counter objections to your position?

- Can you think of the most likely objections to your claim and turn them into your own good reasons?

High school administrators might object to requiring computer literacy because of cost, but schools can now lease computers and put them on a statewide system at a cost less than they now pay for textbooks.

- Can the reverse, or opposite, of an opposing claim be argued?

A proposed expressway through a city is supposed to help traffic, but it also could make traffic worse by encouraging more people to drive to the city.

important when _____ *is not a* _____. Suppose you are taking College Algebra, which is a math course taught by the math department, yet it doesn't count for the math requirement. The reason it doesn't count is because College Algebra is not defined as a college-level math class. So you have to enroll next semester in Calculus I.

Many definitions are not nearly as clear-cut as the math requirement. If you want to argue that figure skaters are athletes, you will need to define what an athlete is. You start thinking. An athlete competes in an activity, but that definition alone is too broad, since many competitions do not require physical activity. Thus, an athlete must participate in a competitive physical activity and must train for it. But that definition is still not quite narrow enough, because soldiers also train for competitive physical activity. You decide to add that the activity must be a sport and that it must require special competence and precision. Your **because clause** turns out as follows: *Figure skaters are athletes because true athletes train for and compete in physical sporting competitions that require special competence and precision.*

If you can get your audience to accept your definitions, you've gone a long way toward convincing them of the validity of your claim. That is why the most controversial issues in our culture—abortion, affirmative action, gay rights, pornography, women's rights, privacy rights, gun control, the death penalty—are argued from definition. Is abortion a crime or a medical procedure? Is pornography protected by the First Amendment, or is it a violation of women's rights? Is the death penalty just or cruel and inhuman? You can see from these examples that definitions often rely on deeply held beliefs.

Because people have strong beliefs about controversial issues, they often don't care about the practical consequences. Arguing that it is much cheaper to execute prisoners who have been convicted of first-degree murder than to keep them in prison for life does not convince those who believe that it is morally wrong to kill. (See Chapter 8.)

Can you argue from value?

A special kind of argument from definition, one that often implies consequences, is the **argument from value**. You can support your claim with a because clause (or several of them) that includes a sense of evaluation. Arguments from value follow from claims like _____ *is a good* _____, or _____ *is not a good* _____.

Evaluation arguments usually proceed from the presentation of certain criteria. These criteria come from the definitions of good and bad, of poor and not so poor, that prevail in a given case. A great burger fulfills certain criteria; so does an outstanding movie, an excellent class, or the best laptop in your price range. Sometimes the criteria are straightforward, as in the burger example. A great burger has to have tasty meat—tender and without gristle, fresh, never frozen—a fresh bun that is the right size, and your favorite condiments.

But if you are buying a laptop computer and want to play the latest games along with your school tasks, you need to do some homework. For realistic graphics the best laptop will have a fast chip, preferably a dual core system. It will be equipped with a wireless modem, so you have access to the Internet at wireless hot spots. The battery life should be at least two hours, the hard drive should be large enough for your needs, the construction should be sturdy, and the warranty should cover the computer for at least three years.

The keys for evaluation arguments are finding the appropriate criteria and convincing your readers that those criteria are the right criteria (see Chapter 10).

Can you compare or contrast?

Evaluation arguments can generate comparisons often enough. But even if they don't generate comparisons, your argument might profit if you get in the habit of thinking in comparative terms—in terms of what things are like or unlike the topic you are discussing. **Claims of comparisons** and **claims of contrast** take the form _____ *is like* _____ or _____ *is not like* _____. If you are having trouble coming up with good reasons, think of comparisons that will help your readers agree with you.

A particular kind of comparison is an analogy. An **analogy** is an extended comparison—one that is developed over several sentences or paragraphs for explanatory or persuasive purposes. Analogies take different forms. A historical analogy compares something that is going on now with a similar case in the past. One of the most frequently used historical analogies is a comparison of a current situation in which one country attacks or threatens another with Germany's seizing Czechoslovakia in 1938 and then invading Poland in 1939, which started World War II. The difficulty with this analogy is that circumstances today are not the same as those in 1939, and it is easy to point out how the analogy fails.

Other analogies make literal comparisons. A literal analogy is a comparison between current situations in which you argue that what is true or works in one situation should be true or should work in another. Most advanced nations provide basic health care to all their citizens either free or at minimal charge. All citizens of Canada are covered for basic medical procedures by the same comprehensive health care system, which is free for both rich and poor. (Canadians pay individually for drugs and adult dental care.) Even though citizens of the United States pay the most expensive health care bills on the planet, Canadians are healthier and live longer than their southern neighbors.

The Canadian analogy has failed to convince members of the U.S. Congress to vote for a similar system in the United States. Opponents of adopting the Canadian system in the United States argue that Canadians are often put on long waiting lists for care, and they lack choice of providers. These opponents believe that the best care can be obtained for the lowest cost if health care is treated like any other service and consumers decide what they are willing to pay. Comparisons can always work both ways.

Analogies are especially valuable when you are trying to explain a concept to a willing listener or reader, but analogies are far from foolproof if the reader does not agree with you from the outset. Using an analogy can be risky if the entire argument depends on the reader's accepting it.

Can you argue from consequence?

Another powerful source of good reasons comes from considering the possible consequences of your position: Can you sketch out the good things that will follow from your position? Can you establish that certain bad things will be avoided if your position is adopted? If so, you will have other good reasons to use.

Causal arguments take the basic form of _____ causes _____ (or _____ does not cause _____). Very often, causal arguments are more complicated, taking the form _____ causes _____ which, in turn, causes _____ and so on. In Chapter 1 we describe how *Silent Spring* makes powerful arguments from consequence. Rachel Carson's primary claim is that *DDT should not be sprayed on a massive scale because it will poison animals and people.* The key to her argument is the causal chain that explains how animals and people are poisoned. Carson describes how nothing exists alone in nature. When a potato field is sprayed with DDT, some of that poison is absorbed by the skin of the potatoes and some washes into the groundwater, where it contaminates drinking water. Other poisonous residue is absorbed into streams, where it is ingested by insect larvae, which in turn are eaten by fish. Fish are eaten by other fish, which are then eaten by waterfowl and people. At each stage, the poisons become more concentrated. (See Chapter 9.)

Proposal arguments are future-oriented arguments from consequence. In a proposal argument, you cannot stop with naming good reasons; you also have to show that these consequences would follow from the idea or course of action that you are arguing. For example, if you are proposing designated lanes for bicycles on the streets of your city, you must argue that they will encourage more people to ride bicycles to work and school, reducing air pollution and traffic congestion for everyone. (See Chapter 13.)

Can you counter objections to your position?

Another good way to find convincing good reasons is to think about possible objections to your position. If you can imagine how your audience might counter or respond to your argument, you will probably include in your argument precisely the points that will address your readers' particular needs and objections. If you are successful, your readers will be convinced that you are right. You've no doubt had the experience of mentally saying to a writer in the course of your reading, "Yeah, but what about this other idea?"—only to have the writer address precisely this objection.

You can impress your readers if you've thought about why anyone would oppose your position and exactly how that opposition would be expressed. If you are writing a proposal argument for a computer literacy requirement for all high school graduates, you might think about why anyone would object, since computers are becoming increasingly important to our jobs and lives. What will the practical objections be? What about philosophical ones? Why hasn't such a requirement been put in place already? By asking such questions in your own arguments, you are likely to develop robust because clauses.

Sometimes, writers pose rhetorical questions such as "You might say, 'But won't paying for computers for all students make my taxes go up?'" Stating objections explicitly can be effective if you make the objections as those of a reasonable person with an alternative point of view. But if the objections you state are ridiculous ones, then you risk being accused of setting up a **straw man**—that is, making the position opposing your own so simplistic that no one would likely identify with it. (See Chapter 12.)

Find Evidence to Support Good Reasons

Good reasons are essential ingredients of good arguments, but they don't do the job alone. You must support or verify good reasons with evidence. **Evidence** consists of hard data, examples, personal experiences, episodes, or tabulations of episodes (known as statistics) that are seen as relevant to the good reasons you are putting forward. Thus, a writer of arguments puts forward not only claims and good reasons but also evidence that those good reasons are true.

How much supporting evidence should you supply? How much evidence is enough? As is usual in the case of rhetoric, the best answer is, "It depends." If a reader is likely to find one of your good reasons hard to believe, then you should be aggressive in offering support. You should present detailed evidence in a patient and painstaking way. As one presenting an argument, you have a responsibility not just to *state* a case but to *make* a case with evidence. Arguments that are unsuccessful tend to fail not because of a shortage of good reasons; more often, they fail because the reader doesn't agree that there is enough evidence to support the good reason that is being presented.

If your good reason isn't especially controversial, you probably should not belabor it. Think of your own experiences as a reader. How often do you recall saying to yourself, as you read a passage or listened to a speaker, "OK! OK! I get the point! Don't keep piling up all of this evidence for me because I don't want it or need it." However, such a reaction is rare, isn't it? By contrast, how often do you recall muttering under your breath, "How can you say that? What evidence do you have to back it up?" When in doubt, err on the side of offering too much evidence. It's an error that is seldom made and not often criticized.

When a writer doesn't provide satisfactory evidence to support a *because* clause, readers might feel that there has been a failure in the reasoning process. In fact, in your previous courses in writing and speaking, you may have learned about various fallacies associated with faulty arguments (pages 27–28).

Strictly speaking, there is nothing false about these so-called logical fallacies. The fallacies most often refer to failures in providing evidence; when you don't provide enough good evidence to convince your audience, you might be accused of committing a fallacy in reasoning. You will usually avoid such accusations if the evidence that you cite is both *relevant* and *sufficient.*

Relevance refers to the appropriateness of the evidence to the case at hand. Some kinds of evidence are seen as more relevant than others for particular audiences. On the one hand, in science and industry, personal testimony is seen as having limited relevance, while experimental procedures and controlled observations have far more credibility. Compare someone who defends the use of a particular piece of computer software because "it worked for me" with someone who defends it because "according to a journal article published last month, 84 percent of the users of the software were satisfied or very satisfied with it." On the other hand, in writing to the general public on controversial issues such as gun control, personal experience is often considered more relevant than other kinds of data.

Sufficiency refers to the amount of evidence cited. Sometimes a single piece of evidence or a single instance will carry the day if it is especially compelling in some way—if it represents the situation well or makes a point that isn't particularly controversial. More often, people expect more than one piece of evidence if they are to be convinced of something. Convincing readers that they should approve a statewide computer literacy requirement for all high school graduates will require much more evidence than the story of a single graduate who succeeded with her computer skills. You will likely need statistical evidence for such a broad proposal.

If you anticipate that your audience might not accept your evidence, face the situation squarely. First, think carefully about the argument you are presenting. If you cannot cite adequate evidence for your assertions, perhaps those assertions must be modified or qualified in some way. If you remain convinced of your assertions, then think about doing more research to come up with additional evidence.

4

Drafting and Revising Arguments

People frequently revise things that they own. What objects have you revised?

Writing is not an assembly-line process of finding ideas, writing a draft, and revising, editing, and proofreading the draft, all in that order. While you write and revise you will often think of additional reasons to support your position. Likely you will work through your paper or project in multiple drafts, strengthening your content, organization, and readability in each successive draft.

State and Evaluate Your Thesis

Once you have identified a topic and have a good sense of how to develop it, the next critical step is to write a **working thesis.** Your **thesis** states your main claim. Much writing that you will do in college and later in your career will require an explicit thesis, usually placed near the beginning.

Focusing your thesis

The thesis can make or break your paper. If the thesis is too broad, you cannot do justice to the argument. Who wouldn't wish for fewer traffic accidents, better medical care, more effective schools, or a cleaner environment? Simple solutions for these complex problems are unlikely.

Stating something that is obvious to everyone isn't an arguable thesis. Don't settle for easy answers. When a topic is too broad, a predictable thesis often results. Narrow your focus and concentrate on the areas where you have the most questions. Those are likely the areas where your readers will have the most questions too.

The opposite problem is less common: a thesis that is too narrow. If your thesis simply states a commonly known fact, then it is too narrow. For example, the growth rate of the population in the United States has doubled since 1970 because of increased immigration. The U.S. Census Bureau provides reasonably accurate statistical information, so this claim is not arguable. But the policies that allow increased immigration and the effects of a larger population—more crowding and higher costs of health care, education, and transportation—are arguable.

Not arguable: The population of the United States grew faster in the 1990s than in any previous decade because Congress increased the rate of legal immigration and the government stopped enforcing most laws against illegal immigration in the interior of the country.

Arguable: Allowing a high rate of immigration helps the United States deal with the problems of an increasingly aging society and helps provide funding for millions of Social Security recipients.

Arguable: The increase in the number of visas to foreign workers in technology industries is the major cause of unemployment in those industries.

Evaluating your thesis

Once you have a working thesis, ask these questions:

- Is it arguable?
- Is it specific?
- Is it manageable given your length and time requirements?
- Is it interesting to your intended readers?

Example 1

Sample thesis

> We should take action to resolve the serious traffic problem in our city.

Is it arguable? The thesis is arguable, but it lacks a focus.

Is it specific? The thesis is too broad.

Is it manageable? Transportation is a complex issue. New highways and rail systems are expensive and take many years to build. Furthermore, citizens don't want new roads running through their neighborhoods.

Is it interesting? The topic has the potential to be interesting if the writer can propose a specific solution to a problem that everyone in the city recognizes.

When a thesis is too broad, it needs to be revised to address a specific aspect of an issue. Make the big topic smaller.

Revised thesis

> The existing freight railway that runs through the center of the city should be converted to a passenger railway because this is the cheapest and quickest way to decrease traffic congestion downtown.

Example 2

Sample thesis

> Over 60 percent of Americans play computer games on a regular basis.

Is it arguable? The thesis states a commonly acknowledged fact. It is not arguable.

Is it specific? The thesis is too narrow.

Is it manageable? A known fact is stated in the thesis, so there is little to research. Several surveys report this finding.

Is it interesting? The popularity of video games is well established. Nearly everyone is aware of the trend.

There's nothing original or interesting about stating that Americans love computer games. Think about what is controversial. One debatable topic is how computer games affect children.

Revised thesis

> Computer games are valuable because they improve children's visual attention skills, literacy skills, and computer literacy skills.

Think About Your Readers

Thinking about your readers doesn't mean telling them what they might want to hear. Instead, imagine yourself in a dialogue with your readers. What questions will they likely have? How might you address any potential objections?

Understanding what your readers know—and do not know

Your readers' knowledge of your subject is critical to the success of your argument. If they are not familiar with the background information, they probably won't understand your argument fully. If you know that your readers will be unfamiliar with your subject, you have to supply background information before attempting to convince them of your position. A good tactic is to tie your new information to what your readers already know. Comparisons and analogies can be very helpful in linking old and new information.

Finding Good Reasons
SHOULD DRIVING WHILE TALKING BE BANNED?

In a movement to improve driving safety, four U.S. states and the District of Columbia have passed laws banning the use of handheld cell phones while driving except for emergency workers and people making 911 calls. Several states are considering similar legislation, while others are considering banning cell phones only for drivers aged 18 and younger.

Proponents of the ban point to a National Highway Traffic Safety Administration study, reporting that approximately 25 to 30 percent of motor vehicle crashes—about 1.2 million accidents each year—are caused by driver distraction. Opponents of the ban argue that anything that distracts the driver—eating potato chips, talking with passengers, spilled coffee—can cause an accident. The answer, they say, is driver education.

Write about it

1. Write a thesis arguing in support of a ban on cell phones while driving, against a ban, or in support of a more limited position such as banning cell-phone use for drivers 18 and under.

2. Think about the audience that would likely oppose your position. For example, if you support a ban on talking while driving, think about the likely responses of high school students, salespeople who spend much of their workdays driving from place to place, and workers who receive assignments by phone. What good reasons would convince readers who hold an opposing view?

3. What reasons would people who oppose your position likely offer in response? What counterarguments could you give to answer these objections?

Understanding your readers' attitudes toward you

To get your readers to take you seriously, you must convince them that they can trust you. You need to get them to see you as

- **Concerned:** Readers want you to be committed to your subject. They also expect you to be concerned about them. After all, if you don't care about them, why should they read what you write?
- **Well informed:** Many people ramble on about any subject without knowing anything about it. College writing requires that you do your homework on a subject.
- **Fair:** Many writers look at only one side of an issue. Readers respect objectivity and an unbiased approach.
- **Ethical:** Many writers use only the facts that support their positions and often distort facts and sources. Critical readers often notice what is being left out. Don't try to conceal what doesn't support your position.

Understanding your readers' attitudes toward your subject

People have prior attitudes about controversial issues. You must take these attitudes into consideration as you write or speak. Imagine, for instance, that you are preparing an argument for a guest editorial in your college newspaper. You are advocating that your state government should provide parents with choices between public and private schools. You plan to argue that the tax dollars that now automatically go to public schools should go to private schools if parents so choose. You have evidence that the sophomore-to-senior dropout rate in private schools is less than half the rate in public schools. Furthermore, students from private schools attend college at nearly twice the rate of public-school graduates. You intend to argue that one of the reasons private schools are more successful is that they spend more money on instruction and less on administration. And you believe that school choice speaks to the American desire for personal freedom.

Not everyone on your campus will agree with your position. How might the faculty at your college or university feel about this issue? How about the administrators, the staff, other students, and interested community members who read the student newspaper? What are their attitudes toward public funding of private schools? How are you going to deal with the objection that many students in private schools do better in school because they come from more affluent families?

Even when you write about a much less controversial subject, you must think carefully about your audience's attitudes toward what you have to say or to write. Sometimes your audience may share your attitudes; other times, your audience may be neutral. At still other times, your audience will have attitudes that differ sharply from your own. Anticipate these various attitudes and act accordingly.

If these attitudes are different from yours, you will have to work hard to counter them without insulting your audience.

Organize Your Argument

Asking a series of questions can generate a list of good reasons, but even if you have plenty, you still have to decide which ones to use and in what order to present them. Thinking about your readers' knowledge, attitudes, and values will help you to decide which reasons to present to your audience.

Writing plans often take the form of outlines, either formal outlines or working outlines. A **formal outline** typically begins with the thesis statement, which anchors the entire outline.

Managing the Risks of Nanotechnology While Reaping the Rewards

THESIS: The revolutionary potential of nanotechnology has arrived in an explosion of consumer products, yet our federal government has yet to recognize the potential risks or to fund research to reduce those risks.

I. Nanotechnology now is in many consumer products.
   A. The promise of nanotechnology to revolutionize medicine, energy production, and communication is years in the future, but consumer products are here now.
   B. Nanotechnology is now in clothing, food, sports equipment, medicines, electronics, and cars.
   C. Experts predict that 15 percent of manufactured products worldwide will contain nanotechnology in 2014.
   D. The question that hasn't been asked: Is nanotechnology safe?
II. Americans have little awareness of nanotechnology.
   A. Companies have stopped mentioning and advertising nanotechnology.
   B. Companies and the insurance industry paid $250 billion in asbestos claims in the United States alone.
   C. Companies fear exposure to lawsuits if nanotechnology is found to be toxic.

A **working outline** is a sketch of how you will arrange the major sections.

Managing the Risks of Nanotechnology While Reaping the Rewards

SECTION 1: Begin by defining nanotechnology—manipulating particles between 1 and 100 nanometers (nanometer is a billionth of a meter). Describe the rapid spread of nanotechnology in consumer products including clothing, food, sports equipment, medicines, electronics, and cars. State projection of 15 percent of global manufactured goods containing nanotechnology in 2014.

SECTION 2: Most Americans know nothing about nanotechnology. Companies have stopped advertising that their products contain nanotechnology because of fear of potential lawsuits. Asbestos, once thought safe, now is known to be toxic and has cost companies $250 billion in lawsuits in the United States alone.

SECTION 3: Almost no research has been done on the safety of nanotechnology, only $11 million in federal research. No testing is required for new products because the materials are common, but materials behave differently at nano-scale (example—aluminum normally inert but combustible at nano-scale).

SECTION 4: Nanoparticles are highly mobile and can cross the blood-brain barrier and through the placenta. They are toxic in brains of fish and may collect in lungs.

SECTION 5: Urge that the federal government develop a master plan for identifying and reducing potential risks of nanotechnology and provide sufficient funding to carry out the plan.

Write an Engaging Title and Introduction

Many writers don't think much about titles, but they are very important. A good title makes the reader want to see what you have to say. Be specific as you can in your title, and if possible, suggest your stance.

Get off to a fast start in your introduction. Convince your reader to keep reading. Cut to the chase. Think about how you can get your readers interested. Consider using one of the following.

- State your thesis concisely.
- Provide a hard hitting fact.
- Ask a question.

- Give a vivid description of a problem.
- Discuss a contradiction or paradox.
- Describe a scenario.

Managing the Risks of Nanotechnology While Reaping the Rewards

The revolutionary potential of nanotechnology for medicine, energy production, and communication is now at the research and development stage, but the future has arrived in consumer products. Nanotechnology has given us products we hardly could have imagined just a few years ago: socks that never stink; pants that repel water yet keep you cool; eyeglasses that won't scratch; "smart" foods that add nutrition and reduce cholesterol; DVDs that are incredibly lifelike; bandages that speed healing; tennis balls that last longer; golf balls that fly straighter; pharmaceuticals that selectively deliver drugs; various digital devices like palm pilots, digital cameras, and cell phones that have longer battery lives and more vivid displays; and cars that are lighter, stronger, and more fuel efficient. These miracle products are now possible because scientists have learned how to manipulate nano-scale particles from 1-100 nanometers (a nanometer is a billionth of a meter; a human hair is about 100,000 nanometers in width). Experts estimate that 15 percent of all consumer products will contain nanotechnology by 2014. In the rush to create new consumer products, however, one question has not been asked: Is nanotechnology safe for those who use the products and the workers who are exposed to nanoparticles daily?

Write a Strong Conclusion

Restating your thesis usually isn't the best way to finish a paper. Conclusions that offer only a summary bore readers. The worst endings say something like "in my paper I've said this." Effective conclusions are interesting and provocative, leaving readers with something to think about. Give your readers something to take away besides a straight summary. Try one of these approaches.

- Issue a call to action.
- Discuss the implications.
- Make recommendations.
- Project into the future.
- Tell an anecdote that illustrates a key point.

> The potential risks of nanotechnology are reasonably well known. Among the more obvious research questions are the following:
>
> - How hazardous are nanoparticles for workers who have daily exposure?
> - What happens to nanoparticles when they are poured down the drain and eventually enter streams, lakes, and oceans?
> - How readily do nanoparticles penetrate the skin?
> - What happens when nanoparticles enter the brain?
> - What effect do airborne nanoparticles have on the lungs?
>
> Nanotechnology promises untold benefits beyond consumer goods in the fields of medicine, energy production, and communication, but these benefits can be realized only if nanotechnology is safe. The federal government is currently spending over $1 billion each year on nanotechnology research, but it spent only $11 million on risk research in 2007. The federal government needs to create a master plan for risk research and to increase spending at least tenfold to ensure sufficient funding to carry out the plan.

When you finish your conclusion, read your introduction again. The main claim in your conclusion should be closely related to the main subject, question, or claim in your introduction. If they do not match, revise the subject, question, or claim in the introduction to match the conclusion. Your thinking evolves and develops as you write, and often your introduction needs some adjusting if you wrote it first.

Evaluate Your Draft

To review and evaluate your draft, pretend you are someone who is either uninformed about your subject or informed but likely to disagree with you. If possible, think of an actual person and imagine yourself as that person.

Read your draft aloud all the way through. When you read aloud, you often hear clunky phrases and catch errors, but just put checks in the margins so you can return to them later. You don't want to get bogged down with the little stuff. What you are after in this stage is an overall sense of how well you accomplished what you set out to do.

Use the questions in the box on the next two pages to evaluate your draft. Note any places where you might make improvements. When you finish, make a list of your goals for the revision. You may have to write another draft before you move to the next stage.

CHECKLIST FOR EVALUATING YOUR DRAFT

Does your paper or project meet the assignment?

- Look again at your assignment, especially at key words such as *define, analyze causes, evaluate,* and *propose.* Does your paper or project do what the assignment requires? If not, how can you change it?

- Look again at the assignment for specific guidelines including length, format, and amount of research. Does your work meet these guidelines?

Can you better focus your thesis and your supporting reasons?

- You may have started out with a large topic and ended up writing about one aspect of it. Can you make your thesis even more precise?

- Can you find the exact location where you link each reason to your thesis?

Are your main points adequately developed?

- Can you explain your reasons in more detail?

- Can you add evidence to better support your main points?

- Do you provide enough background on your topic?

Is your organization effective?

- Is the order of your main points clear? (You may want to make a quick outline of your draft if you have not done so already.)

- Are there any abrupt shifts or gaps?

- Are there sections or paragraphs that should be rearranged?

Are your key terms adequately defined?

- What are your key terms?

- Can you define these terms more precisely?

Do you consider other points of view?

- Where do you acknowledge views besides your own? If you don't acknowledge other views, where can you add them?

- How can you make your discussion of opposing views more acceptable to readers who hold those views?

(continued)

CHECKLIST FOR EVALUATING YOUR DRAFT *(continued)*

Do you represent yourself effectively?

- Forget for the moment that you wrote what you are reading. What is your impression of the writer?

- Is the tone of the writing appropriate for the subject?

Can you improve your title and introduction?

- Can you make your title more specific and indicate your stance?

- Can you think of a way to start faster and to get your readers interested in what you have to say?

Can you improve your conclusion?

- Can you think of an example that sums up your position?

- Can you discuss an implication of your argument that will make your readers think more about the subject?

- If you are writing a proposal, can you end with a call for action?

Can you improve your visual presentation?

- Is the type style easy to read and consistent?

- Would headings and subheadings help to mark the major sections of your argument?

- If you have statistical data, do you use charts?

- Would illustrations, maps, or other graphics help to explain your main points?

Respond to the Writing of Others

Your instructor may ask you to respond to the drafts of your classmates. Responding to other people's writing requires the same careful attention you give to your own draft. To write a helpful response, you should go through the draft more than once.

First reading

Read at your normal rate the first time through without stopping. When you finish you should have a clear sense of what the writer is trying to accomplish. Try writing the following:

- **Main idea and purpose:** Write a sentence that summarizes what you think is the writer's main idea in the draft.
- **Purpose:** Write a sentence that states what you think the writer is trying to accomplish in the draft.

Second reading

In your second reading, you should be most concerned with the content, organization, and completeness of the draft. Make notes in pencil as you read.

You can get one-on-one help in developing your ideas, focusing your topic, and revising your paper or project at your writing center.

- **Introduction:** Does the writer's first paragraph effectively introduce the topic and engage your interest?
- **Thesis:** What exactly is the writer's thesis? Is it clear? Note in the margin where you think the thesis is located.
- **Focus:** Does the writer maintain focus on the thesis? Note any places where the writer seems to wander off to another topic.
- **Organization:** Are the sections and paragraphs arranged effectively? Do any paragraphs seem to be out of place? Can you suggest a better order for the paragraphs?
- **Completeness:** Are there sections or paragraphs that lack key information or adequate development? Where do you want to know more?
- **Sources:** Are outside sources cited accurately? Are quotations used correctly and worked into the fabric of the draft?

Third reading

In your third reading, turn your attention to matters of audience, style, and tone.

- **Audience:** Who are the writer's intended readers? What does the writer assume the audience knows and believes?
- **Style:** Is the writer's style engaging? How would you describe the writer's voice?
- **Tone:** Is the tone appropriate for the writer's purpose and audience? Is the tone consistent throughout the draft? Are there places where another word or phrase might work better?

When you have finished the third reading, write a short paragraph on each bulleted item above. Refer to specific paragraphs in the draft by number. Then end by answering these two questions:

- What does the writer do especially well in the draft?
- What one or two things would most improve the draft in a revision?

Edit and proofread carefully

When you finish revising, you are ready for one final careful reading with the goals of improving your style and eliminating errors.

Edit for style

- **Check connections between sentences and paragraphs.** Notice how your sentences flow within each paragraph and from paragraph to paragraph. If you need to signal the relationship from one sentence or paragraph to the next, use a transitional word or phrase (e.g., *in addition, moreover, similarly, however, nevertheless*).
- **Check your sentences.** Often you will pick up problems with individual sentences by reading aloud. If you notice that a sentence doesn't sound right, think about how you might rephrase it. If a sentence seems too long, consider breaking it into two or more sentences. If you notice a string of short sentences that sound choppy, consider combining them.
- **Eliminate wordiness.** Look for wordy expressions such as *because of the fact that* and *at this point in time*, which can easily be shortened to *because* and *now*. Reduce unnecessary repetition such as *attractive in appearance* or *visible to the eye* to *attractive* and *visible*. Remove unnecessary words like *very, really*, and *totally*. See how many words you can remove without losing the meaning.

■ **Use active verbs.** Make your style more lively by replacing forms of *be* (*is, are, was, were*) or verbs ending in *–ing* with active verbs. Sentences that begin with *There is (are)* and *It is* can often be rewritten with active verbs.

Proofread carefully

In your final pass through your text, eliminate as many errors as you can. To become an effective proofreader, you have to learn to slow down. Some writers find that moving from word to word with a pencil slows them down enough to find errors. Others read backwards to force them to concentrate on each word.

■ **Know what your spelling checker can and can't do.** Spelling checkers are the greatest invention since peanut butter. They turn up many typos and misspellings that are hard to catch. But spelling checkers do not catch wrong words (*to much for too much*), missing endings (*three dog*), and other similar errors.

■ **Check for grammar and punctuation.** Nothing hurts your credibility more than leaving errors in what you write. Many job application letters get tossed in the reject pile because of a single, glaring error. Readers probably shouldn't make such harsh judgments when they find errors, but often they do. Keep a grammar handbook beside your computer, and use it when you are uncertain about what is correct.

PART 2

Analyzing Arguments

5

Analyzing Written Arguments

"Well, it all depends. Where are these huddled masses coming from?"

What makes a cartoon funny? Is it the drawing, the caption, the readers' knowledge of the context, or all three?

What Is Rhetorical Analysis?

To many people, the term *rhetoric* means speech or writing that is highly ornamental or deceptive or manipulative. You might hear someone say, "That politician is just using a bunch of rhetoric" or "The rhetoric of that advertisement is very deceptive." But the term *rhetoric* is also used in a positive or neutral sense to describe human communication; for instance, *Silent Spring* is one of the most influential pieces of environmental rhetoric ever written. As a subject of study, rhetoric is usually associated with effective communication, following Aristotle's classic definition of rhetoric as "the art of finding in any given case the available means of persuasion."

Rhetoric is not just a means of *producing* effective communication but also a way of *understanding* communication. The two aspects mutually support one another: becoming a better writer makes you a better interpreter, and becoming a better interpreter makes you a better writer.

Rhetorical analysis can be defined as an effort to understand how people attempt to influence others through language and more broadly every kind of important symbolic action—not only speeches, articles, and books, but also architecture, movies, television shows, memorials, Web sites, advertisements, photos and other images, dance, and popular songs. It might be helpful to think of rhetorical analysis as the kind of critical reading discussed in Chapter 2. Critical reading—rhetorical analysis, that is—involves studying carefully any kind of persuasive action in order to understand it better and to appreciate the tactics involved.

Build a Rhetorical Analysis

Rhetorical analysis examines how an idea is shaped and presented to an audience in a particular form for a specific purpose. There are many approaches to rhetorical analysis and no one "correct" way to do it. Generally, though, approaches to rhetorical analysis can be placed between two broad extremes—not mutually exclusive categories but extremes at the ends of a continuum.

At one end of the continuum are analyses that concentrate more on texts than on contexts. They typically use rhetorical concepts to analyze the features of texts. Let's call this approach **textual analysis.** At the other extreme are approaches that emphasize **context** over text. These focus on reconstructing the cultural environment, or context, that existed when a particular rhetorical event took place. That reconstruction provides clues about the persuasive tactics and appeals. Those who undertake **contextual analysis**—as we'll call this second approach—regard particular rhetorical acts as parts of larger communicative chains, or "conversations."

Now let's examine these two approaches in detail.

The statue of Castor stands at the entrance of the Piazza del Campidoglio in Rome. A textual analysis focuses on the statue itself. The size and realism of the statue makes it a masterpiece of classical Roman sculpture.

Analyze the Rhetorical Features

Just as expert teachers in every field of endeavor—from baseball to biology—devise vocabularies to facilitate specialized study, rhetoricians too have developed a set of key concepts to describe rhetorical activities. A fundamental concept in rhetoric is audience. But there are many others. Classical rhetoricians in the tradition of Aristotle, Quintilian, and Cicero developed a range of terms around what they called the canons of rhetoric in order to describe some of the actions of communicators: *inventio* (invention—the finding or creation of information for persuasive acts, and the planning of strategies), *dispostio* (arrangement), *elocutio* (style), *memoria* (the recollection of rhetorical resources that one might call upon, as well as the memorization of what has been invented and arranged), and *pronuntiatio* (delivery). These five canons generally describe the actions of any persuader, from preliminary planning to final delivery.

A contextual analysis focuses on the surroundings and history of the statue. According to legend, Castor (left of staircase) and his twin brother Pollux (right of staircase), the mythical sons of Leda, assisted Romans in an early battle. Romans built a large temple in the Forum to honor them. The statues were discovered in the sixteenth century and in 1583 were brought to stand at the top of the Cordonata, a staircase designed by Michelangelo as part of a renovation of the Piazza del Campidoglio commissioned by Pope Paul III Farnese in 1536.

Over the years, as written discourse gained in prestige against oral discourse, four canons (excepting *memoria*) led to the development of concepts and terms useful for rhetorical analysis. Terms like *ethos, pathos,* and *logos,* all associated with invention, account for features of texts related to the trustworthiness and credibility of the writer or speaker (ethos), for the persuasive good reasons in an argument that derive from a community's mostly deeply held values (pathos), and for the good reasons that emerge from intellectual reasoning (logos). Fundamental to the classical approach to rhetoric is the concept of *decorum,* or "appropriateness": Everything within a persuasive act can be understood as reflecting a central rhetorical goal that governs consistent choices according to occasion and audience.

An example will make textual rhetorical analysis clearer. If you have not done so already, read "The Border Patrol State" by Leslie Marmon Silko in Chapter 11 (pp. 182–187). In the pages that follow, we use the concepts of classical rhetoric to better understand this essay.

Silko's purpose and argument

What is the purpose of Silko's essay? She wrote the essay well over a decade ago, but you probably find it to be interesting and readable still because it concerns the perennial American issue of civil rights. In this case, Silko takes issue with practices associated with the Border Patrol of the Immigration and Naturalization Service (INS). She feels they are reenacting the long subjugation of native peoples by the white majority. Silko proposes that the power of the Border Patrol be sharply reduced so that the exploitation of her people might be curtailed, and she supports that thesis with an essay that describes and condemns the Border Patrol's tactics.

Essentially Silko's argument comes down to two good reasons: the Border Patrol must be reformed because "the Immigration and Naturalization Service and Border Patrol have implemented policies that interfere with the rights of U.S. citizens to travel freely within our borders" (para. 8), and because efforts to restrict immigration are ineffective and doomed to fail ("It is no use; borders haven't worked, and they won't work," para. 16). Silko's essay amounts to an evaluation of the Border Patrol's activities, an evaluation that finds those activities lacking on ethical and practical grounds.

Silko's use of logos, pathos, and ethos

Logos

When Silko condemns the unethical actions of the Border Patrol early in the essay, she combines ample evidence with other appeals, including our sense of what is legal, constitutional, fair, and honorable. When she explains the futility of trying to stop immigration, she appeals again to her readers' reasonableness: Constructing walls across the border with Mexico is foolish because "border entrepreneurs have already used blowtorches to cut passageways through the fence" (para. 15), because "a mass migration is already under way" (para. 16), and because "The Americas are Indian country, and the 'Indian problem' is not about to go away" (para. 17).

The bulk of "The Border Patrol State" amounts to an argument by example. The single case—Silko's personal experience, as a Native American, with the border police—stands for many such cases. This case study persuades as other case studies and narratives do—by serving as a representative example that stands for the treatment of many Native Americans.

good reasons from intellectual reasoning

Pathos

The logical appeals in Silko's essay are reinforced by her emotional appeals.

- The Border Patrol is constructing an "Iron Curtain" that is as destructive of human rights as the Iron Curtain that the Soviet Union constructed around Eastern Europe after World War II (para. 15).
- "Proud" and "patriotic" Native Americans are being harassed: "old Bill Pratt used to ride his horse 300 miles overland . . . every summer to work as a fire lookout" (para. 1).
- Border police terrify American citizens in a way that is chillingly reminiscent of "the report of Argentine police and military officers who became addicted to interrogation, torture, and murder" (paras. 3–5).

The essay's most emotional moment may be when Silko describes how the Border Patrol dog, trained to find illegal drugs and other contraband, including human contraband, seems to sympathize with her and those she is championing: "I saw immediately from the expression in her eyes that the dog hated them" (para. 6); "The dog refused to accuse us: She had an innate dignity that did not permit her to serve the murderous impulses of those men" (para. 7). Clearly the good reasons in "The Border Patrol State" appeal in a mutually supportive way to both the reason and the emotions of Silko's audience. She appeals to the whole person.

Ethos

Why do we take Silko's word about the stories she tells? It is because she establishes her *ethos*, or trustworthiness, early in the essay. Silko reminds her readers that she is a respected, published author who has been on a book tour to publicize her novel *Almanac of the Dead* (para. 3). She buttresses her trustworthiness in other ways too:

- She quotes widely, if unobtrusively, from books and reports to establish that she has studied the issues thoroughly. Note how much she displays her knowledge of INS policies in paragraph 9, for instance.
- She tells not only of her own encounters with the border police (experiences that are a source of great credibility), but also of the encounters of others whom she lists, name after careful name, in order that we might trust her account.
- She demonstrates knowledge of history and geography.
- She connects herself to America generally by linking herself to traditional American values such as freedom (para. 1), ethnic pride, tolerance, and even a love of dogs.

This essay, because of its anti-authoritarian strain, might seem to display politically progressive attitudes at times, but overall, Silko comes off as hardworking, honest, educated, even patriotic. And definitely credible.

Silko's arrangement

Silko arranges her essay appropriately as well. In general the essay follows a traditional pattern. She begins with a long concrete introductory story that hooks the reader and leads to her thesis in paragraph 8. Next, in the body of her essay, she supports her thesis by evaluating the unethical nature of INS policies. She cites their violation of constitutional protections, their similarity to tactics used in nations that are notorious for violating the rights of citizens, and their fundamental immorality. She also emphasizes how those policies are racist in nature (paras. 11–13).

After completing her moral evaluation of INS policy, she turns to the practical difficulties of halting immigration in paragraph 14. The North American Free Trade Agreement (NAFTA) permits the free flow of goods, and even drugs are impossible to stop, so how can people be stopped from crossing borders? Efforts to seal borders are "pathetic" in their ineffectiveness (para. 15). These points lay the groundwork for Silko's surprising and stirring conclusions: "The great human migration within the Americas cannot be stopped; human beings are natural forces of the earth, just as rivers and winds are natural forces" (para. 16); "the Americas are Indian country, and the 'Indian problem' is not about to go away" (para. 17). The mythic "return of the Aztlan" is on display in the box cars that go by as the essay closes. In short, this essay unfolds in a conventional way: it has a standard beginning, middle, and end.

Silko's style

What about Silko's style? How is it appropriate to her purposes? Take a look at paragraphs 3 and 4. You will notice that nearly all of the fourteen sentences in these paragraphs are simple in structure. There are only five sentences that use any form of subordination (clauses that begin with *when, that,* or *if*). Many of the sentences consist either of one clause or of two clauses joined by simple coordination (connection with conjunctions such as *and* or *but* or a semicolon). Several of the sentences and clauses are unusually short. Furthermore, in these paragraphs Silko never uses metaphors or other sorts of poetic language. Her choice of words is as simple as her sentences. It all reminds you of the daily newspaper, doesn't it? Silko chooses a style similar to one used in newspaper reporting—simple, straightforward, unadorned—because she wants her readers to accept her narrative as credible and trustworthy. Her tone and voice reinforce her ethos.

There is more to say about the rhetorical choices that Silko made in crafting "The Border Patrol State," but this analysis is enough to illustrate our main point. Textual rhetorical analysis employs rhetorical terminology—in this case, terms borrowed from classical rhetoric such as ethos, pathos, logos, arrangement, style, and tone—as a way of helping us to understand how a writer makes choices to achieve certain effects. And textual analysis cooperates with contextual analysis.

Analyze the Rhetorical Context

Communication as conversation

Notice that in the previous discussion the fact that Leslie Marmon Silko's "The Border Patrol State" was originally published in the magazine *The Nation* did not matter too much. Nor did it matter when the essay was published (October 17, 1994), who exactly read it, what their reaction was, or what other people were saying at the time. Textual analysis can proceed as if the item under consideration "speaks for all time," as if it is a museum piece unaffected by time and space. There's nothing wrong with museums, of course; they permit people to observe and appreciate objects in an important way. But museums often fail to reproduce an artwork's original context and cultural meaning. In that sense museums can diminish understanding as much as they contribute to it. Contextual rhetorical analysis is an attempt to understand communications through the lens of their environments, examining the setting or scene out of which any communication emerges.

Similar to textual analysis, contextual analysis may be conducted in any number of ways. But contextual rhetorical analysis always proceeds from a description of the **rhetorical situation** that motivated the event in question. It demands an appreciation of the social circumstances that call rhetorical events into being and that orchestrate the course of those events. It regards communications as anything but self-contained:

- Each communication is considered as a response to other communications and to other social practices.
- Communications, and social practices more generally, are considered to reflect the attitudes and values of the communities that sustain them.
- Analysts seek evidence of how those other communications and social practices are reflected in texts.

Rhetorical analysis from a contextualist perspective understands individual pieces as parts of ongoing conversations.

The challenge is to reconstruct the conversation surrounding a specific piece of writing or speaking. Sometimes it is easy to do so. You may have appropriate background information on the topic, as well as a feel for what is behind what people are writing or saying about it. People who have strong feelings about the environment, stem cell research, same-sex marriage, or any number of other current issues are well informed about the arguments that are converging around those topics.

But other times it takes some research to reconstruct the conversations and social practices related to a particular issue. If the issue is current, you need to see how the debate is conducted in current magazines, newspapers, talk shows, movies and TV shows, Web sites, and so forth. If the issue is from an earlier time, you must do archival research into historical collections of newspapers, magazines, books, letters, and other documentary sources. Archival research usually involves libraries, special research collections, or film and television archives where it is possible to learn quite a bit about context.

An example will clarify how contextual analysis works to open up an argument to analysis. Let's return to a discussion of Silko's "The Border Patrol State" on pages 182–187. It will take a bit of research to reconstruct some of the "conversations" that Silko is participating in, but the result will be an enhanced understanding of the essay as well as an appreciation for how you might do a contextual rhetorical analysis.

Silko's life and works

You can begin by learning more about Silko herself. The essay provides some facts about her (e.g., that she is a Native American writer of note who is from the Southwest). The headnote on page 182 gives additional information (that her writing usually develops out of Native American traditions and tales). You can learn more about Silko using the Internet and your library's Web site. Silko's credibility, her ethos, is established not just by her textual decisions but also by her prior reputation, especially for readers of *The Nation* who would recognize and appreciate her accomplishments.

Perhaps the most relevant information on the Web is about *Almanac of the Dead*, the novel Silko refers to in paragraph 3. The novel, set mainly in Tucson, involves a Native American woman psychic who is in the process of transcribing the lost histories of her dead ancestors into "an almanac of the dead"—a history of her people. This history is written from the point of view of the conquered, not the conqueror. "The Border Patrol State," it seems, is an essay version of *Almanac of the Dead* in that Silko protests what has been lost—and what is still being lost—in the clash between white and Native American cultures. It is a protest against the tactics of the border police. Or is it?

The context of publication

Through a consideration of the conversations swirling around it, contextual analysis actually suggests that "The Border Patrol State" is just as much about immigration policy as it is about the civil rights of Native Americans. The article first appeared in *The Nation*, a respected, politically progressive magazine that has been appearing weekly for decades. Published in New York City, it is a magazine of public opinion that covers theater, film, music, fiction, and other arts; politics and public affairs; and contemporary culture. If you want to know what left-leaning people are thinking about an issue, *The Nation* is a good magazine to consult. You can imagine that Silko's essay therefore reached an audience of sympathetic readers— people who would be receptive to her message. They would be inclined to sympathize with Silko's complaints and to heed her call for a less repressive Border Patrol.

What is more interesting is that Silko's essay appeared on October 17, 1994 in a special issue of *The Nation* devoted to "The Immigration Wars," a phrase prominent on the magazine's cover. Silko's essay was one of several articles that appeared under that banner, an indication that Silko's argument is not just about the violation of the civil rights of Native Americans but also about the larger issue of immigration policy. "The Border Patrol State" appeared after David Cole's "Five Myths about Immigration," Elizabeth Kadetsky's "Bashing Illegals in California," Peter Kwong's "China's Human Traffickers," two editorials about immigration policy, and short columns on immigration by *Nation* regulars Katha Pollitt, Aryeh Neier, and Christopher Hitchens. Together the articles in this issue of *The Nation* mounted a sustained argument in favor of a liberal immigration policy.

The larger conversation

Why did *The Nation* entitle its issue "The Immigration Wars"? Immigration was a huge controversy in October 1994, just before the 1994 elections. When the 1965 Immigration Act was amended in 1990, the already strong flow of immigrants to the United States became a flood. While many previous immigrants came to the United States from Europe, most recent immigrants have come from Asia, Latin America, the Caribbean islands, and Africa. While earlier immigrants typically passed through Ellis Island and past the Statue of Liberty that welcomed them, most recent immigrants in 1994 were coming to Florida, Texas, and California. The arrival of all those new immigrants revived old fears that have been in the air for decades (that they take away jobs from native-born Americans, that they undermine national values by resisting assimilation and clinging to their own cultures, that they reduce standards of living by putting stress on education and social-welfare budgets). Many people countered those fears by pointing out that immigrants create jobs and wealth, enhance the vitality of American culture, become among the proudest of Americans, and contribute to the tax base of their communities. But those counterarguments were undermined when a tide of illegal immigrants—up to 500,000 per year—was arriving at the time Silko was writing.

The Immigration Wars were verbal wars. In the 1994 election, Republicans had united under the banner of a "Contract with America." Some 300 Republican congressional candidates, drawn together by conservative leader Newt Gingrich, agreed to run on a common platform in an ultimately successful effort to gain control of the House of Representatives. The Contract with America offered a number of conservative initiatives, including a reduction in the size of government, a balanced-budget amendment, crime legislation, a reduction in welfare benefits and capital gains taxes, and benefits increases for seniors on Social Security. More to the point here, it also proposed changes in laws in order to curtail immigration, to reduce illegal immigration, and to deny benefits such as health care, social services, and education to illegal residents.

The Contract with America offered support for California's Proposition 187, another important 1994 proposal. This so-called "Save Our State" initiative was designed to "prevent California's estimated 1.7 million undocumented immigrants from partaking of every form of public welfare including non-emergency medical care, pre-natal clinics and public schools," as Kadetsky explained in her essay in *The Nation*. In the words of the proposition itself, "The People of California find and declare as follows: That they have suffered and are suffering economic hardship caused by the presence of illegal aliens in this state. That they have suffered and are suffering personal injury and damage caused by the criminal conduct of illegal aliens. That they have a right to the protection of their government from any person or persons entering this country illegally." The Republican Contract for America and California's Proposition 187 together constituted the nation's leading domestic issue in October 1994. The war of words about the issue was evident in the magazines, books, newspapers, talk shows, barber shops, and hair salons of America—much as it is today.

Silko's political goals

In this context, it is easy to see that Silko's essay is against more than the Border Patrol. It is an argument in favor of relatively unrestricted immigration, especially for Mexicans and Native Americans. Moreover, it is a direct refutation of the Contract for America and Proposition 187. Proposition 187 states "that [the People of California] have suffered and are suffering economic hardship caused by the presence of illegal aliens in this state, that they have suffered and are suffering personal injury and damage caused by the criminal conduct of illegal aliens, [and] that they have a right to the protection of their government from any person or persons entering this country illegally."

Silko turns the claim around. It is the Border Patrol that is behaving illegally. It is the Border Patrol that is creating economic hardship. It is the border police that are inflicting personal injury and damage through criminal conduct. Finally, it is the U.S. government that is acting illegally by ignoring the treaty of Guadalupe Hidalgo, which "recognizes the right of the Tohano O'Odom (Papago) people to move freely across the U.S.-Mexico border without documents," as Silko writes in a footnote. Writing just before the election of 1994 and in the midst of a spirited national debate, Silko had specific political goals in mind. A contextual analysis of "The Border Patrol State" reveals that the essay is, at least in part, an eloquent refutation of the Contract for America and Proposition 187—two items that are not even named explicitly in the essay!

   We could do more contextual analysis here. We could cite many more articles, books, reports, and TV broadcasts that can be compared with "The Border Patrol State," including speeches and TV interviews by Pat Buchanan, who ran for the Republican presidential nomination in 1992 and 1996 on an anti-immigration stance. A discussion of the conversation about immigration in 1994 and about specific contribution to that conversation could be extended for a long time—indefinitely, in fact. There is no need to belabor the point, however; our purpose has been simply to illustrate that contextual analysis of a piece of rhetoric can enrich our understanding.

Write a Rhetorical Analysis

Effective rhetorical analysis, as we have seen, can be textual or contextual in nature. But we should emphasize again that these two approaches to rhetorical analysis are not mutually exclusive. Indeed, many if not most analysts operate between these two extremes; they consider the details of the text, but they also attend to the particulars of context. Textual analysis and contextual analysis inevitably complement each other. Getting at what is at stake in "The Border Patrol State" or any other sophisticated argument takes patience and intelligence. Many arguments appeal to the attitudes and beliefs of audiences. Rhetorical analysis, as a way of understanding how people argue, is both enlightening and challenging.

   Try to use elements of both kinds of analysis whenever you want to understand a rhetorical event more completely. Rhetoric is "inside" texts, but it is also "outside" them. Specific rhetorical performances are an irreducible mixture of text and context, and so interpretation and analysis of those performances must account for both as well. Remember, however, the limitations of your analysis. Realize that your analysis will always be somewhat partial and incomplete, ready to be deepened, corrected, modified, and extended by the insights of others. Rhetorical analysis can itself be part of an unending conversation—a way of learning and teaching within a community.

Barbara Jordan

Statement on the Articles of Impeachment

Barbara Jordan (1936–1996) grew up in Houston and received a law degree from Boston University in 1959. Working on John F. Kennedy's 1960 presidential campaign stirred an

interest in politics, and Jordon became the first African-American woman elected to the Texas State Senate in 1966. In 1972 she was elected to the United States House of Representatives and thus became the first African-American woman from the South ever to serve in Congress. Jordan was appointed to the House Judiciary Committee. Soon she was in the national spotlight when that committee considered articles of impeachment against President Richard Nixon, who had illegally covered up a burglary of Democratic Party headquarters during the 1972 election. When Nixon's criminal acts reached to the Judiciary Committee, Jordan's opening speech on July 24, 1974, set the tone for the debate and established her reputation as a moral beacon for the nation. Nixon resigned as president on August 9, 1974, when it was evident that he would be impeached.

T hank you, Mr. Chairman.

Mr. Chairman, I join my colleague Mr. Rangel in thanking you for giving the junior members of this committee the glorious opportunity of sharing the pain of this inquiry. Mr. Chairman, you are a strong man, and it has not been easy but we have tried as best we can to give you as much assistance as possible.

2   Earlier today, we heard the beginning of the Preamble to the Constitution of the United States: "We, the people." It's a very eloquent beginning. But when that document was completed on the seventeenth of September in 1787, I was not included in that "We, the people." I felt somehow for many years that George Washington and Alexander Hamilton just left me out by mistake. But through the process of amendment, interpretation, and court decision, I have finally been included in "We, the people."

3   Today I am an inquisitor. An hyperbole would not be fictional and would not overstate the solemnness that I feel right now. My faith in the Constitution is whole; it is complete; it is total. And I am not going to sit here and be an idle spectator to the diminution, the subversion, the destruction, of the Constitution.

4   "Who can so properly be the inquisitors for the nation as the representatives of the nation themselves?" "The subjects of its jurisdiction are those offenses which proceed from the misconduct of public men." And that's what

we're talking about. In other words, [the jurisdiction comes] from the abuse or violation of some public trust.

5   It is wrong, I suggest, it is a misreading of the Constitution for any member here to assert that for a member to vote for an article of impeachment means that that member must be convinced that the President should be removed from office. The Constitution doesn't say that. The powers relating to impeachment are an essential check in the hands of the body of the legislature against and upon the encroachments of the executive. The division between the two branches of the legislature, the House and the Senate, assigning to the one the right to accuse and to the other the right to judge, the framers of this Constitution were very astute. They did not make the accusers and the judgers the same person.

6   We know the nature of impeachment. We've been talking about it awhile now. It is chiefly designed for the President and his high ministers to somehow be called into account. It is designed to "bridle" the executive if he engages in excesses. "It is designed as a method of national inquest into the conduct of public men." The framers confided in the Congress the power if need be, to remove the President in order to strike a delicate balance between a President swollen with power and grown tyrannical, and preservation of the independence of the executive.

7   The nature of impeachment: a narrowly channeled exception to the separation-of-powers maxim. The Federal Convention of 1787 said that. It limited impeachment to high crimes and misdemeanors and discounted and opposed the term *maladministration*. "It is to be used only for great misdemeanors," so it was said in the North Carolina ratification convention. And in the Virginia ratification convention: "We do not trust our liberty to a particular branch. We need one branch to check the other."

8   "No one need be afraid"—the North Carolina ratification convention— "No one need be afraid that officers who commit oppression will pass with immunity." "Prosecutions of impeachments will seldom fail to agitate the passions of the whole community," said Hamilton in the Federalist Papers, number 65. "We divide into parties more or less friendly or inimical to the accused." I do not mean political parties in that sense.

9   The drawing of political lines goes to the motivation behind impeachment; but impeachment must proceed within the confines of the constitutional term "high crime[s] and misdemeanors." Of the impeachment process, it was Woodrow Wilson who said that "Nothing short of the grossest offenses against the plain law of the land will suffice to give them speed and effectiveness. Indignation so great as to overgrow party interest may secure a conviction; but nothing else can."

10   Common sense would be revolted if we engaged upon this process for petty reasons. Congress has a lot to do: Appropriations, Tax Reform, Health Insurance, Campaign Finance Reform, Housing, Environmental Protection, Energy Sufficiency, Mass Transportation. Pettiness cannot be allowed to stand

in the face of such overwhelming problems. So today we are not being petty. We are trying to be big, because the task we have before us is a big one.

11   This morning, in a discussion of the evidence, we were told that the evidence which purports to support the allegations of misuse of the CIA by the President is thin. We're told that that evidence is insufficient. What that recital of the evidence this morning did not include is what the President did know on June the 23rd, 1972.

12   The President did know that it was Republican money, that it was money from the Committee for the Re-Election of the President, which was found in the possession of one of the burglars arrested on June the 17th. What the President did know on the 23rd of June was the prior activities of E. Howard Hunt, which included his participation in the break-in of Daniel Ellsberg's psychiatrist, which included Howard Hunt's participation in the Dita Beard ITT affair, which included Howard Hunt's fabrication of cables designed to discredit the Kennedy Administration.

13   We were further cautioned today that perhaps these proceedings ought to be delayed because certainly there would be new evidence forthcoming from the President of the United States. There has not even been an obfuscated indication that this committee would receive any additional materials from the President. The committee subpoena is outstanding, and if the President wants to supply that material, the committee sits here. The fact is that on yesterday, the American people waited with great anxiety for eight hours, not knowing whether their President would obey an order of the Supreme Court of the United States.

14   At this point, I would like to juxtapose a few of the impeachment criteria with some of the actions the President has engaged in. Impeachment criteria: James Madison, from the Virginia ratification convention. "If the President be connected in any suspicious manner with any person and there be grounds to believe that he will shelter him, he may be impeached."

15   We have heard time and time again that the evidence reflects the payment to defendants' money. The President had knowledge that these funds were being paid and these were funds collected for the 1972 presidential campaign. We know that the President met with Mr. Henry Petersen 27 times to discuss matters related to Watergate, and immediately thereafter met with the very persons who were implicated in the information Mr. Petersen was receiving. The words are: "If the President is connected in any suspicious manner with any person and there be grounds to believe that he will shelter that person, he may be impeached."

16   Justice Story: "Impeachment" is attended—"is intended for occasional and extraordinary cases where a superior power acting for the whole people is put into operation to protect their rights and rescue their liberties from violations." We know about the Huston plan. We know about the break-in of the psychiatrist's office. We know that there was absolute complete direction on September 3rd when the President indicated that a surreptitious entry had

been made in Dr. Fielding's office, after having met with Mr. Ehrlichman and Mr. Young. "Protect their rights." "Rescue their liberties from violation."

17   The Carolina ratification convention impeachment criteria: those are impeachable "who behave amiss or betray their public trust." Beginning shortly after the Watergate break-in and continuing to the present time, the President has engaged in a series of public statements and actions designed to thwart the lawful investigation by government prosecutors. Moreover, the President has made public announcements and assertions bearing on the Watergate case, which the evidence will show he knew to be false. These assertions, false assertions, impeachable, those who misbehave. Those who "behave amiss or betray the public trust."

18   James Madison again at the Constitutional Convention: "A President is impeachable if he attempts to subvert the Constitution." The Constitution charges the President with the task of taking care that the laws be faithfully executed, and yet the President has counseled his aides to commit perjury, willfully disregard the secrecy of grand jury proceedings, conceal surreptitious entry, attempt to compromise a federal judge, while publicly displaying his cooperation with the processes of criminal justice. "A President is impeachable if he attempts to subvert the Constitution."

19   If the impeachment provision in the Constitution of the United States will not reach the offenses charged here, then perhaps that 18th-century Constitution should be abandoned to a 20th-century paper shredder.

20   Has the President committed offenses, and planned, and directed, and acquiesced in a course of conduct which the Constitution will not tolerate? That's the question. We know that. We know the question. We should now forthwith proceed to answer the question. It is reason, and not passion, which must guide our deliberations, guide our debate, and guide our decision.

21   I yield back the balance of my time, Mr. Chairman. ■

Sample Student Rhetorical Analysis

T. Jonathan Jackson

Dr. Netaji

English 1101

5 December 2008

An Argument of Reason and Passion: Barbara Jordan's

"Statement on the Articles of Impeachment"

On March 9, 1974, the U.S. House Judiciary Committee began an impeachment hearing against President Richard Nixon for his role in the cover-up of the Watergate scandal. On July 25, 1974, Congresswoman Barbara Jordan stood before this committee and delivered an 11-minute speech known as "Statement on the Articles of Impeachment." The argument of this speech is that the president should be impeached because his actions threaten both the Constitution and the people of the United States. Jordan states, "It is reason, and not passion, which must guide our deliberation, guide our debate, and guide our decision." Subsequently, she uses a strong logical argument that she supports with appeals to both her credibility and the audience's feelings of patriotism for the Constitution.

The context of Jordan's speech is important for three reasons. First, the charges against Nixon and his impeachment case were controversial because he was a Republican president and the committee was mostly Democratic. The burden was on Jordan to show that the case for impeachment was not a partisan issue. Second, the speech was televised. Jordan was speaking not only to the committee—an audience well informed about the topic and mostly in support of her argument— but also to a television audience that was not as informed and potentially hostile. Finally, although Jordan was already known in Texas politics, she was new to Congress, and she was a low-ranking member of the committee. Consequently, she had to prove her ethos to both the committee and the wider television audience who did not know her.

At the heart of Jordan's argument is her insistence that the Constitution is important because it protects the rights of the American people. Therefore the Constitution itself should be protected. Thus impeachment is the proper punishment for a president or other leaders who upset the balance of power and act against the Constitution. Using evidence from the North Carolina and Virginia Constitutional

Conventions, she shows that impeachment is used only for "great misdemeanors" and that we need the branches of government to check the powers of each other. Her next task is to show what these misdemeanors are and to show that Nixon has committed them. Here she appeals to logic in that she not only explains each misdemeanor in full and matches the president's actions to each one, but she also cites reputable sources such as James Madison, who wrote the Federalist Papers; the South Carolina Ratification Convention; and Justice Joseph Story, who as a justice under Madison was known for his work explaining the states' powers under the Constitution. In addition, she emphasizes each point by starting with a key quotation by one of these figures, such as James Madison: "A President is impeachable if he attempts to subvert the Constitution." Then she describes the president's actions that illustrate this quotation—in this case, he told his associates to commit perjury, to hide evidence, and to bribe a judge—and stresses the point with the same quotation she used earlier: "A President is impeachable if he attempts to subvert the Constitution." This repetition of the quotation makes the connection both clearer and more memorable to the audience.

Jordan shows that she has an extensive knowledge of the Constitution and of the facts in the impeachment case, which gains her credibility as someone who can speak knowledgeably on the subject. She also shows her credibility as a citizen, as well as an African-American woman who relies on the Constitution and the Constitutional process for protection. She says that when the Constitution was completed, "I was not included in that 'We, the People.' I felt somehow for many years that George Washington and Alexander Hamilton just left me out by mistake. But through the process of amendment, interpretation, and court decision I have finally been included in 'We, the People.'"

Jordan also addresses the concern that the impeachment case is partisan, an allegation that could damage the credibility of the committee. She recognizes that "the drawing of political lines goes to the motivation behind impeachment," but such a large crime should transcend party lines. She backs this assertion by quoting Woodrow Wilson, who said, "Indignation so great as to overthrow party interest may secure a conviction; but nothing else can." Jordan continues, "Thus, party pettiness cannot, and will not, stand in the way of the committee member's jobs as representatives of the nation: We are trying to be *big*, because the task we have before us is a big one."

Jordan claims that passion should not be a part of the impeachment proceedings, but she uses her passion for the Constitution to connect to her audience's emotions and sense of patriotism: "My faith in the Constitution is whole, it is complete, it is total. And I am not going to sit here and be an idle spectator to the diminution, the subversion, the destruction of the Constitution." She stirs her audience's emotions by repeatedly creating the sense that the Constitution is in physical danger of being destroyed. Not only is it in danger of being figuratively destroyed by Nixon's crimes, but also a failure to impeach him could also destroy the document's integrity. She makes this destruction literal when she says, "If the impeachment provisions will not reach the offenses charged here, then perhaps that eighteenth-century Constitution should be abandoned to a twentieth-century paper shredder." This dramatic image encourages the audience to imagine Nixon actually shredding the Constitution as he ordered the shredding of documents that could link him to crimes. In addition, she makes the American people responsible; "we," meaning both the committee and the television audience, might as well be shredding the Constitution to bits if Nixon is not impeached.

Jordan makes a strong case for impeachment by first appealing to logic and then using her passion for the Constitution to connect to her audience's patriotism. Significantly, because this speech was also televised, Jordan also emerged to a national audience as a powerful speaker. Her clear, rhythmic style is both dramatic and easy to follow. Jordan's reputation as a powerful speaker continues to this day, as does the importance of her speeches, such as this one and other keynote addresses she made throughout her career. In particular, this argument for exercising the checks and balances within our government in order to protect the Constitution and the American people from possible tyranny is an argument that resonates with events today.

Works Cited

Jordan, Barbara. "Statement on the Articles of Impeachment." *American Rhetoric: Top 100 Speeches*. American Rhetoric, 25 July 1974. Web. 21 Nov. 2007.

Steps to Writing a Rhetorical Analysis

Step 1 Select an Argument to Analyze

Find an argument to analyze—a speech or sermon, an op-ed in a newspaper, an ad in a magazine designed for a particular audience, or a commentary on a talk show.

Examples

- Editorial pages of newspapers (but not letters to the editor unless you can find a long and detailed letter)
- Opinion features in magazines such as *Time, Newsweek,* and *U.S. News & World Report*
- Magazines that take political positions such as *National Review, Mother Jones, New Republic, Nation,* and *Slate*
- Web sites of activist organizations (but not blog or newsgroup postings unless they are long and detailed)

Step 2 Analyze the Context

Who is the author?

Through research in the library or on the Web, learn all you can about the author of the argument.

- How does the argument you are analyzing repeat arguments previously made by the author?
- Does the author borrow arguments and concepts from previous pieces he or she has written?
- What motivated the author to write? What is the author's purpose for writing this argument?

Who is the audience?

Through research, learn all you can about the place where the argument appeared and the audience.

- Who is the anticipated audience?
- How do the occasion and forum for writing affect the argument?
- How would the argument have been written differently if it had appeared elsewhere?
- What motivated the newspaper or magazine (or other venue) to publish it?

What is the larger conversation?

Through research, find out what else was being said about the subject of your selection. Track down any references made in the text you are examining.

- When did the argument appear?
- Why did it get published at that particular moment?
- What other concurrent pieces of "cultural conversation" (e.g., TV shows, other articles, speeches, Web sites) does the item you are analyzing respond to or "answer"?

Step 3 Analyze the Text

Summarize the argument

- What is the main claim?
- What reasons are given in support of the claim?
- How is the argument organized? What are the components, and why are they presented in that order?

What is the medium and genre?

- What is the medium? A newspaper? a scholarly journal? a Web site? or something else?
- What is the genre? An editorial? an essay? a speech? an advertisment? What expectations does the audience have about this genre?

What appeals are used?

- Analyze the ethos. How does the writer represent himself or herself? Does the writer have any credentials as an authority on the topic? Do you trust the writer? Why or why not?
- Analyze the logos. Where do you find facts and evidence in the argument? What kinds of facts and evidence does the writer present? Direct observation? statistics? interviews? surveys? secondhand sources such as published research? quotations from authorities?
- Analyze the pathos. Does the writer attempt to invoke an emotional response? Where do you find appeals to shared values? You are a member of that audience, so what values do you hold in common with the writer? What values do you not hold in common?

How would you characterize the style?

- Is the style formal, informal, satirical, or something else?
- Are any metaphors used?

Step 4 Write a Draft

Introduction

- Describe briefly the argument you are analyzing, including where it was published, how long it is, and who wrote it.
- If the argument is about an issue unfamiliar to your readers, supply the necessary background.

Body

- Analyze the context, following Step 2.
- Analyze the text, following Step 3.

Conclusion

- Do more than simply summarize what you have said. You might, for example, end with an example that typifies the argument.
- You don't have to end by either agreeing or disagreeing with the writer. Your task in this assignment is to analyze the strategies the writer uses.

Step 5 Revise, Edit, Proofread

For detailed instructions, see Chapter 4.
For a checklist to evaluate your draft, see pages 61–62.

6

Analyzing Visual Arguments

The Stata Center is a controversial building at the Massachusetts Institute of Technology. Why do you think MIT wanted a building so different and whimsical on its campus?

What Is a Visual Argument?

We live in a world flooded with images. They pull on us, compete for our attention, push us to do things. But how often do we think about how they work?

Arguments in written language are visual in one sense: we use our eyes to read the words on the page. But without words, can there be a visual argument? Certainly some visual symbols take on conventional meanings. Signs in airports or other public places, for example, are designed to communicate with speakers of many languages.

Some visual symbols even make explicit claims. A one-way street sign says that drivers should travel only in the one direction. But are such signs arguments? In Chapter 3 we point out that scholars of argument do not believe that everything *is* an argument. Most scholars define an argument as a claim supported by one or more reasons. A one-way sign has a claim: all drivers should go in the same direction. But is there a reason? We all know an unstated reason the sign carries: drivers who go the wrong way violate the law and risk a substantial fine (plus they risk a head-on collision with other drivers).

Visual arguments often are powerful because they invite viewers to create claims and links. For example, the artists who decorated medieval cathedrals taught religious lessons. The facade of the Last Judgment on the front pillar of the Duomo in Orvieto, Italy, shown on the next page, depicts Christ as judge damning sinners to hell. The facade makes a powerful visual argument about the consequences that await the unfaithful.

Facade of Last Judgment, Orvieto, Italy. ca. 1310–1330.

Eighteen-year-old mother from Oklahoma, now a California migrant. Photo by Dorothea Lange. March 1937.

Other visual arguments cannot be explained this easily—even ones that are intended to make claims. Beginning in 1935, the U.S. Farm Security Administration hired photographers to document the effects of the Great Depression and the drought years on Americans. One of the photographers, Dorothea Lange, shot a series of photographs of homeless and destitute migrant workers in California. Her photographs have become some of the most familiar images of the United States in the 1930s. Lange had an immediate goal—getting the government to build a resettlement camp for the homeless workers. She wrote to her boss in Washington that her images were "loaded with ammunition."

Lange titled one of her images "Eighteen-year-old mother from Oklahoma, now a California migrant." The young woman and child in the photograph are obviously quite poor if we assume the tent is where they live. Yet the image doesn't seem to be one of suffering. Lange was a portrait photographer before becoming a documentary photographer, and her experience shows. She takes advantage of the highlighting of the woman's hair from the sun contrasted with the dark interior of the tent to draw our eyes to the woman's face. She doesn't appear to be distressed—just bored. Only later do we notice the dirty face of the child and other details. With another caption—perhaps "Young mother on a camping trip left behind while her husband went for a hike"—we might read the photograph to say something else. And even if we take the image as evidence of poverty, Lange's claim is not evident, just as images of homeless people today do not necessarily make arguments.

Analyze Visual Persuasion

For many years the Italian clothing retailer Benetton has run ad campaigns intended to raise public awareness on issues including AIDS, hunger, pollution, and racism. In 2003, Benetton launched a "Food for Life" campaign codeveloped with the United Nations World Food Programme, with photographs by James Mollison. According to Benetton, "Setting the scene is the symbol for the Food for Life campaign: a man with a mutilated arm, whose metal prosthesis is a spoon." The image is memorable, but it does not make a claim that can be put into words easily.

Advertisements often work in complex ways. Benetton advertises for the same reason other companies advertise—to get consumers to buy their products. The question then becomes how the controversial ads influence consumers to purchase Benetton clothing. Perhaps consumers identify with the messages in

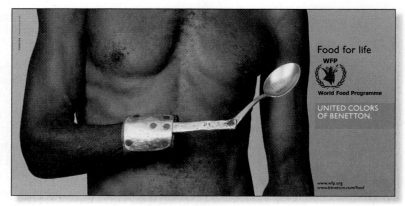

Food for Life. Benetton Ad Campaign. 2003.

Benetton's ads and consequently identify with their clothing. Benetton says on its Web site that its ad campaigns "have succeeded in attracting the attention of the public and in standing out amid the current clutter of images." At the very least the ads give Benetton name recognition. You may have other ideas about why the Benetton ads have been successful, but the point we are making is that explicit claims and reasons are often hard to extract from images.

Analyze Visual Evidence

Photographs

Images and graphics seldom make arguments on their own, but they are frequently used to support arguments. Photographs are commonly used as factual evidence, but as with other kinds of evidence, the significance of images can be contested. In 1936, 21-year-old Arthur Rothstein worked as a photographer for the Resettlement Administration, a federal agency created to help people living in rural poverty. Rothstein sent a photograph of a bleached cow's skull lying on cracked dirt to Roy Stryker, his boss in Washington, D.C. Stryker saw the image as representing the plight of Midwestern plains states in the midst of a severe drought.

But not all people living in plains states found this image—or others like it—representative. A newspaper in Fargo, North Dakota, published one of Rothstein's photographs on the front page under the headline, "It's a fake!" The newspaper accused journalists of making the situation on the plains appear worse than it was and accused Rothstein in particular of using a movable prop to make a cheap point.

Close examination of the set of photographs revealed the skull had been moved about 10 feet, which Rothstein admitted. But he protested that the drought was real enough and there were plenty of cow bones on the ground. Rothstein had followed a long practice among photographers of altering a scene for the purpose of getting a better photograph.

Photographers often manipulated their images in the darkroom, but realistic results required a high skill level. More recently, digital photography

The bleached skull of a steer on the dry, sun-baked earth of the South Dakota Badlands, 1939. Photo by Arthur Rothstein.

has made it relatively easy to alter photographs. You've no doubt seen many of the thousands of altered images that circulate daily—photographs that put heads on different bodies and put people in different places, often within historical images.

The ease of cropping digital photographs reveals an important truth about photography: a photograph represents reality from a particular viewpoint. A high-resolution picture of a crowd can be divided into many smaller images that each say something different about the event. The act of pointing the camera in one direction and not in another shapes how photographic evidence will be interpreted.

Tables, charts, and other graphics

Statistical information is frequently used as evidence in arguments. The problem with giving many statistics in sentence form, however, is that readers shortly lose track of the numbers. Readers require formats such as tables, which allow them to take in an array of numerical data at once. Below is a table on the costs of cancer drugs, which can run up to $100,000 for a few months' treatment.

Charts and graphs present the magnitude and proportion of data with more visual impact than tables. A bar chart showing the number of unredeemed frequent-flyer miles, such as the example opposite, illustrates the problem airlines face in offering free seats to fulfill their mileage redemption obligations much more clearly than a description would.

The Price of Fighting Cancer

The estimated costs of some of a new wave of cancer drugs, which aim at the disease without the side effects of traditional chemotherapy.

CANCER DRUG	MANUFACTURER	APPROVED FOR USE	TYPE OF CANCER TREATED	EST. ANNUAL COST PER PATIENT
Erbitux	ImClone/Bristol-Myers	2004	Colorectal	$ 111,000
Avastin	Genentech	2004	Colorectal	54,000
Herceptin	Genentech	1998	Breast	38,000
Tarceva	Genentech	2004	Lung	35,000

Source: Sanford C. Bernstein & Co.

The New York Times

A table allows a quick comparison of numeric data such as the price of fighting cancer with expensive drugs.

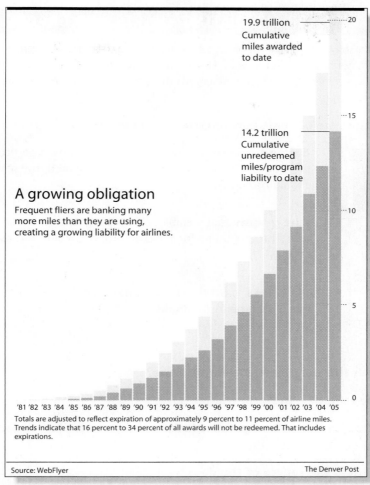

A growing obligation

Frequent fliers are banking many
more miles than they are using,
creating a growing liability for airlines.

19.9 trillion
Cumulative
miles awarded
to date

14.2 trillion
Cumulative
unredeemed
miles/program
liability to date

'81 '82 '83 '84 '85 '86 '87 '88 '89 '90 '91 '92 '93 '94 '95 '96 '97 '98 '99 '00 '01 '02 '03 '04 '05

Totals are adjusted to reflect expiration of approximately 9 percent to 11 percent of airline miles.
Trends indicate that 16 percent to 34 percent of all awards will not be redeemed. That includes
expirations.

Source: WebFlyer   The Denver Post

Bar charts are useful to represent the magnitude and proportion of data such as the
enormous growth of frequent-flyer miles.

Charts can also be misleading. For example, a chart that compares the
amounts of calories in competing brands of cereal might list one with 70 calories
and another with 80 calories. If the chart begins at zero, the difference looks small.
But if the chart starts at 60, the brand with 80 calories appears to have twice the
calories of the brand with 70. Furthermore, the chart is worthless if the data is
inaccurate or comes from an unreliable source. Creators of charts and graphs have
an ethical obligation to present data as fairly and accurately as possible and to
provide the sources of the data.

CHECKLIST FOR EVALUATING CHARTS AND GRAPHS

Computer software makes it simple to create charts and graphs. This software, however, does not help you decide which kind of chart or graph is best to use or tell you the purpose of including a chart or graph. Ask these questions when you are analyzing charts and graphs.

- **Is the type of chart appropriate for the information presented?**

 Bar and column charts make comparisons in particular categories. If two or more charts are compared, the scales should be consistent.

 Line graphs plot variables on a vertical and a horizontal axis. They are useful for showing proportional trends over time.

 Pie charts show the proportion of parts in terms of the whole. Segments must add up to 100 percent of the whole.

- **Does the chart have a clear purpose?**

- **Does the title indicate the purpose?**

- **What do the units represent** (dollars, people, voters, percentages, and so on)?

- **What is the source of the data?**

- **Is there any distortion of information?** A bar chart can exaggerate small differences if intervals are manipulated (for example, 42 can look twice as large as 41 if the numbering begins at 40).

Build a Visual Analysis

It's one thing to construct a visual argument yourself; it's another thing to analyze visual arguments that are made by someone else. Fortunately, analyzing arguments made up of images and graphics is largely a matter of following the same strategies for rhetorical analysis that are outlined in Chapter 5—except that you must analyze

Ad for Hofstra University, 1989.

images instead of (or in addition to) words. To put it another way, when you analyze a visual argument, think about the image itself as well as its relationship to other images (and discourses). The arguments implied by visual images, like the arguments made through text alone, are carried both by the context and by the image.

Analyzing context

A critical analysis of a visual image, like the analyses of written arguments that we discussed in the previous chapter, must include a consideration of context. Consider, for example, the above advertisement for Hofstra University. The context for the ad is not difficult to uncover through a bit of research. The ad appeared in 1989 and 1990 when Hofstra, located on Long Island 25 miles from New York City, was celebrating its fiftieth anniversary and hoping to use the occasion to enhance its esteem. At the time, Hofstra enjoyed a good reputation for its professional programs, particularly in education and business (which one-third of the 7500 students were majoring in). However, it was not as highly regarded in the core science and humanities disciplines that are often associated with institutional prestige. In addition, Hofstra was quite well known in the New York metropolitan area—half its students were commuting to school rather than living in dormitories—but it was not attracting many students from outside the region, and its campus life was consequently regarded as mediocre. Its student body was generally well prepared, hardworking, and capable, but its most outstanding applicants were too often choosing other universities.

Feeling that its performance was exceeding its reputation and that it was capable of attracting a more diverse and talented student body, Hofstra conceived of a national ad campaign designed to change the opinions of prospective students and their parents, as well as the general public. It placed the ads—the ad reproduced here is one of a series—in several magazines and newspapers in order to persuade people that Hofstra was an outstanding university not just in the professions but in all fields, and that the opportunities available to its students were varied and valuable.

Analyzing visual and textual elements

Ads make arguments, and the message of the Hofstra ad is something like this: "Hofstra is a prestigious, high-quality institution that brings out the best in students because of its facilities, its academic reputation, its student body, and the strength of its faculty and academic programs." The text of the Hofstra ad expresses that argument specifically: "The best" and "we teach success" are prominently displayed; the size of the print visually reinforces the message; and the fine print supports the main thesis by mentioning Hofstra's facilities (the large library with "a collection [of volumes] larger than that of 95% of American universities," the "television facility . . . with broadcast quality production capability"); its reputation (its ranking in *Barron's Guide to the Most Prestigious Colleges* and its "professionally accredited programs"); and its faculty and students. As we emphasized in the previous chapter, the ad works by offering good reasons and supporting arguments that are based on logical reasoning and evidence, as well as appeals to our most fervently held values. By placing the ad in prestigious publications, Hofstra enhanced its credibility even further.

In this chapter, however, we are emphasizing visuals in arguments. What kind of argument is made and supported by the image of the young girl with the flute? The photo of the girl is black and white, so that it can be printed easily and inexpensively in newspapers and magazines. But the black and white format also contributes a sense of reality and truthfulness, in the manner of black and white photos or documentary films. (Color images, on the other hand, can imply flashiness or commercialism.) Even in black and white, the image is quite arresting. In the context of an ad for Hofstra, the image is particularly intriguing. The girl is young—does she seem about ten or twelve years of age?—and her readiness for distinguished performance suggests that she is a prodigy, a genius—in other words, the kind of person that Hofstra attracts and sustains. The ad implies that you might encounter her on the Hofstra campus sometime: if she is not a student at Hofstra now, she soon will be. Come to Hofstra, and you too can acquire the traits associated with excellence and success.

The girl is dressed up for some kind of musical performance, and the details of her costume imply that the performance is of a high order: it is not just any costume, but one associated with professional performances of the most rarefied kind, a concert that calls for only the best musicians. The delicacy and refinement of the girl are implied by the posture of her fingers, the highly polished flute that she holds with an upright carriage, and the meticulousness of her tie, shirt, and coat. The girl's expression suggests that she is serious, sober, disciplined, but comfortable—the kind of student (and faculty member) that Hofstra features. (The layout and consistent print style used in the ad reinforce that impression: by offering a balanced and harmonious placement of elements and by sticking to the same type style throughout, the ad stands for the values of balance, harmony, consistency, and order.) The girl is modest and unpretentious in expression, yet she looks directly at the viewer with supreme self-confidence. Her age suggests innocence, yet her face proclaims ambition; her age and the quasi-masculine costume (note that she wears neither a ring nor earrings) give her a sexual innocence that is in keeping with the contemplative life. Come to Hofstra, the image proclaims, and you will meet people who are sober and graceful, self-disciplined and confident, ambitious without being arrogant. The ad is supporting its thesis with good reasons implied by its central image—good reasons that we identified with logos and pathos in the previous chapter.

Speaking of pathos, what do you make of the fact that the girl is Asian? On one hand, the Asian girl's demeanor reinforces cultural stereotypes. Delicate, small, sober, controlled, even humorless, she embodies characteristics that recall other Asian-American icons (particularly women), especially icons of success through discipline and hard work. On the other hand, the girl speaks to the Asian community. It is as if she is on the verge of saying, "Come and join me at Hofstra, where you too can reach the highest achievement. And read the copy below me to learn more about what Hofstra has to offer." In this way the girl participates in Hofstra's ambition to attract highly qualified, highly motivated, and high-performing minority students—as well as any other high-performing student, regardless of ethnicity or gender, who values hard work, academic distinction, and the postponement of sensual gratification in return for long-term success.

If she is Asian, the girl is also thoroughly American. She appears not to be an international student but an American of immigrant stock. Her costume, her controlled black hair, and her unmarked face and fingers identify her as achieving the American dream of material success, physical health and well being, and class advancement. If her parents or grandparents came to New York or California as immigrants, they (and she) are now naturalized—100 percent American, completely successful. The social class element to the image is unmistakable: the entire ad speaks of Hofstra's ambition to be among the best, to achieve an elite status. When the ad appeared in 1989, Hofstra was attracting few of the nation's elite students. The girl signals a change. She displays the university's aspiration to become among the nation's elite—those who enjoy material success as well as the leisure, education, and sophistication to appreciate the finest music. That ambition is reinforced by the university's emblem in the lower right-hand corner of the ad. It resembles a coat of arms and is associated with royalty. Hofstra may be a community that is strong in the professions, but it also values the arts.

No doubt there are other aspects of the image that work to articulate and to support the complex argument of the ad. There is more to be said about this ad, and you may disagree with some of the points we have offered. But consider this: By 2007, almost 20 years after the ad was run, college guides were reporting that Hofstra's enrollment had climbed above 8000. Its admissions were more selective, its student body was more diverse and less regional in character, its graduation rate had improved, its sports teams had achieved national visibility, and its minority student population had grown. Many factors contributed to the university's advancement, but it seems likely that this ad was one such factor.

Write a Visual Analysis

Like rhetorical analysis, effective visual analysis takes into account the context of the image as well as its visual elements and any surrounding text. When you analyze a visual image, look carefully at its details and thoroughly consider its context. What visual elements grab your attention first, and how do other details reinforce that impression—what is most important and less important? How do color and style influence impressions? How does the image direct the viewer's eyes and reinforce what is important? What is the relationship between the image and any text that might accompany it? Consider the shapes, colors, and details of the image, as well as how the elements of the image connect with different arguments and audiences.

Consider also what you know or can learn about the context of an image and the design and text that surround it. Try to determine why and when it was created, who created it, where it appeared, and the target audience. Think about how the context of its creation and publication affected its intended audience. What elements have you seen before? Which elements remind you of other visuals?

Sample Student Visual Analysis

Yamashita 1

Angela Yamashita
Dr. Sanchez
English 15
13 October 2008

Got Roddick?

Andy Roddick is one of the hottest up-and-coming athletes of today. In 2003 he became the youngest American to finish ranked number one in the ATP rankings, and he's known not only for his excellent playing skills but also for his good looks and easygoing attitude. Ex-boyfriend to popular singer Mandy Moore, Roddick has been thrown into the spotlight and is now a teenage crush. It was his picture that stopped me while leafing through *Seventeen* and made me take a longer look. Roddick stands staring at the viewer, racquet over his shoulder, leaning against the net on the court. More prominent than his white pants, white tennis shirt, and white towel draped around his neck is the white milk mustache above his upper lip. The ad reads, "Now serving. I'm into power. So I drink milk. It packs 9 essential nutrients into every glass. Which comes in handy whether

"Got Milk?" ad featuring Andy Roddick

you're an athlete or an energetic fan." At the bottom of the page is the ad slogan (also in white) "Got Milk?"

The "Got Milk?" campaign has been going on since 1993. Its numerous ads try to convince adults to drink more milk. Everyone from rock groups to actors to athletes have participated in this campaign. In today's caffeine-obsessed society of coffee and soda drinkers, America's Dairy Farmers and Milk Processors (the association that sponsors the "Got Milk?" campaign) felt the need to reverse the decline in milk consumption by advertising milk in a new way. The catchy "Got Milk?" proved to be highly successful, and the campaign has been mimicked by many others, including "Got cookies?" "Got fish?" "Got sports?" and even "Got Jesus?" (Philpot). The Andy Roddick ad is typical of the "Got Milk?" series, urging people young and old to drink milk to remain healthy and strong. The Roddick ad primarily uses the appeals ethos and pathos to persuade its audience. (The one gesture toward logos in the ad is the fact that milk has nine nutrients.)

America's Dairy Farmers and Milk Processors uses celebrity endorsements to establish the ethos of their ads. The "Got Milk?" campaign has enlisted a range of celebrities popular with young audiences from Amy Grant to Austin Powers, Britney Spears to Brett Favre, T-Mac (Tracy McGrady) to Bernie Mac. Andy Roddick, the dominant young male player in American tennis, fits squarely in this lineup. Admired by a strong following of young adults (girls for his looks, boys for his athletic ability), Roddick is an ideal spokesman for establishing that milk is a healthy drink. Implicit in the ad is that milk will help you become a better athlete and better looking too.

The ad conveys pathos not simply through Roddick's good looks. His pose is casual, almost slouching, yet his face is serious, one that suggests that he means business not only about playing tennis but also about his drink of choice. The words "I'm into power" don't mess around. They imply that you too can be more powerful by drinking milk. "Now serving" is also in your face, making a play on the word *serving* both as a tennis and a drink term.

The effectiveness of the "Got Milk?" campaign is demonstrated in gallons of milk sold. The campaign began in California in 1993 at a time when milk sales were rapidly eroding. A San Francisco ad agency developed the milk mustache idea, which is credited for stopping the downward trend in milk consumption in California. In 1995 the campaign went national. By 2000 national sales of milk remained consistent in contrast to annual declines in the early 1990s (Stamler). "Got Milk?" gave milk a brand identity that it previously had lacked, allowing it to compete with the well-established identities of Pepsi and Coca-Cola. Milk now has new challengers with more and more people going out to Starbucks and other breakfast bars. Nonetheless, the original formula of using celebrities like Andy Roddick who appeal to younger audiences continues to work. Milk isn't likely to go away soon as a popular beverage.

Works Cited

"Got Milk?" Advertisement. Milk Processor Education Program, 2007. Web. 3 Oct. 2008.

Philpot, Robert. "Copycats Mimic 'Got Milk' Ads." *Milwaukee Journal Sentinel* 12 May 2002, final ed.: D3. *LexisNexis Academic*. Web. 6 Oct. 2008.

Stamler, Bernard. "Got Sticking Power?" *New York Times* 30 July 2001, late ed.: C11. *LexisNexis Academic*. Web. 6 Oct. 2008.

Steps to Writing a Visual Analysis

Step 1 Select an Example of Visual Persuasion to Analyze

Many visual objects and images intend to persuade. Of course, all forms of advertising fall into the category of persuasion.

Examples

- Car ads: What draws you to look at and read some ads and skip others? How can you tell whether or not you are the intended audience for a particular ad?
- Maps: What is represented on a map? What is most prominent? What is left out? Maps most often do not make explicit claims, but they are persuasive nonetheless.
- Popular consumer products such as iPods, cell phones, or computers: Why did the iPod become the hottest-selling MP3 player? What makes it or any other popular product stand out?
- Public buildings or parks in your city or town: What messages do they convey?
- Images on an online real estate site: Why are particular pictures of a house displayed? What arguments do those images make?
- Cartoons: What about a cartoon makes it funny—the image, the caption, or the historical context?

Step 2 Analyze the Context

What is the context?

- Why was this image or object created?
- What was the purpose?
- Where did it come from?

Who is the audience?

- What can you infer about the intended audience?
- What did the designer(s) assume the audience knew or believed?

Who is the designer?

- Do you know the identity of the author?
- What else has the designer done?

Step 3 Analyze the Image

What is the subject?

- Can you describe the content?
- How is the image or object arranged?

What is the medium? the genre?

- What is the medium? A printed photograph? an oil painting? an outdoor sign? a building?
- What is the genre? An advertisement? a monument? a portrait? a cartoon? What expectations does the audience have about this genre?

Are words connected to the image or object?

- Is there a caption attached to the image, or are there words in the image?
- Are there words on the building or object?

What appeals are used?

- Are there appeals to ethos—the character of what is represented?
- Are there appeals to logos—the documentation of facts?
- Are there appeals to pathos—the values of the audience? Are there elements that can be considered as symbolic?

How would you characterize the style?

- Is the style formal, informal, comic, or something else?
- Are any visual metaphors used?

Step 4 Write a Draft

- Introduce the image or object and provide the background.

- Make a claim about the image or object you are analyzing. For example, the "Got Milk?" ad featuring Andy Roddick relies on the appeals of ethos and pathos.
- Support your claim with close analysis of the image or object. Describe key features.

Step 5 Revise, Edit, Proofread

- For detailed instructions, see Chapter 4.
- For a checklist to use to evaluate your draft, see pages 61–62.

Writing
Arguments

7

Putting Good Reasons into Action

For decades police used breathalyzers to combat drunk driving, but alcohol-related traffic deaths recently began to rise after a period of decline. Law enforcement officials now want alcohol detection devices in every vehicle, like seat belts. Do you think these devices should be required?

Imagine that you bought a new car in June and you are taking some of your friends to your favorite lake over the Fourth of July weekend. You have a great time until, as you are heading home, a drunk driver—a repeat offender—swerves into your lane and totals your new car. You and your friends are lucky not to be hurt, but you're outraged because you believe that repeat offenders should be prevented from driving, even if that means putting them in jail. You also remember going to another state that had sobriety checkpoints on holiday weekends. If such a checkpoint had been at the lake, you might still be driving your new car. You live in a town that encourages citizens to contribute to the local newspaper, and you think you could get a guest editorial published. The question is, how do you want to write the editorial?

- You could tell your story about how a repeat drunk driver endangered the lives of you and your friends.
- You could define driving while intoxicated (DWI) as a more legally culpable crime.
- You could compare the treatment of drunk drivers in your state with the treatment of drunk drivers in another state.
- You could cite statistics that alcohol-related accidents killed 17,941 people in 2006, an increase from 2005.
- You could evaluate the present drunk-driving laws as insufficiently just or less than totally successful.
- You could propose taking vehicles away from repeat drunk drivers and forcing them to serve mandatory sentences.
- You could argue that your community should have sobriety checkpoints at times when drunk drivers are likely to be on the road.
- You could do several of the above.

You're not going to have much space in the newspaper, so you decide to argue for sobriety checkpoints. You know that they are controversial. One of your friends who was in the car with you said that the checkpoints are unconstitutional because they involve search without cause. However, after doing some research to find out whether checkpoints are defined as legal or illegal, you learn that on June 14, 1990, the U.S. Supreme Court upheld the constitutionality of using checkpoints as a deterrent and enforcement tool against drunk drivers.

But you still want to know whether most people would agree with your friend that sobriety checkpoints are an invasion of privacy. You find opinion polls and surveys going back to the 1980s that show that 70 to 80 percent of those polled support sobriety checkpoints. You also realize that you can argue by analogy that security checkpoints for alcohol are similar in many ways to airport security checkpoints that protect passengers. You decide you will finish by making an argument from consequence. If people who go to the lake with plans to drink know in advance that there will be checkpoints, they will find a designated driver or some other means of safe transportation, and everyone else will also be a safer.

The point of this example is that people very rarely set out to define something in an argument for the sake of definition, to compare for the sake of comparison, or to adopt any of the other ways of structuring an argument. Instead, they have a purpose in mind, and they use the kinds of arguments that are discussed in Chapters 8-13—most often in combination—as means to an end. Most arguments use multiple approaches and multiple sources of good reasons. Proposal arguments in particular often analyze a present situation with definition, causal, and evaluative arguments before advancing a course of future action to address that situation. The advantage of thinking explicitly about the structure of arguments is that you often find other ways to argue. Sometimes you just need a way to get started writing about complex issues.

Use Different Approaches to Construct An Argument

An even greater advantage of thinking explicitly about specific kinds of arguments is that they can often give you a sequence for constructing arguments. Take affirmative action policies for granting admission to college as an example. No issue has been more controversial on college campuses during the last ten years.

Definition

What exactly does *affirmative action* mean? It is a policy that attempts to address the reality of contemporary social inequality based on past injustice. But injustice

Finding Good Reasons
WHAT DO WE MEAN BY DIVERSITY?

Colleges and universities talk a great deal about diversity nowadays, but what exactly do they mean by diversity? If diversity is connected with people, do they mean diversity of races and ethnicities? Is it diversity of nations and cultures represented among the students? Should the numbers of students of different races, ethnicities, or family income levels be roughly equal to the population of the state where the school is located? Is a campus diverse if about 60 percent of the students are women and 40 percent men, as many campuses now are? Or if diversity is connected with ideas, what makes for a diverse intellectual experience on a college campus?

Write about it

1. Formulate your own definition of what diversity means on a college campus (see Chapter 8).

2. Evaluate diversity on your campus according to your definition. Is your campus good or bad in its diversity (see Chapter 10)?

3. What are the effects of having a diverse campus, however you define diversity (see Chapter 9)? What happens if a campus isn't diverse?

4. If you consider diversity desirable, write a proposal that would increase diversity on your campus, whether it's interacting with people of different backgrounds or encountering a variety of ideas (see Chapter 13). Or if you think too much emphasis is being placed on diversity, write a rebuttal argument against proponents of diversity (see Chapter 12).

to whom and by whom? Do all members of minorities, all women, and all people with disabilities have equal claims for redress of past injustices? If not, how do you distinguish among them? And what exactly does affirmative action entail? Should all students who are admitted by affirmative action criteria automatically receive scholarships? Clearly, you need to define affirmative action first before proposing any changes in the policy.

Cause and effect

Since affirmative action policies have been around for a few years, you might next investigate how well they have worked. If you view affirmative action as a cause, then what have been its effects? You might find, for example, that the percentage of African Americans graduating from college dropped from 1991 to 2001 in many states. Furthermore, affirmative action policies have created a backlash attitude among many whites who believe, rightly or wrongly, that they are victims of reverse racism. But you might find that enrollment of minorities at your university has increased substantially since affirmative action policies were instituted. And you might come across a book by the then-presidents of Princeton and Harvard, William G. Bowen and Derek Bok, entitled *The Shape of the River: Long-Term Consequences of Considering Race in College and University Admissions*, which examines the effects of affirmative action policies at 28 of the nation's most select universities. They found that African-American graduates of elite schools were more likely than their white counterparts to earn graduate degrees and to take on civic responsibilities after graduation.

Evaluation

With a definition established and evidence collected, you can move to evaluation. Is affirmative action fair? Is the goal of achieving diversity through affirmative action admissions policies a worthy one because white people enjoyed preferential treatment until the last few decades? Or are affirmative action admissions policies bad because they continue the historically bad practice of giving preference to people of certain races and because they cast the people they are trying to help into the role of victims?

Proposal

When you have provided a definition with evidence and have made an evaluation, you have the groundwork for making a recommendation in the form of a proposal. A proposal argues what should be done in the future or what should not be done. It also outlines the good or bad consequences that will follow.

8
Definition Arguments

Is graffiti vandalism? Or is it art?

The continuing controversies about what art is, free speech, pornography, and hate crimes (to name just a few) illustrate why definitions often matter more than we might think. People argue about definitions because of the consequences of something being defined in a certain way. The controversies about certain subjects also illustrate three important principles that operate when definitions are used in arguments.

First, people make definitions that benefit their interests. Early in life you learned the importance of defining actions as "accidents." Windows can be broken through carelessness, especially when you are tossing a ball against the side of the house, but if it's an accident, well, accidents just happen (and don't require punishment).

Second, most of the time when you are arguing about a definition, your audience will either have a different definition in mind or be unsure of the definition. Your mother or father probably didn't think breaking the window was an accident, so you had to convince Mom or Dad that you were really being careful, and the ball just slipped out of your hand. It's your job to get them to accept your definition.

Third, if you can get your audience to accept your definition, then usually you succeed. For this reason, definition arguments are the most powerful arguments.

Understand How Definition Arguments Work

Definition arguments set out criteria and then argue that whatever is being defined meets or does not meet those criteria.

> **Something is (is not) a _____ because it has (does not have) features A, B, and C (or more).**

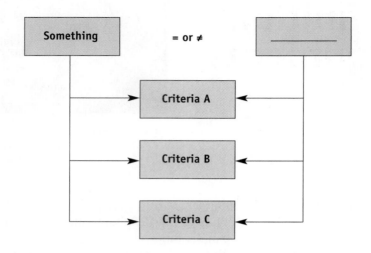

Graffiti is art because it is a means of self expression, it shows an understanding of design principles, and it stimulates both the senses and the mind.

Recognize Kinds of Definitions

Rarely do you get far into an argument without having to define something. Imagine that you are writing an argument about the decades-old and largely ineffective "war on drugs" in the United States. We all know that the war on drugs is being waged against drugs that are illegal, like cocaine and marijuana, and not against the legal drugs produced by the multibillion-dollar drug industry. Our society classifies drugs into two categories: "good" drugs, which are legal, and "bad" drugs, which are illegal.

How exactly does our society arrive at these definitions? Drugs would be relatively easy to define as good or bad if the difference could be defined at the molecular level. Bad drugs would contain certain molecules that define them as bad. The history of drug use in the United States, however, tells us that it is not so simple. In the twentieth century alcohol was on the list of illegal drugs for over a decade, while opium was considered a good drug and was distributed in many patent medicines by pharmaceutical companies. Similarly, LSD and MDMA (methylenedioxymethamphetamine, known better by its street name *ecstasy*) were developed by the pharmaceutical industry but later made illegal. In a few states marijuana is now legal for medicinal use.

If drugs cannot be classified as good or bad by their molecular structure, then perhaps society classifies them by their effects. It might be reasonable to assume that addictive drugs are illegal, but that's not the case. Nicotine is highly addictive and is a legal drug, as are many prescription medicines. Drugs taken for the purpose of pleasure are not necessarily illegal (think of alcohol and Viagra), nor are drugs that alter consciousness or change personality (such as Prozac).

How a drug is defined as legal or illegal apparently is determined by example. The nationwide effort to stop Americans from drinking alcohol during the first decades of the twentieth century led to the passage of the Eighteenth Amendment and the ban on sales of alcohol from 1920 to 1933, known as Prohibition. Those who argued for Prohibition used examples of drunkenness, especially among the poor, to show how alcohol broke up families and left mothers and children penniless in the street. Those who opposed Prohibition initially pointed to the consumption of beer and wine in many cultural traditions. Later they raised examples of the bad effects of Prohibition—the rise of organized crime, the increase in alcohol abuse, and the general disregard for laws.

When you make a definition argument, it's important to think about what kind of definition you will use. Descriptions of three types follow.

Formal definitions

Formal definitions typically categorize an item into the next-higher classification and provide criteria that distinguish the item from other items within that classification. Most dictionary definitions are formal definitions. For example, fish are cold-blooded aquatic vertebrates that have jaws, fins, and scales and are distinguished from other cold-blooded aquatic vertebrates (such as sea snakes) by the presence of gills. If you can construct a formal definition with specific criteria that your audience will accept, then likely you will have a strong argument. The key is to get your audience to agree to your criteria.

Operational definitions

Many concepts cannot be easily defined by formal definitions. Researchers in the natural and social sciences must construct **operational definitions** that they use for their research. For example, researchers who study binge drinking among college students define a binge as five or more drinks in one sitting for a man, and four or more drinks for a woman. Some people think this standard is too low and should be raised to six to eight drinks to distinguish true problem drinkers from the general college population. No matter what the number, researchers must argue that the particular definition is one that suits the concept.

Definitions from example

Many human qualities such as honesty, courage, creativity, deceit, and love must be defined by examples that the audience accepts as representative of the concept. Few would not call the firefighters who entered the World Trade Center on September 11, 2001, courageous. Most people would describe someone with a diagnosis of terminal cancer who refuses to feel self-pity as courageous. But what about a student who declines to go to a concert with her friends so she can study for an exam? Her behavior might be admirable, but most people would hesitate to call it courageous. The key to arguing a **definition from example** is that the examples must strike the audience as typical of the concept, even if the situation is unusual.

When Avenue Café's lease expired, the owners of the building refused to renew the restaurant's lease so they could tear down the building to make room for a hotel complex. The restaurant's owners appealed to the city for historic landmark status and received a generous settlement for relocating. What defines a building as a historic landmark?

Finding Good Reasons

WHAT IS PARODY?

The Adbusters Media Foundation, a Canadian media activist group, takes on specific advertising campaigns with clever spoofs of well-known ads. At the top of the Adbusters sabotage list have been alcohol and cigarette ads, among them the above parody of Absolut Vodka ads. (The caption quotes William Shakespeare: "Drink provokes the desire but takes away the performance.")

Because ads are in the public domain, their copyright status is questionable, and Adbusters has pushed that line. In 1992 Absolut threatened to sue Adbusters, but Absolut quickly backed down when the company recognized that the suit would lead to a public debate about protecting advertisers who sell dangerous products. Had the suit gone forward, the legal definition of parody—a work that comments upon or criticizes a prior work—would likely have been key to the Adbusters defense.

Write about it

1. Which of the following criteria do you think must be present for a work to be considered a parody? Are there any criteria you might change or add?

   - the work criticizes a previous work
   - the work copies the same structure, details, or style of the previous work
   - the connections to the previous work are clear to the audience
   - the work is humorous
   - the title is a play on the previous work
   - the work is presented in either a print, visual, or musical medium

2. Does the "Absolut Impotence" ad meet the criteria above? Would you define it as a parody? Why or why not?

Build a Definition Argument

Because definition arguments are the most powerful arguments, they are often at the center of the most important debates in American history. The major arguments of the civil rights movement were definition arguments, none more eloquent than Martin Luther King Jr.'s "Letter from Birmingham Jail." From 1957 until his assassination in April 1968, King served as president of the Southern Christian Leadership Conference, an organization of primarily African-American clergymen dedicated to bringing about social change. King, who was a Baptist minister, tried to put into practice Mahatma Gandhi's principles of nonviolence in demonstrations, sit-ins, and marches throughout the South. During Holy Week in 1963, King led demonstrations and a boycott of downtown merchants in Birmingham, Alabama, to end racial segregation at lunch counters and discriminatory hiring practices.

On Wednesday, April 10, the city obtained an injunction directing the demonstrations to cease until their legality could be argued in court. After meditation, King decided, against the advice of his associates, to defy the court order and proceed with the march planned for Good Friday morning. On Friday morning, April 12, King and 50 followers were arrested. King was held in solitary confinement until the end of the weekend. He was allowed neither to see his attorneys nor to call his wife. On the day of his arrest, King read in the newspaper a statement objecting to the demonstrations signed by eight white Birmingham clergymen of Protestant, Catholic, and Jewish faiths, urging that the protests stop and that grievances be settled in the courts.

On Saturday morning, King started writing an eloquent response that addresses the criticisms of the white clergymen, who are one primary audience of his response. But King intended his response to the ministers for widespread publication, and he clearly had in mind a larger readership. The clergymen gave him the occasion to address moderate white leaders in the South as well as religious and educated people across the nation and supporters of the civil rights movement. King begins "Letter from Birmingham Jail" by addressing the ministers as "My Dear Fellow Clergymen," adopting a conciliatory and tactful tone from the outset but at the same time offering strong arguments for the

Martin Luther King, Jr.

necessity of acting now rather than waiting for change. A critical part of King's argument is justifying disobedience of certain laws. The eight white clergymen asked that laws be obeyed until they were changed.

King argues that there are two kinds of laws: just and unjust. He maintains that people have a moral responsibility to obey just laws and, by the same logic, "a moral responsibility to disobey unjust laws." The cornerstone of his argument is the ability to distinguish just and unjust laws on clear moral and legal criteria. Otherwise people could selectively disobey any law they choose.

Here's how King makes the distinction:

> A just law is a man-made code that squares with the moral law or the law of God. An unjust law is a code that is out of harmony with the moral law. To put it in the terms of St. Thomas Aquinas: An unjust law is a human law that is not rooted in eternal law and natural law. Any law that uplifts human personality is just. Any law that degrades human personality is unjust. All segregation statutes are unjust because segregation distorts the soul and damages the personality. It gives the segregator a false sense of superiority and the segregated a false sense of inferiority. Segregation, to use the terminology of the Jewish philosopher Martin Buber, substitutes an "I-it" relationship and ends up relegating persons to the status of things. Hence segregation is not only politically, economically and sociologically unsound, it is morally wrong and sinful.

King's analysis of just and unjust laws is a classic definitional argument. According to King, a just law possesses the criteria of being consistent with moral law and uplifting human personality. Just as important, King sets out the criteria of an unjust law, which has the criteria of being out of harmony with moral law and damaging to human personality. The criteria are set out in because clauses: _____ *is a* _____ *because it has these criteria.* The criteria provide the link shown in Figure 8.1. The negative argument can be made in the same way, as shown in Figure 8.2.

An extended definition argument like King's is a two-step process. First you have to determine the criteria. Then you have to argue that what you are defining possesses these criteria. If you want to argue that housing prisoners in unheated and non-air-conditioned tents is cruel and unusual punishment, then you have to make exposing prisoners to hot and cold extremes one of the criteria of cruel and unusual punishment. The keys to a definitional argument are getting your audience to accept your criteria and getting your audience to accept that the case in point meets those criteria. King's primary audience was the eight white clergymen; therefore, he used religious criteria and cited theologians as his authorities. His second criterion, that just laws uplift the human personality, was a less familiar concept than the idea of moral law. King therefore offered a more detailed explanation.

But King also knew that not all of his potential readers would put quite so much stock in religious authorities. Therefore, in his letter he follows the religious criteria with two other criteria that appeal to definitions of democracy. First, King

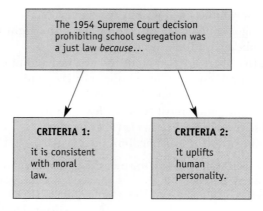

Figure 8.1

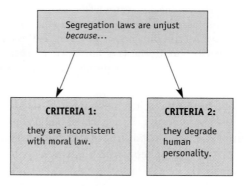

Figure 8.2

argues that "An unjust law is a code that a numerical or power majority group compels a minority group to obey but does not make binding on itself." Just laws, according to King, are ones that everyone should follow. Second, King points out that many African Americans were denied the right to vote in Alabama, and consequently the Alabama legislature that passed the segregation laws was not elected democratically. In all, King sets out four major criteria for defining just and unjust laws (see Figure 8.3).

King's "Letter from Birmingham Jail" draws much of its rhetorical power from its reliance on a variety of arguments that are suited for different readers. An atheist could reject the notion of laws made by God but could still be convinced by the criteria that segregation laws are undemocratic and therefore unjust. To make definitional arguments work, often you must put much effort into identifying and explaining your criteria. You must convince your readers that your criteria are the best ones for what you are defining and that they apply to the case you are arguing.

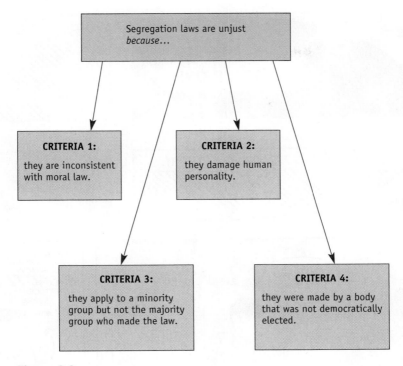

Figure 8.3

Scott McCloud

Setting the Record Straight

Scott McCloud is the pseudonym of Scott Willard McLeod, who was born in Boston in 1960 and graduated from Syracuse University in 1982. After a short stint in the production department at DC Comics, he quickly became a highly regarded writer and illustrator of comics. His works include Reinventing Comics: How Imagination and Technology Are Revolutionizing an Art Form *(2000),* Making Comics: Storytelling Secrets of Comics, Manga and Graphic Novels *(2006), and* Understanding Comics: The Invisible Art *(1993), from which this selection is taken.*

Understanding Comics is a brilliant explanation of how comics combine words and pictures to achieve effects that neither words nor pictures can do alone. At the beginning of the book, McCloud finds it necessary to define what comics are and are not before he can begin to analyze the magic of comics. Notice how he has to refine his criteria several times before he has an adequate definition. ■

Understanding Comics Copyright © 1993, 1994 by Scott McCloud. Published by Kitchen Sink Press. Reprinted by permission of HarperCollins Publishers Inc.

THE ARTFORM -- THE *MEDIUM* -- KNOWN AS COMICS IS A *VESSEL* WHICH CAN HOLD ANY *NUMBER* OF *IDEAS* AND *IMAGES*.

THE *"CONTENT"* OF THOSE IMAGES AND IDEAS IS, OF COURSE, UP TO *CREATORS*, AND WE ALL HAVE DIFFERENT *TASTES*.

GLUG
GLUG

PTUI!!!

GAAK
WHEEEEZ
KAF! KAF!
GLUGH-GGH...

ahem
THE *TRICK* IS TO NEVER MISTAKE THE *MESSAGE* --

-- FOR THE *MESSENGER*.

COMICS

AT ONE TIME OR ANOTHER VIRTUALLY *ALL* THE GREAT MEDIA HAVE RECEIVED *CRITICAL EXAMINATION*, IN AND OF *THEMSELVES*.

WRITTEN WORD   MUSIC   VIDEO
THEATRE   VISUAL ART   FILM

BUT FOR *COMICS*, THIS ATTENTION HAS BEEN *RARE*.*

LET'S SEE IF WE CAN HELP *RECTIFY* THE SITUATION.

*EISNER'S OWN *COMICS AND SEQUENTIAL ART* BEING A HAPPY EXCEPTION.

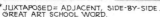

*JUXTAPOSED= ADJACENT, SIDE-BY-SIDE.
GREAT ART SCHOOL WORD.

Sample Student Definition Argument

Chris Nguyen
Professor Conley
GOV 322
24 March 2009

Speech Doesn't Have to Be Pretty to Be Protected

Last month six students on our campus were ejected from a university auditorium for wearing T-shirts with WAR CRIMINAL on the front. Was the university justified in removing our fellow students who were not disruptive in any other way?

The First Amendment to the Constitution of the United States of America guarantees the right to freedom of expression. This important right is one of the foundations of our democracy. Yet many Americans do not understand what the right to free speech really means. Free speech is your right to say what you think—within limits. It is not the right to cause mayhem, to threaten violence, or to incite others to violence. Authority figures also need to understand the limits on free speech. Generally, courts have found that, in order for the restriction of free speech to be justified, the speech must incite imminent lawless action (such as a riot), and it must take place on public property. Even in public high schools, where the government has an obligation to protect minors, "imminent lawless action" must be threatened before speech can be repressed.

Clearly, it's not always easy to tell when restriction of free speech is justified. Consider these recent controversies over free speech:

- A student at Warren Hills Regional High School in New Jersey was suspended for wearing a T-shirt that featured the word *redneck* ("Federal Court").
- Jeff and Nicole Rank attended an official visit by President Bush at the West Virginia capitol and were charged with trespassing when they refused to remove T-shirts that read "Love America, Hate Bush" (Bundy).
- Six students were removed from a university auditorium and charged with trespassing during a speech by former U.S. Secretary of State Henry Kissinger for wearing T-shirts that referred to the speaker as a "war criminal."

In the first two cases, it has been established that authorities did not have the right to curtail the speech of the people involved: A federal appeals court decided the first case in favor of the student, and the prosecutor in the second case dropped the charges, admitting that no law had been broken. If we examine the similarities and differences among these three cases, it becomes clear that in the third case, which happened on our own campus last month, the administration's ejection of the students was unconstitutional.

These are the factors the three cases have in common:

1. In each case, the wearers of the shirts did not express themselves in any way other than by wearing the shirts. They did not speak, shout, hold up banners or signs, or call attention to themselves.
2. None of the events where the shirts were worn were disrupted by the shirts. Any disruption that occurred was due to the removal of the wearers by authority figures.
3. None of the T-shirts featured obscene language or imagery.
4. All took place in government-funded venues: a public school, a state capitol, and a state-funded university.

These similarities are important because they show how, in each case, the T-shirt wearers acted within their constitutionally protected right to free expression.

The first two factors above show how each of these cases fails to meet the standard of "imminent lawless action," set in the 1969 case of *Brandenburg v. Ohio*. In that case, the Supreme Court ruled that in order to ban forms of expression, the government had to prove the expression was "directed to and likely to incite imminent lawless action." If the act of expression did not seem likely to cause a riot, for example, it could not be restricted. Simply making people angry or uncomfortable is not justification for censorship.

In the first case, at Warren Hills High School, the only person who objected to the T-shirt was a vice principal, who claimed the term *redneck* was offensive to minority students and violated the school's racial harassment policy ("Federal Court"). The U.S. Court of Appeals for the Third Circuit, however, ruled that the school failed to prove "that the shirt might genuinely threaten disruption or, indeed, that it violated any of the particular provisions of the harassment policy." This decision followed the precedent of another landmark case, *Tinker v. Des Moines*, in which the Supreme Court ruled that, even in public schools, the government must provide evidence that the speech would cause "(a.) a substantial disruption of the school environment, or (b.) an invasion of the rights of others" (Haynes).

In the second case, the government never even made a claim that the T-shirts worn by Jeff and Nicole Rank were inciting lawlessness. The only people who were upset by the Ranks' T-shirts were two Secret Service officers, who ordered the couple to remove the shirts. When they refused, the officers ordered Charleston city police to arrest them, which the police did. The Ranks were charged with trespassing ("Secret Service"). The irony of arresting U.S. citizens for standing peacefully on public, state-owned property was even clear to the prosecutor, who dropped the charges (Bundy).

Moreover, none of the cases met the test for "vulgar or obscene" language. Vulgar and obscene language can be regulated, to some extent, without violating the First Amendment. In 1986, the Supreme Court ruled in the case of *Bethel v. Fraser* that public school officials could prohibit vulgar speech at a school assembly. The court said that "[T]he undoubted freedom to advocate unpopular and controversial views in schools and classrooms must be balanced against the society's countervailing interest in teaching students the boundaries of socially appropriate behavior." The vice principal in the Warren Hills case was the only one who thought *redneck* was offensive, and the fact that the word is used constantly on television and other media shows that it is not considered obscene by society at large.

The Ranks' arrest is a better comparison to the situation at our school, because their shirts were clearly singled out for their political content, not for vulgarity. They carried a message that might have been offensive to some of the president's supporters who were present, but under no circumstances could the content of the shirts be considered obscene. The same is true of the shirts that got my fellow students kicked out of a public event. Calling someone a war criminal is a serious accusation, but it is not obscene.

Finally, public versus private venue is an important factor in the protection of free speech. The Constitution guarantees that the state will not infringe the right to free expression. Private entities are free to do so, however. For example, protestors can be thrown out of a private meeting of club members. Even a shopping mall owner can deny entry to protesters or even to people without shoes. Of course, anyone with private property also has to consider the economic impact of limiting speech. Recently a shopping mall owner had police arrest a man wearing a "Give Peace a Chance" T-shirt ("Man Arrested") that he had just bought in the mall. Not surprisingly, the mall owner received a great deal of bad publicity about this decision. Concerned citizens who felt this action by the mall owner went too far wrote letters to newspapers publicizing the act. They even wrote letters to the police who arrested the man ("Big Support"). The trespassing charges against the man were dropped. This incident illustrates how free speech is negotiated in the marketplace.

In the Ranks' case, the trespassing charges against them were dropped because they were on the statehouse grounds. How can a citizen trespass on public property? In the same vein, how can students be trespassing on their own campus? The six people arrested at our school were students, whose tuition and fees helped pay for the building they were in. What's more, the event was advertised in flyers and newspaper ads as "free and open to the public." How can anyone be charged with trespassing at a public event?

The Warren Hills case was decided in favor of the student, even though the expression took place in a public school. As *Bethel v. Fraser* shows, courts generally rule that schools can take special steps to protect minors: vulgar or obscene speech can be censored, and school-sponsored forms of expression, like newspapers, can be censored. But these actions are justified because the students are minors. Presumably, they need more guidance as they learn about the boundaries of socially acceptable behavior. But most college students are legally adults, so it does not make sense to say our school was "teaching students the boundaries of socially appropriate behavior" by throwing them out of a public event because of their shirts. It is not the job of a college administration to teach manners.

Our school administrators violated the Constitutional rights of six students last month. They forcibly removed them from a public event in a public building. The students were not causing a commotion in any way before their arrests; there was no indication whatsoever that "imminent lawless action" might be provoked by their T-shirts. Because the students in this case were clearly exercising their Constitutional right to free speech, the university administration should immediately drop the trespassing charges against the students. Evidence from prior cases indicates the charges will not stand up in court in any case, so the legal battle will be a waste of money for the college. Furthermore, as an institution of learning that supposedly safeguards the free exchange of ideas, the college should offer a sincere apology to the arrested students. The administrators would send an important message to all students by doing this: Your right to free speech is respected at this school.

Works Cited

Bethel School Dist. v. Fraser. 478 US 675. Supreme Court of the US. 1986. *Supreme Court Collection*. Legal Information Inst., Cornell U Law School, n.d. Web. 7 Mar. 2009.

"Big Support for 'Peace' T-shirt Arrestees." *The Smoking Gun*. Turner Entertainment Digital Network, 25 Mar. 2003. Web. 10 Mar. 2009.

Brandenburg v. Ohio. 395 US 444. Supreme Court of the US. 1969. *Supreme Court Collection*. Legal Information Inst., Cornell U Law School, n.d. Web. 7 Mar. 2009.

Bundy, Jennifer. "Trespass Charges Dropped Against Bush Protesters." *CommonDreams.org Newscenter*. CommonDreams.org, 15 July 2004. Web. 18 Mar. 2009.

"Federal Court Says NJ School Can't Ban Redneck T-shirt." *Center for Individual Rights*. Center for Individual Rights, 6 Nov. 2003. Web. 11 Mar. 2009.

Haynes, Charles C. "T-shirt Rebellion in the Land of the Free." *First Amendment*. First Amendment Center, 14 Mar. 2004. Web. 18 Mar. 2009.

"Man Arrested for 'Peace' T-shirt." *CNN.com*. Cable News Network, 4 Mar. 2003. Web. 15 Mar. 2009.

"Secret Service and White House Charged with Violating Free Speech Rights in ACLU Lawsuit." *ACLU*. American Civil Liberties Union, 14 Sept. 2004. Web. 19 Mar. 2009.

Steps to Writing a Definition Argument

Step 1 Make a Claim

Make a definitional claim on a controversial issue that focuses on a key term.

Template

- _____ is (or is not) a _____ because it has (or does not have) features A, B, and C (or more).

Examples

- Hate speech (or pornography, literature, films, and so on) is (or is not) free speech protected by the First Amendment because it has (or does not have) these features.
- Hunting (or using animals for cosmetics testing, keeping animals in zoos, wearing furs, and so on) is (or is not) cruelty to animals because it has (or does not have) these features.
- A pharmacist who denies a patient birth control (or the morning-after pill) based on his or her religious beliefs is (or is not) in violation of the Hippocratic oath.
- Displaying pinup calendars (or jokes, innuendo, rap lyrics, and so on) is (or is not) an example of sexual harassment.

Step 2 Think About What's at Stake

- Does nearly everyone agree with you? If so, then your claim probably isn't interesting or important. If you can think of people who disagree, then something is at stake.
- Who argues the opposite of your claim?
- Why or how do they benefit from a different definition?

Step 3 List the Criteria

- Which criteria are necessary for _____ to be a _____?
- Which are not necessary?
- Which are the most important?
- Does your case in point meet all the criteria?

Step 4 Analyze Your Potential Readers

- Who are your readers?
- How does the definitional claim you are making affect them?
- How familiar are they with the issue, concept, or controversy that you're writing about?
- What are they likely to know and not know?
- Which criteria are they most likely to accept with little explanation, and which will they disagree with?
- Which criteria will you have to argue for?

Step 5 Write a Draft

Introduction

- Set out the issue, concept, or controversy.
- Explain why the definition is important.
- Give the background that your intended readers need.

Body

- Set out your criteria and argue for the appropriateness of the criteria.
- Determine whether the criteria apply to the case in point.
- Anticipate where readers might question either your criteria or how they apply to your subject.
- Address opposing viewpoints by acknowledging how their definitions differ and by showing why your definition is better.

Conclusion

■ Do more than simply summarize. You can, for example, go into more detail about what is at stake or the implications of your definition.

Step 6 Revise, Edit, Proofread

■ For detailed instructions, see Chapter 4.
■ For a checklist to use to evaluate your draft, see pages 61–62.

9

Causal
Arguments

Why is the number of women studying computer science shrinking at a time when the number of women studying science and engineering is increasing?

Why did the driver who passed you on a blind curve risk his life to get one car ahead at the next traffic light? Why is it hard to recognize people you know when you run into them unexpectedly in an unfamiliar setting? Why does your mother or father spend an extra hour, plus the extra gas, driving to a supermarket across town just to save a few pennies on one or two items on sale?

Life is full of big and little mysteries, and people spend a lot of time speculating about the causes. Most of the time, however, they don't take the time to analyze in depth what causes a trend, event, or phenomenon. But in college and in the workplace, you likely will have to write causal arguments that require in-depth analysis. In a professional career you will have to make many detailed causal analyses: Why did a retail business fail when it seemed to have an ideal location? What causes cost overruns in the development of a new product? What causes people in some circumstances to prefer public transportation over driving?

Understand How Causal Arguments Work

Causal arguments take three basic forms.

1. One cause leads to one or more effects.

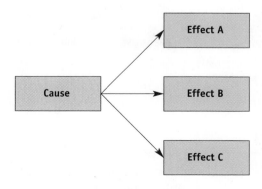

137

The invention of the telegraph led to the commodities market, the establishment of standard time zones, and news reporting as we know it today.

2. One effect has several causes.

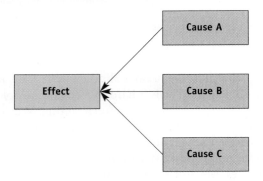

Hurricanes are becoming more financially destructive to the United States because of the greater intensity of recent storms, an increase in the commercial and residential development of coastal areas, and a reluctance to enforce certain construction standards in coastal residential areas.

3. Something causes something else to happen, which in turn causes something else to happen.

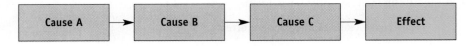

Making the HPV vaccination mandatory for adolescent girls will make unprotected sex seem safer, leading to greater promiscuity, and resulting in more teenage pregnancies.

Find Causes

The causal claim is at the center of a causal argument. Therefore, to get started on a causal argument, you need to propose one or more causes. The big problem with causal arguments is that any topic worth writing about is likely to be complex, making identifying causes difficult. The philosopher John Stuart Mill recognized this problem long ago and devised four methods for finding causes:

- **The Common Factor Method.** When the cause-and-effect relationship occurs more than once, look for something in common in the events and circumstances of each effect; any common factor could be the cause. Scientists have used this method to explain how seemingly different phenomena are associated. There were a variety of explanations of fire until, in the 1700s, Joseph Priestley in England and Antoine Lavoisier in France discovered that oxygen was a separate element and that burning was caused by oxidation.

- **The Single Difference Method.** This method works only when there are at least two similar situations, one that leads to an effect and one that does not. Look for something that was missing in one case and present in another—the single difference. The writer assumes that if everything is substantially alike in both cases, then the single difference is the (or a) cause. At the Battle of Midway in 1942, the major naval battle of World War II in the Pacific, the Japanese Navy had a 4-to-1 advantage over the U.S. Navy. Both fleets were commanded by competent, experienced leaders. But the U.S. commander, Admiral Nimitz, had a superior advantage in intelligence, which proved to be decisive.

- **Concomitant Variation.** This tongue twister is another favorite method of scientists. If an investigator finds that a possible cause and a possible effect have a similar pattern of variation, then one can suspect that a relationship exists. For example, scientists noticed that peaks in the 11-year sunspot cycle have predictable effects on high-frequency radio transmission on the earth.

- **Process of Elimination.** Many possible causes can be proposed for most trends and events. If you are a careful investigator, you have to consider all causes that you can think of and eliminate the ones that cannot be causes.

To understand how these methods might work for you, consider this example. Suppose you want to research the causes of the increase in legalized lotteries in the United States. You might discover that lotteries go back to colonial times. Harvard and Yale universities have been longtime rivals in football, but the schools' rivalry goes back much further. Both schools ran lotteries before the Revolutionary War! In 1747 the Connecticut legislature voted to allow Yale to conduct a lottery to raise money to build dormitories, and in 1765 the Massachusetts legislature gave Harvard permission for a lottery. Lotteries were common before and after the American Revolution, but they eventually ran into trouble because they were run by private companies that failed to pay the winners. After 1840, laws against lotteries were passed, but they came back in the South after the Civil War.

Finding Good Reasons
WHY ARE AMERICANS GAINING WEIGHT?

Eric Schlosser, author of *Fast Food Nation* (2001), chows down on a grilled cheese sandwich, fries, and a soda. *Fast Food Nation* traces the rise of fast food restaurants against the background of American culture based on the automobile. Schlosser claims that one of the effects of fast food is the increase of overweight Americans. For an example of his writing on another topic, see pages 520-523.

There is no doubt that Americans have grown larger. A 2004 survey of Americans published in *JAMA: The Journal of the American Medical Association* found that nearly one-third (32.5 percent) of adults are obese and two-thirds (66.3 percent) are overweight. An especially disturbing aspect of this trend is that children are increasingly obese. The Center for Disease Control and Prevention reports that the percentage of obese children aged 6 to 11 almost quadrupled from 4 percent in 1974 to 15 percent in 2000, and the percentage of obese children aged 12 to 19 increased from 6 percent in 1974 to 15 percent in 2000.

Write about it

To what extent do you think fast food is the cause of the trend toward excess weight? To what extent do you think lifestyle changes and the content of food are causes? In addition to the amount of fast food Americans consume, consider the following:

- more sedentary lifestyle with more driving and less walking
- more time spent watching television, using computers, and playing video games
- introduction of high-fructose corn syrup in many foods, from ketchup and peanut butter to chocolate milk and yogurt
- inadequate physical education and reduced outdoor recess periods in schools
- more food advertising directed at children

The defeated states of the Confederacy needed money to rebuild the bridges, buildings, and schools that were destroyed in the Civil War, and they turned to selling lottery tickets throughout the nation (ironically, the tickets were very popular in the North). Once again, the lotteries were run by private companies, and scandals eventually led to their being banned.

In 1964 the voters in New Hampshire approved a lottery as a means of funding education—in preference to an income tax or a sales tax. Soon other northeastern states followed this lead and establishing lotteries with the reasoning that if people were going to gamble, the money should remain at home. During the 1980s, other states approved not only lotteries but also other forms of state-run gambling such as keno and video poker. By 1993 only Hawaii and Utah had no legalized gambling of any kind.

If you are analyzing the causes of the spread of legalized gambling, you might use the **common factor method** to investigate what current lotteries have in common with earlier lotteries. That factor is easy to identify: It's economic. The early colonies and later the states have turned to lotteries again and again as a way of raising money that avoids unpopular tax increases. But why have lotteries spread so quickly and seemingly become so permanent since 1964, when before that, they were used only sporadically and were banned eventually? The **single difference method** points us to the major difference between the lotteries of today and those of previous eras: Lotteries in the past were run by private companies, and inevitably someone took off with the money instead of paying it out. Today's lotteries are owned and operated by state agencies or contracted under state control, and while they are not immune to scandals, they are much more closely monitored than lotteries were in the past.

The controversies over legal gambling now focus on casinos. In 1988 Congress passed the Indian Gaming Regulatory Act, which started a new era of casino gambling in the United States. The world's largest casino, Foxwoods Casino in Connecticut, owned by the Mashantucket Pequot Tribe, became a huge money-maker. Along with nearby Mohegan Sun Casino, Foxwoods paid over $400 million into the Connecticut state treasury. Other tribes and other states were quick to cash in on casino gambling. Iowa legalized riverboat gambling in 1989, followed shortly by Louisiana, Illinois, Indiana, Mississippi, and Missouri. As with lotteries, the primary justification for approving casino gambling has been economic. States have been forced to fund various programs that the federal government used to pay for. Especially in states where lottery revenues had begun to sag, legislatures and voters turned to casinos to make up the difference.

Casinos, however, have been harder to sell to voters than lotteries. For many voters, casinos are a NIMBY ("not in my back yard") issue. They may believe that people should have the right to gamble, but they don't want a casino in their town. Casino proponents have tried to overcome these objections by arguing that casinos bring added tourist dollars, benefiting the community as a whole. Opponents argue the opposite: that people who go to casinos spend their money on gambling and not on tourist attractions. The cause-and-effect benefit of casinos to community businesses can be examined by **concomitant variation.** Casino supporters argue that people who come to gamble spend a lot of money elsewhere. Opponents of casinos claim that people who come for gambling don't want to spend money elsewhere. Furthermore, they point out that gambling represents another entertainment option for people within easy driving distance and can hurt area businesses such as restaurants, amusement parks, and bowling alleys. So far, the record has been mixed, some businesses being helped and others being hurt when casinos are built nearby.

Many effects don't have causes as obvious as the spread of legalized gambling. The **process of elimination method** can be a useful tool when several possible causes are involved. Perhaps you have had the experience of your computer not turning on. If you checked first to see if it was plugged in, then plugged it into another socket to make sure the socket was on, and then checked the surge suppressor to see if it worked, you used a process of elimination to diagnose the cause of the problem. Major advances in science and medicine have resulted from the process of elimination. For centuries soldiers on long campaigns and sailors on long sea voyages suffered horrible deaths from scurvy until 1747, when James Lind demonstrated that scurvy could be treated and prevented with a diet that includes lemons and limes. Nevertheless, people proposed various causes for scurvy including poor hygiene, lack of exercise, and tainted canned food. Finally, in 1932, the cause of scurvy was proven to be a vitamin C deficiency.

Build a Causal Argument

Effective causal arguments move beyond the obvious to get at underlying causes. The great causal mystery today is global warming. Scientists generally agree that the average surface temperature on Earth has gone up by 1 degree Fahrenheit or 0.6 degrees Celsius over the last hundred years and that the amount of carbon dioxide has increased by 25 percent. But the causes of those facts are much disputed. Some people believe that the rise in temperature is a naturally occurring climate variation and that the increase in carbon dioxide is only minimally the cause or not related at all. Others argue that the burning of fossil fuels and the cutting of tropical forests have led to the increase in carbon dioxide, which in turn traps heat in the atmosphere, thus increasing the temperature of the earth. The major problem for all participants in the global warming debate is that the causation is not simple and direct.

Arctic and subarctic regions have been affected more dramatically than elsewhere. In Iceland, average summer temperatures have risen by 0.5 to 1.0 degree Celsius since the early 1980s. All of Iceland's glaciers, except a few that surge and ebb independent of weather, are now in rapid retreat, a pattern observed throughout

Glaciers in many parts of the world are melting at rates faster than scientists thought possible just a few years ago. Even major oil companies have acknowledged that global warming is real. Yet the American public has taken little notice of world climate change—perhaps because it's difficult to get excited about the mean temperature rising a few degrees and the sea level rising a few feet. What would get Americans thinking seriously about global warming?

regions in the far north. Arctic sea ice shrank by 14 percent—an area the size of Texas—from 2004 to 2005, and Greenland's massive ice sheet has been thinning by more than 3 feet a year. Environmentalists today point to the melting of the glaciers and sea ice as proof that human-caused global warming is taking place.

Scientists, however, are not so certain. Their difficulty is to sort human causes from naturally recurring climate cycles. Much of the detailed data about the great melt in the north goes back only to the early 1990s—not long enough to rule out short-term climate cycles. If we are in a regular, short-term warming cycle, then the question becomes, how does greenhouse warming interact with that cycle? Computer models suggest there is a very low probability that such rapid change could occur naturally. But the definitive answers to the causes of the Great Melt are probably still a long way off.

Another pitfall common in causal arguments using statistics is mistaking correlation for causation. For example, the FBI reported that in 1995 criminal victimization rates in the United States dropped 13 percent for personal crimes and 12.4 percent for property crimes—the largest decreases ever. During that same year, the nation's prison and jail populations reached a record high of 1,085,000 and 507,000 inmates, respectively. The easy inference is that putting more people behind bars lowers the crime rate, but there are plenty of examples to the contrary. The drop in crime rates in the 1990s remains quite difficult to explain.

Others have argued that the decline in SAT verbal scores during the late 1960s and 1970s reflected a decline in literacy skills caused by an increase in television viewing. But the fact that the number of people who took the SAT during the 1970s greatly increased suggests that there was not an actual decline in literacy skills, only a great expansion in the population who wanted to go to college.

Annie Murphy Paul

The Real Marriage Penalty

Annie Murphy Paul is a freelance journalist who writes about mental health issues for publications such as Salon, Discover, *and* Self. *She is also the author of* The Cult of Personality: How Personality Tests Are Leading Us to Miseducate Our Children, Mismanage Our Companies, and Misunderstand Ourselves *(2004).*

In this article, which appeared in the New York Times Magazine *on November 19, 2006, Paul explores the possibility that the greater prevalence of egalitarian marriages in our society is leading to a less egalitarian society overall. She also asks why egalitarian marriages are on the rise: Are there more opportunities than ever before for singles to find a partner matched in education and earning potential? Or, has there been a change in the qualities women and men look for in a life partner?*

"Some of us are becoming the men we wanted to marry," Gloria Steinem proclaimed 25 years ago. She meant, of course, that women in large numbers were seizing the places in higher education and the professions that had formerly been closed to them, becoming the doctors, lawyers and executives that they once hoped only to wed. Over the past generation, the liberal notion of egalitarian marriage—in which wives are in every sense their husbands' peers—has gone from pie-in-the-sky ideal to unremarkable reality. But this apparently progressive shift has been shadowed by another development: America's growing gap between rich and poor. Even as husbands and wives have moved closer together on measures of education and income, the divide between well-educated, well-paid couples and their less-privileged counterparts has widened, raising an awkward possibility: are we achieving more egalitarian marriages at the cost of a more egalitarian society?

2   Once, it was commonplace for doctors to marry nurses and executives to marry secretaries. Now the wedding pages are stocked with matched sets, men and women who share a tax bracket and even an alma mater. People, like other members of the animal kingdom, have always been prone to "assortative mating," or choosing to have babies with a reassuringly similar partner. But observers like Geoffrey Miller, an evolutionary psychologist at the University of New Mexico and author of "The Mating Mind," suggest that the innovations of modern society—from greater geographic mobility to specialized work environments to Internet dating—have made this matching process much more efficient. "Assortative mating is driven by our personal preferences, but also by whom we meet, and these days we have many more opportunities to meet others like ourselves," he says. (As with most contemporary sociological phenomena, "Seinfeld" was there first: a 1996 episode featured the comedian finding "the female Jerry.")

3   In particular, Americans are increasingly pairing off by education level, according to the sociologists Christine Schwartz and Robert Mare. In an article published last year in the journal *Demography*, they reported that the odds of a high-school graduate marrying someone with a college degree declined by 43 percent between 1940 and the late 1970s. In our current decade, the researchers wrote, the percentage of couples who are "educationally homogamous"—that is, share the same level of schooling—reached its highest point in 40 years. Assortative mating by income also seems to be on the rise. In a 2004 study of couples wed in the 1970s through the early 1990s, the researchers Megan Sweeney and Maria Cancian found an increasingly strong association between women's wages before marriage and the occupational status and future earnings prospects of the men they married.

4   Why is this happening? For one thing, more couples are meeting in college and other educational settings, where prospective mates come pre-screened by admissions committees as discerning as any yenta. Husbands and wives who begin their relationships during their school years are more likely to have comparable education (and, presumably, income) levels. Secondly, men and women have become more alike in what they want from a marriage partner. This convergence is both cultural—co-ed gyms and bars have replaced single-sex sewing circles and Elks clubs—and economic. Just as women have long sought to marry a good breadwinner, men, too, now find earning potential sexy. "There are fewer Cinderella marriages these days," says Stephanie Coontz, author of "Marriage, a History." "Men are less interested in rescuing a woman from poverty. They want to find someone who will pull her weight." For this reason, the "marriage penalty" once paid by highly educated women has all but disappeared: among women born after 1960, a college graduate is more likely to marry than her less-educated counterpart. And finally, there's

what Schwartz calls the growing "social and economic distance" between the well educated and the less so, a gulf even ardent romantics may find difficult to bridge.

5   This last theory holds that disparities in wealth influence whom we marry, but there's reason to think that our mating patterns could be producing economic inequality as well as reflecting it. A model constructed by the economists Raquel Fernandez and Richard Rogerson, published in 2001 in *The Quarterly Journal of Economics,* led them to conclude that "increased marital sorting"—high earners marrying high earners and low earners marrying low earners—"will significantly increase income inequality." A 2003 analysis by Gary Burtless, an economist at the Brookings Institution, found that a rising correlation of husband-and-wife earnings accounted for 13 percent of the considerable growth in economic inequality between 1979 and 1996.

6   Burtless himself does not think that assortative mating is necessarily becoming more prevalent. In fact, he says he believes that "the tendency of like to marry like has remained roughly unchanged over time. What have changed are the labor-market opportunities and behavior of women." In this conception, men have always married women of their own social class, but such stratification was obscured by the fact that the female halves of these couples often did not work or pursue advanced degrees. Now that women who are in a position to do so are attending college and graduate school and joining the professions, the economic consequences of Americans' assortative mating habits are becoming clearer.

7   If assortative mating does contribute to our growing gap between rich and poor, does that matter? Few people would question any individual's romantic preferences. And yet as the current clash over gay marriage demonstrates, private choices about whom we marry—or don't marry, or can't marry—can have loud public reverberations. Not long ago, the marriages of whites and blacks, and the lifting of laws that once prohibited such unions, revealed a nation beginning to open its mind on matters of race; likewise, rates of marriage across lines of education and income provide an index of social mobility. If there are fewer such marriages, then there are "fewer sources of intimate ties" between groups, Schwartz says, making marriage one more brick in the wall that separates America's haves and have-nots.

8   Of course, men and women don't choose each other on the basis of education and income alone. Putting love aside, as men's and women's roles continue to shift, other standards for selecting a partner may come to the fore. Indeed, the sociologist Julie Press recently offered what she called "a gynocentric theory of assortative mating," moving the focus from what men now desire in a marriage partner to the evolving preferences of women. What would-be wives may be seeking now, she proposed in *The Journal of Marriage and Family,* is "cute butts and housework"—that is, a man with an appealing physique and a willingness to wash dishes. Could this be a feminist slogan for our time? ■

Emily Raine

Why Should I Be Nice to You? Coffeeshops and the Politics of Good Service

Emily Raine recently received a master's degree in communication studies at McGill University in Montreal. She also writes about graffiti and street art. This article appeared in the online journal Bad Subjects *in 2005.*

*   In this article, Raine explains why work in a coffee chain is worse than work in other kinds of service jobs. She also outlines the causes for what she sees as a destructive dynamic in the coffee chain culture and provides a possible alternative.*

> "There is no more precious commodity than the relationship
> of trust and confidence a company has with its employees."
> —*Starbucks Coffee Company chairman Howard Schultz*

I actually like to serve. I'm not sure if this comes from some innate inclination to mother and fuss over strangers, or if it's because the movement and sociability of service work provides a much-needed antidote to the solitude of academic research, but I've always found something about service industry work satisfying. I've done the gamut of service jobs, from fine dining to cocktail waitressing to hip euro-bistro counter work, and the only job where I've ever felt truly whipped was working as a barista at one of the now-ubiquitous specialty coffee chains, those bastions of jazz and public solitude that have spread through urban landscapes over the last ten years or so. The pay was poor, the shifts long and oddly dispersed, the work boring and monotonous, the managers demanding, and the customers regularly displayed that unique spleen that emerges in even the most pleasant people before they've had the morning's first coffee. I often felt like an aproned Coke machine, such was the effect my sparkling personality had on the clientele. And yet, some combination of service professionalism, fear of termination and an imperative to be "nice" allowed me to suck it up, smile and continue to provide that intangible trait that the industry holds above all else, good service.

2   Good service in coffee shops doesn't amount to much. Unlike table service, where interaction with customers spans a minimum of half an hour, the average contact with a café customer lasts less than ten seconds. Consider how specialty cafés are laid out: the customer service counter is arranged in a long line that clients move along to "use" the café. The linear coffee bar resembles an assembly line, and indeed, café labor is heavily grounded in the rationalism of Fordist manufacturing principles, which had already been tested for use in hospitality services by fast food chains. Each of the café workers is assigned a specific stage in the service process to perform exclusively, such as taking orders, using the cash registers, or handing clients cups of brewed coffee.

3   The specialization of tasks increases the speed of transactions and limits the duration of any one employee's interaction with the clientele. This means that in a given visit a customer might order from one worker, receive food from the next, then brewed coffee or tea from yet another, then pay a cashier before proceeding down the line of the counter, finishing the trip at the espresso machine which is always situated at its end. Ultimately, each of the café's products is processed and served by a different employee, who repeats the same preparation task for hours and attends to each customer only as they receive that one product.

4   Needless to say, the productive work in cafés is dreary and repetitive. Further, this style of service severely curtails interaction with the clientele, and the very brevity of each transaction precludes much chance for authentic friendliness or conversation—even asking about someone's day would slow the entire operation. The one aspect of service work that can be unpredictable—people—becomes redundant, and interaction with customers is reduced to a fatiguing eight-hour-long smile and the repetition of sentiments that allude to good service, such as injunctions to enjoy their purchases or to have a nice day. Rather than friendly exchanges with customers, barista workers' good service is reduced to a quick rictus in the customer's direction between a great deal of friendly interaction with the espresso machine.

5   As the hospitality industry really took off in the sixties, good service became one of the trademarks of its advertising claims, a way for brands to distinguish themselves from the rest of the pack. One needn't think too hard to come up with a litany of service slogans that holler the good graces of their personnel—at Starbucks where the baristas make the magic, at Pacific Southwest Airlines where smiles aren't just painted on, or at McDonald's where smiles are free. Employee friendliness emerged as one of the chief distinguishing brand features of personal services, which means that the workers themselves become an aspect of the product for sale.

6   Our notions of good service revolve around a series of platitudes about professionalism—we're at your service, with a smile, where the customer's always right—each bragging the centrality of the customer to everything "we" do. Such claims imply an easy and equal exchange between two parties: the "we" that gladly serves and the "you" that happily receives. There is, however, always a third party involved in the service exchange, and that's whoever has hired the server, the body that ultimately decides just what the dimensions of good service will be.

7   Like most employees, a service worker sells labor to an employer at a set rate, often minimum wage, and the employer sells the product of that labor, the service itself, at market values. In many hospitality services, where gratuities make up the majority of employment revenue, the worker directly benefits from giving good service, which of course translates to good tips. But for the vast majority of service staff, and particularly those employed in venues yielding little or no gratuities—fast food outlets, café chains, cleaning and

maintenance operations—this promises many workers little more than a unilateral imperative to be perpetually bright and amenable.

8 The vast majority of service personnel do not spontaneously produce an unaffected display of cheer and good will continuously for the duration of a shift. When a company markets its products on servers' friendliness, they must then monitor and control employees' friendliness, so good service is defined and enforced from above. Particularly in chains, which are premised upon their consistent reproduction of the same experience in numerous locations, organizations are obliged to impose systems to manage employees' interaction their customers. In some chains, namely the fast food giants such as McDonald's and Burger King, employee banter is scripted into cash registers, so that as soon as a customer orders, workers are cued to offer, "would you like a dessert with that?" (an offer of dubious benefit to the customer) and to wish them a nice day. Ultimately, this has allowed corporations to be able to assimilate "good service"—or, friendly workers—into their overall brand image.

9 While cafés genuflect toward the notion of good service, their layouts and management styles preclude much possibility of creating the warmth that this would entail. Good service is, of course, important, but not if it interferes with throughput. What's more, these cafés have been at the forefront of a new wave of organizations that not only market themselves on service quality but also describe employees' job satisfaction as the seed from which this flowers.

10 Perhaps the most glaring example of this is Starbucks, where cheerful young workers are displayed behind elevated counters as they banter back and forth, calling out fancy Italian drink names and creating theatre out of their productive labor. Starbucks' corporate literature gushes not only about the good service its customers will receive, but about the great joy that its "partners" take in providing it, given the company's unique ability to "provide a great work environment and treat each other with respect and dignity," and where its partners are "emotionally and intellectually committed to Starbucks success." In the epigraph to this essay, Starbucks' chairman even describes the company's relationship with its workers as a commodity. Not only does Starbucks offer good service, but it attempts to guarantee something even better: good service provided by employees that are genuinely happy to give it.

11 Starbucks has branded a new kind of worker, the happy, wholesome, perfume-free barista. The company offers unusual benefits for service workers, including stock options, health insurance, dental plans and other perks such as product discounts and giveaways. Further, they do so very, very publicly, and the company's promotional materials are filled with moving accounts of workers who never dreamed that corporate America could care so much. With the other hand, though, the company has smashed unionization drives in New York, Vancouver and at its Seattle roaster; it schedules workers at oddly timed shifts that never quite add up to full-time hours; the company pays only

nominally more than minimum wage, and their staffs are still unable to subsist schlepping lattes alone.

12   Starbucks is not alone in marketing itself as an enlightened employer. When General Motors introduced its Saturn line, the new brand was promoted almost entirely on the company's good relations with its staff. The company's advertising spots often featured pictures of and quotes from the union contract, describing their unique partnership between manufacturer, workers and union, which allowed blue-collar personnel to have a say in everything from automobile designs to what would be served for lunch. The company rightly guessed that this strategy would go over well with liberal consumers concerned about the ethics of their purchases. Better yet, Saturn could market is cars based on workers' happiness whether personnel were satisfied or not, because very few consumers would ever have the chance to interact with them.

13   At the specialty coffee chains, however, consumers *have* to talk to employees, yet nobody ever really asks. The café service counter runs like a smooth piece of machinery, and I found that most people preferred to pretend that they were interacting with an appliance. In such short transactions, it is exceedingly difficult for customers to remember the humanity of each of the four to seven people they might interact with to get their coffees. Even fast food counters have one server who processes each customer's order, yet in cafés the workers just become another gadget in the well-oiled café machine. This is a definite downside for the employees—clients are much ruder to café staff than in any other sector of the industry I ever worked in. I found that people were more likely to be annoyed than touched by any reference to my having a personality, and it took no small amount of thought on my part to realize why.

14   Barista workers are hired to represent an abstract category of worker, not to act as individuals. Because of the service system marked by short customer interaction periods and a homogenous staff, the services rendered are linked in the consumer imagination to the company and not to any one individual worker. Workers' assimilation into the company image makes employees in chain service as branded as the products they serve. The chain gang, the workers who hold these eminently collegiate after-school jobs, are proscribed sales scripts and drilled on customer service scenarios to standardize interactions with customers. The company issues protocols for hair length, color and maintenance, visible piercings and tattoos as well as personal hygiene and acceptable odorific products. Workers are made more interchangeable by the use of uniforms, which, of course, serve to make the staff just that. The organization is a constant intermediary in every transaction, interjecting its presence in every detail of the service experience, and this standardization amounts to an absorption of individuals' personalities into the corporate image.

15   Many of the measures that chains take to secure the homogeneity of their employees do not strike us as particularly alarming, likely because similar

restrictions have been in place for several hundred years. Good service today has inherited many of the trappings of the good servant of yore, including prohibitions against eating, drinking, sitting or relaxing in front the served, entering and exiting through back doors and wearing uniforms to visually mark workers' status. These measures almost completely efface the social identities of staff during work hours, providing few clues to workers' status in their free time. Contact between service workers and their customers is thus limited to purely functional relations, so that the public only see them as workers, as makers of quality coffee, and never as possible peers.

16   Maintaining such divisions is integral to good service because this display of class distinctions ultimately underlies our notions of service quality. Good service means not only serving well, but also allowing customers to feel justified in issuing orders, to feel okay about being served—which, in turn, requires demonstrations of class difference and the smiles that suggest servers' comfort with having a subordinate role in the service exchange.

17   Unlike the penguin-suited household servant staffs whose class status was clearly defined, service industry workers today often have much more in common from a class perspective with those that they serve. This not only creates an imperative for them to wear their class otherness on their sleeves, as it were, but also to accept their subordinate role to those they serve by being unshakably tractable and polite.

18   Faith Popcorn has rather famously referred to the four-dollar latte as a "small indulgence," noting that while this is a lot to pay for a glass of hot milk, it is quite inexpensive for the feeling of luxury that can accompany it. In this service climate, the class status of the server and the served—anyone who can justify spending this much on a coffee—is blurry, indeed. Coffee shops that market themselves on employee satisfaction assert the same happy servant that allows politically conscientious consumers who are in many cases the workers' own age and class peers, to feel justified in receiving good service. Good service—as both an apparent affirmation of subordinate classes' desire to serve and as an enforced one-sided politeness—reproduces the class distinctions that have historically characterized servant-served relationships so that these are perpetuated within the contemporary service market.

19   The specialty coffee companies are large corporations, and for the twenty-somethings who stock their counters, barista work is too temporary to bother fighting the system. Mostly, people simply quit. Dissatisfied workers are stuck with engaging in tactics that will change nothing but allow them to make the best of their lot. These include minor infractions such as taking liberties with the uniforms or grabbing little bits of company time for their own pleasure, what Michel de Certeau calls *la perruque* and the companies themselves call "time theft." As my time in the chain gang wore on, I developed my own tactic, the only one I found that jostled the customers out of their complacency and allowed me to be a barista and a person.

20   There is no easy way to serve without being a servant, and I have always found that the best way to do so is to show my actual emotions rather than affecting a smooth display of interminable patience and good will. For café customers, bettering baristas' lots can be as simple as asking about their day, addressing them by name—any little gesture to show that you noticed the person behind the service that they can provide. My tactic as a worker is equally simple, but it is simultaneously an assertion of individual identity at work, a refusal of the class distinctions that characterize the service environment and a rebuttal to the companies that would promote my satisfaction with their system: be rude. Not arbitrarily rude, of course—customers are people, too, and nobody gains anything by spreading bad will. But on those occasions when customer or management behavior warranted a zinging comeback, I would give it.

21   Rudeness, when it is demanded, undermines companies' claims on workers' personal warmth and allows them to retain their individuality by expressing genuine rather than affected feelings in at-work interpersonal exchanges. It is a refusal of the class distinctions that underlie consumers' unilateral prerogative of rudeness and servers' unilateral imperative to be nice. It runs contrary to everything that we have been taught, not only about service but about interrelating with others. But this seems to be the only method of asserting one's person-hood in the service environment, where workers' personalities are all too easily reduced to a space-time, conflated with the drinks they serve. Baristas of the world, if you want to avoid becoming a green-aproned coffee dispensary, you're just going to have to tell people off about it. ■

Steps to Writing a Causal Argument

Step 1 Make a Claim

Make a causal claim on a controversial trend, event, or phenomenon.

Template

- SOMETHING does (or does not) cause SOMETHING ELSE.

  —or—

- SOMETHING causes SOMETHING ELSE, which, in turn, causes SOMETHING ELSE.

Examples

- One-parent families (or television violence, bad diet, and so on) are (or are not) the cause of emotional and behavioral problems in children.
- Firearms control laws (or right-to-carry-handgun laws) reduce (or increase) violent crimes.
- The trend toward home schooling (or private schools) is (or is not) improving the quality of education.
- The length of U.S. presidential campaigns forces candidates to become too much influenced by big-dollar contributors (or prepares them for the constant media scrutiny that they will endure as president).
- Putting grade school children into competitive sports teaches them how to succeed in later life (or puts undue emphasis on winning and teaches many who are slower to mature to have a negative self-image).

Step 2 What's at Stake in Your Claim?

- If the cause is obvious to everyone, then it probably isn't worth writing about.

Step 3 Think of Possible Causes

- Which are the immediate causes?
- Which are the background causes?
- Which are the hidden causes?
- Which are the causes that most people have not recognized?

Step 4 Analyze Your Potential Readers

- Who are your readers?
- How familiar will they be with the trend, event, or phenomenon that you're writing about?
- What are they likely to know and not know?
- How likely are they to accept your causal explanation?
- What alternative explanation might they argue for?

Step 5 Write a Draft

Introduction

- Describe the controversial trend, event, or phenomenon.
- Give the background that your intended readers will need.

Body

- Explain the cause or chain of causation of a trend, event, or phenomenon that is unfamiliar to your readers. Remember that providing facts is not the same thing as establishing causes, although facts can help to support your causal analysis.
- Set out the causes that have been offered and reject them one by one. Then you can present the cause that you think is most important.
- Treat a series of causes one by one, analyzing the importance of each.

Conclusion

- Do more than simply summarize. Consider describing additional effects beyond those that have been noted previously.

Step 6 Revise, Edit, Proofread

- For detailed instructions, see Chapter 4.
- For a checklist to use to evaluate your draft, see pages 61-62.

10

Evaluation Arguments

Why is it good to send humans on long space missions when probes and robots can gather the same data without risking lives?

Whenever people debate whether or not something is a good idea, like sending people into space, they are making an evaluation argument. People make evaluations all the time. Newspapers and magazines have picked up on this love of evaluation by running "best of" polls. They ask their readers to vote on the best Chinese restaurant, the best pizza, the best local band, the best coffeehouse, the best dance club, the best neighborhood park, the best swimming hole, the best bike ride (scenic or challenging), the best volleyball court, the best place to get married, and so on. If you ask one of your friends who voted in a "best" poll why she picked a particular restaurant as the best of its kind, she might respond by saying simply, "I like it." But if you ask her why she likes it, she might start offering good reasons such as these: the food is good, the service prompt, the prices fair, and the atmosphere comfortable. It's really not a mystery why these polls are often quite predictable or why the same restaurants tend to win year after year. Many people think that evaluations are matters of personal taste, but when we begin probing the reasons, we often discover that different people use similar criteria to make evaluations.

People opposed to sending humans into space, for example, use the criteria of cost and safety. Those who argue for sending people into space use the criteria of expanding human presence and human experience. The key to convincing other people that your judgment is sound is establishing the criteria you will use to make your evaluation. Sometimes it will be necessary to argue for the validity of the criteria that you think your readers should consider. If your readers accept your criteria, it's likely they will agree with your conclusions.

Understand How Evaluation Arguments Work

Evaluation arguments set out criteria and then judge something to be good or bad or best or worst according to those criteria.

Something is a good (bad, the best, the worst) _____ if measured by certain criteria (practicality, aesthetics, ethics).

156

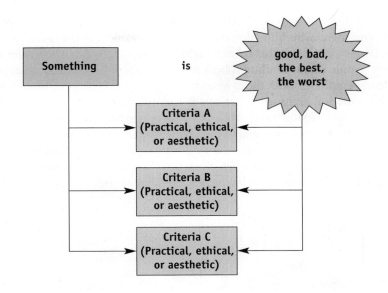

Google Maps is the best mapping program because it is easy to use, it is accurate, and it provides entertaining and educational features such as Google Earth.

Recognize Kinds of Evaluations

Arguments of evaluation are structured much like arguments of definition. Recall that the criteria in arguments of definition are set out in because clauses: SOME-THING is a _____ because it has these criteria. The key move in writing most evaluative arguments is first deciding what kind of criteria to use.

Imagine that the oldest commercial building in your city is about to be torn down. Your goal is to get the old store converted to a museum by making a proposal argument. First you will need to make an evaluative argument that will form the basis of your proposal. You might argue that a downtown museum would be much better than more office space because it would draw more visitors. You might argue that the stonework in the building is of excellent quality and deserves preservation. Or you might argue that it is only fair that the oldest commercial building be preserved because the oldest house and other historic buildings have been saved.

Each of these arguments uses different criteria. An argument that a museum is better than an office building because it would bring more visitors to the downtown area is based on **practical criteria.** An argument that the old building is beautiful and that beautiful things should be preserved uses **aesthetic criteria**. An argument that the oldest commercial building deserves the same treatment as the oldest house is based on fairness, a concept that relies on **ethical criteria**. The debate over the value of sending people versus sending robots into space employs all these criteria but with different emphases. Both those who favor and those who oppose human space travel make practical arguments that much scientific knowledge and many other benefits result from space travel. Those who favor sending humans use aesthetic arguments: space travel is essential to the way we understand ourselves as humans and Americans. Those who oppose sending humans question the ethics of spending so much money for manned space vehicles when there are pressing needs at home, and they point out that robots can be used for a fraction of the cost. (See Figure 10.1.)

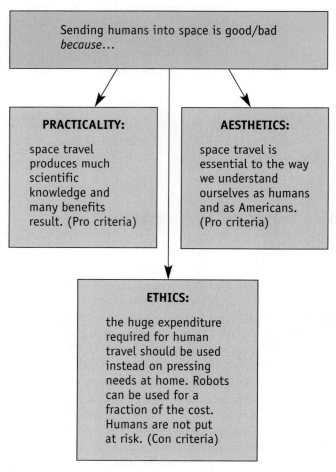

Figure 10.1

Finding Good Reasons

WHAT'S THE BEST ALTERNATIVE FUEL?

Since the 1990s automakers have produced flex-fuel cars, which burn ethanol (E-85) and gasoline, and hybrid vehicles, which combine electric and gasoline engines. More recently, spurred on by the federal government's 2003 $1.2-billion hydrogen initiative, automakers also have built fuel-cell prototypes. In a fuel-cell car, hydrogen reacts with oxygen to produce water and electricity, which then is used to power an electric motor. Hydrogen burns cleanly, emitting only water vapor, and can be produced from both renewable and nonrenewable energy sources, including solar, water, wind, and nuclear power.

But is hydrogen a realistic solution to the world's dependence on fossil fuels? The automaker Honda says yes. It plans to bring the first fuel-cell car, the FCX, to the market in 2008. Detractors say no. According to former U.S. Department of Energy official Joseph Romm, "A hydrogen car is one of the least efficient, most expensive ways to reduce greenhouse gases."

Write about it

1. One way to assess a complicated issue like alternative fuel technologies is to evaluate each technology against a set of common criteria. Which of the following criteria are useful for evaluating fuel-efficient cars? Why are they useful?

   - cost of development and production
   - sticker price of cars using the technology
   - how long it takes for cars to reach the market
   - efficiency and reliability of cars using the technology
   - environmental impact
   - convenience of refueling and maintenance
   - driver's aesthetic experience

2. Are any of the above criteria more important than the others? If so, how would you rank them? Why? Are there any criteria you would add?

Build an Evaluation Argument

Most people have a lot of practice making consumer evaluations, and when they have enough time to do their homework, they usually make an informed decision. Sometimes, criteria for evaluations are not so obvious, however, and evaluations are much more difficult to make. Sometimes one set of criteria favors one choice, while another set of criteria favors another. You might have encountered this problem when you chose a college. If you were able to leave home to go to school, you had a potential choice of over 1400 accredited colleges and universities. Until 20 years ago, there wasn't much information about choosing a college other than what colleges said about themselves. You could find out the price of tuition and what courses were offered, but it was hard to compare one college with another.

In 1983 the magazine *U.S. News & World Report* began ranking U.S. colleges and universities from a consumer's perspective. These rankings have remained highly controversial ever since. Many college officials have attacked the criteria that *U.S. News* uses to make its evaluations. In an August 1998 *U.S. News* article, Gerhard Casper, the president of Stanford University (which is consistently near the top of the rankings), writes, "Much about these rankings—particularly their specious formulas and spurious precision—is utterly misleading." Casper argues that using graduation rates as a criterion of quality rewards easy schools. Other college presidents have called for a national boycott of the *U.S. News* rankings (without much success).

U.S. News replies in its defense that colleges and universities themselves do a lot of ranking. Schools rank students for admissions, using SAT or ACT scores, high school GPA, high school class rank, quality of high school, and other factors, and then grade the students and rank them against each other when they are enrolled in college. Furthermore, schools also evaluate faculty members and take great interest in the national ranking of their departments. They care very much about where they stand in relation to each other. Why, then, *U.S. News* argues, shouldn't people be able to evaluate colleges and universities, since colleges and universities are so much in the business of evaluating people?

Arguing for the right to evaluate colleges and universities is one thing; actually doing comprehensive and reliable evaluations is quite another. *U.S. News* uses a formula in which 25 percent of a school's ranking is based on a survey of reputation in which the president, provost, and dean of admissions at each college rate the quality of schools in the same category, and the remaining 75 percent is based on statistical criteria of quality. These statistical criteria fall into six major categories: retention of students, faculty resources, student selectivity, financial resources, alumni giving, and (for national universities and liberal arts colleges only) graduation rate performance—the difference between the number of

Windmills produce energy without pollution and reduce dependence on foreign oil. Do you agree or disagree with people who do not want windmills built near them because they find them ugly?

students who are expected to graduate and the number that actually do. These major categories are made up of factors that are weighted according to their importance. For example, the faculty resources category is determined by the size of classes (the proportion of classes with fewer than 20 students to classes with 50 or more students), the average faculty pay weighted by the cost of living in different regions of the country, the percentage of professors with the highest degree in their field, the overall student–faculty ratio, and the percentage of faculty who are full-time.

Those who have challenged the *U.S. News* rankings argue that the magazine should use different criteria or weight the criteria differently. *U.S. News* explains its ranking system on its Web site (www.colleges.usnews.rankingsandreviews.com/college). If you are curious about where your school ranks, take a look.

Michael Eric Dyson

Gangsta Rap and American Culture

Michael Eric Dyson is a Baptist minister and professor of religious studies at the University of Pennsylvania. He is one of the first academics to defend rap music as an art form. This essay, from the 2004 collection The Michael Eric Dyson Reader, *is based on a 1994 editorial Dyson wrote for the* New York Times. *In this essay, Dyson responds to those in Congress and to social activists who wish to censor gangsta rap because of its tendency to feature violent and obscene lyrics.*

The recent attacks on the entertainment industry, especially gangsta rap, by Senator Bob Dole, former Education Secretary William Bennett, and political activist C. Delores Tucker, reveal the fury that popular culture can evoke in a wide range of commentators. As a thirty-five-year-old father of a sixteen-year-old son and as a professor and ordained Baptist minister who grew up in Detroit's treacherous inner city, I too am disturbed by many elements of gangsta rap. But I'm equally anguished by the way many critics have used its artists as scapegoats. How can we avoid the pitfall of unfairly attacking black youth for problems that bewitched our culture long before they gained prominence? First, we should understand what forces drove the emergence of rap. Second, we should place the debate about gangsta rap in the context of a much older debate about "negative" and "positive" black images. Finally, we should acknowledge that gangsta rap crudely exposes harmful beliefs and practices that are often maintained with deceptive civility in much of mainstream society, including many black communities.

2   If the fifteen-year evolution of hip-hop teaches us anything, it's that history is made in unexpected ways by unexpected people with unexpected results. Rap is now safe from the perils of quick extinction predicted at its humble start. But its birth in the bitter belly of the '70s proved to be a Rosetta stone of black popular culture. Afros, "blunts," funk music, and carnal eruptions define a "back-in-the-day" hip-hop aesthetic. In reality, the severe '70s busted the economic boom of the '60s. The fallout was felt in restructured automobile industries and collapsed steel mills. It was extended in exported employment to foreign markets. Closer to home, there was the depletion of social services to reverse the material ruin of black life. Later, public spaces for black recreation were gutted by Reaganomics or violently transformed by lethal drug economies.

3   Hip-hop was born in these bleak conditions. Hip-hoppers joined pleasure and rage while turning the details of their difficult lives into craft and capital. This is the world hip-hop would come to "represent": privileged persons speaking for less visible or vocal peers. At their best, rappers shape the tortuous twists of urban fate into lyrical elegies. They represent lives swallowed by too little love or opportunity. They represent themselves and their

peers with aggrandizing anthems that boast of their ingenuity and luck in surviving. The art of "representin" that is much ballyhooed in hiphop is the witness of those left to tell the afflicted's story.

4 As rap expands its vision and influence, its unfavorable origins and its relentless quest to represent black youth are both a consolation and challenge to hip-hoppers. They remind rappers that history is not merely the stuff of imperial dreams from above. It isn't just the sanitizing myths of those with political power. Representing history is within reach of those who seize the opportunity to speak for themselves, to represent their own interests at all costs. Even rap's largest controversies are about representation. Hip-hop's attitudes toward women and gays continually jolt in the unvarnished malevolence they reveal. The sharp responses to rap's misogyny and homophobia signify its central role in battles over the cultural representation of other beleaguered groups. This is particularly true of gangsta rap.

5 While gangsta rap takes the heat for a range of social maladies from urban violence to sexual misconduct, the roots of our racial misery remain buried beneath moralizing discourse that is confused and sometimes dishonest. There's no doubt that gangsta rap is often sexist and that it reflects a vicious misogyny that has seized our nation with frightening intensity. It is doubly wounding for black women who are already beset by attacks from outside their communities to feel the thrust of musical daggers to their dignity from within. How painful it is for black women, many of whom have fought valiantly for black pride, to hear the dissonant chord of disdain carried in the angry epithet "bitch."

6 The link between the vulgar rhetorical traditions expressed in gangsta rap and the economic exploitation that dominates the marketplace is real. The circulation of brutal images of black men as sexual outlaws and black females as "ho's" in many gangsta rap narratives mirrors ancient stereotypes of black sexual identity. Male and female bodies are turned into commodities. Black sexual desire is stripped of redemptive uses in relationships of great affection or love.

7 Gangsta rappers, however, don't merely respond to the values and visions of the marketplace; they help shape them as well. The ethic of consumption that pervades our culture certainly supports the rapacious materialism shot through the narratives of gangsta rap. Such an ethic, however, does not exhaust the literal or metaphoric purposes of material wealth in gangsta culture. The imagined and real uses of money to help one's friends, family, and neighborhood occupy a prominent spot in gangsta rap lyrics and lifestyles.

8 Equally troubling is the glamorization of violence and the romanticization of the culture of guns that pervades gangsta rap. The recent legal troubles of Tupac Shakur, Dr. Dre, Snoop Doggy Dogg, and other gangsta rappers chastens any defense of the genre based on simplistic claims that these artists are merely performing roles that are divorced from real life. Too often for gangsta rappers, life does indeed imitate and inform art.

9 But gangsta rappers aren't *simply* caving in to the pressure of racial stereotyping and its economic rewards in a music industry hungry to exploit

their artistic imaginations. According to this view, gangsta rappers are easily manipulated pawns in a chess game of material dominance where their consciences are sold to the highest bidder. Or else gangsta rappers are viewed as the black face of white desire to distort the beauty of black life. Some critics even suggest that white record executives discourage the production of "positive rap" and reinforce the desire for lewd expressions packaged as cultural and racial authenticity.

10   But such views are flawed. The street between black artists and record companies runs both ways. Even though black artists are often ripe for the picking—and thus susceptible to exploitation by white and black record labels—many of them are quite sophisticated about the politics of cultural representation. Many gangsta rappers helped to create the genre's artistic rules. Further, they have figured out how to financially exploit sincere and sensational interest in "ghetto life." Gangsta rap is no less legitimate because many "gangstas" turn out to be middle-class blacks faking homeboy roots. This fact simply focuses attention on the genre's essential constructedness, its literal artifice. Much of gangsta rap makes voyeuristic whites and naive blacks think they're getting a slice of authentic ghetto life when in reality they're being served colorful exaggerations. That doesn't mean, however, that the best of gangsta rappers don't provide compelling portraits of real social and economic suffering.

11   Critics of gangsta rap often ignore how hip-hop has been developed without the assistance of a majority of black communities. Even "positive" or "nation-conscious" rap was initially spurned by those now calling for its revival in the face of gangsta rap's ascendancy. Long before white record executives sought to exploit transgressive sexual behavior among blacks, many of us failed to lend support to politically motivated rap. For instance, when political rap group Public Enemy was at its artistic and popular height, most of the critics of gangsta rap didn't insist on the group's prominence in black cultural politics. Instead, Public Enemy, and other conscientious rappers, were often viewed as controversial figures whose inflammatory racial rhetoric was cause for caution or alarm. In this light, the hue and cry directed against gangsta rap by the new defenders of "legitimate" hip-hop rings false.

12   Also, many critics of gangsta rap seek to curtail its artistic freedom to transgress boundaries defined by racial or sexual taboo. That's because the burden of representation falls heavily on what may be termed the race artist in a far different manner than the one I've described above. The race artist stands in for black communities. She represents millions of blacks by substituting or sacrificing her desires and visions for the perceived desires and visions of the masses. Even when the race artist manages to maintain relative independence of vision, his or her work is overlaid with, and interpreted within, the social and political aspirations of blacks as a whole. Why? Because of the appalling lack of redeeming or nonstereotypical representations of black life that are permitted expression in our culture.

13   This situation makes it difficult for blacks to affirm the value of nontraditional or transgressive artistic expressions. Instead of viewing such cultural products through critical eyes—seeing the good and the bad, the productive and destructive aspects of such art—many blacks tend to simply dismiss such work with hypercritical disdain. A suffocating standard of "legitimate" art is thus produced by the limited public availability of complex black art. Either art is seen as redemptive because it uplifts black culture and shatters stereotypical thinking about blacks, or it is seen as bad because it reinforces negative perceptions of black culture.

14   That is too narrow a measure for the brilliance and variety of black art and cultural imagination. Black folk should surely pay attention to how black art is perceived in our culture. We must be mindful of the social conditions that shape perceptions of our cultural expressions and that stimulate the flourishing of one kind of art versus another. (After all, die-hard hip-hop fans have long criticized how gangsta rap is eagerly embraced by white record companies while "roots" hip-hop is grossly underfinanced.)

15   But black culture is too broad and intricate—its artistic manifestations too unpredictable and challenging—for us to be *obsessed* with how white folk view our culture through the lens of our art. And black life is too differentiated by class, sexual identity, gender, region, and nationality to fixate on "negative" or "positive" representations of black culture. Black culture is good and bad, uplifting and depressing, edifying and stifling. All of these features should be represented in our art, should find resonant voicing in the diverse tongues of black cultural expressions.

16   Gangsta rappers are not the first to face the grueling double standards imposed on black artists. Throughout African-American history, creative personalities have sought to escape or enliven the role of race artist with varying degrees of success. The sharp machismo with which many gangsta rappers reject this office grates on the nerves of many traditionalists. Many critics argue that since gangsta rap is often the only means by which many white Americans come into contact with black life, its pornographic representations and brutal stereotypes of black culture are especially harmful. The understandable but lamentable response of many critics is to condemn gangsta rap out of hand. They aim to suppress gangsta rap's troubling expressions rather than critically engage its artists and the provocative issues they address. Thus the critics of gangsta rap use it for narrow political ends that fail to enlighten or better our common moral lives.

17   Tossing a moralizing *j'accuse* at the entertainment industry may have boosted Bob Dole's standing in the polls over the short term. It did little, however, to clarify or correct the problems to which he has drawn dramatic attention. I'm in favor of changing the moral climate of our nation. I just don't believe that attacking movies, music, and their makers is very helpful. Besides, rightwing talk radio hosts wreak more havoc than a slew of violent films. They're the ones terrorist Timothy McVeigh was inspired by as he planned to bomb the federal building in Oklahoma City.

18   A far more crucial task lies in getting at what's wrong with our culture and what it needs to get right. Nailing the obvious is easy. That's why Dole, along with William Bennett and C. Delores Tucker, goes after popular culture, especially gangsta rap. And the recent attempts of figures like Tucker and Dionne Warwick, as well as national and local lawmakers, to censor gangsta rap or to outlaw its sale to minors are surely misguided. When I testified before the U.S. Senate's Subcommittee on Juvenile Justice, as well as the Pennsylvania House of Representatives, I tried to make this point while acknowledging the need to responsibly confront gangsta rap's problems. Censorship of gangsta rap cannot begin to solve the problems of poor black youth. Nor will it effectively curtail their consumption of music that is already circulated through dubbed tapes and without the benefit of significant airplay.

19   A crucial distinction needs to be made between censorship of gangsta rap and edifying expressions of civic responsibility and community conscientiousness. The former seeks to prevent the sale of vulgar music that offends mainstream moral sensibilities by suppressing the First Amendment. The latter, however, is a more difficult but rewarding task. It seeks to oppose the expression of misogynistic and sexist sentiments in hip-hop culture through protest and pamphleteering, through community activism, and through boycotts and consciousness raising.

20   What Dole, Bennett, and Tucker shrink from helping us understand—and what all effective public moralists must address—is why this issue now? Dole's answer is that the loss of family values is caused by the moral corruption of popular culture, and therefore we should hold rap artists, Hollywood moguls, and record executives responsible for our moral chaos. It's hard to argue with Dole on the surface, but a gentle scratch reveals that both his analysis and answer are flawed.

21   Too often, "family values" is a code for a narrow view of how families work, who gets to count as a legitimate domestic unit, and consequently, what values are crucial to their livelihood. Research has shown that nostalgia for the family of the past, when father knew best, ignores the widespread problems of those times, including child abuse and misogyny. Romantic portrayals of the family on television and the big screen, anchored by the myth of the Benevolent Patriarch, hindered our culture from coming to grips with its ugly domestic problems.

22   To be sure, there have been severe assaults on American families and their values, but they have not come mainly from Hollywood, but from Washington with the dismantling of the Great Society. Cruel cuts in social programs for the neediest, an upward redistribution of wealth to the rich, and an unprincipled conservative political campaign to demonize poor black mothers and their children have left latter-day D. W. Griffiths in the dust. Many of gangsta rap's most vocal black critics (such as Tucker) fail to see how the alliances they forge with conservative white politicians such as Bennett and Dole are plagued with problems. Bennett and Dole have put up roadblocks to many legislative and

political measures that would enhance the fortunes of the black poor they now claim in part to speak for. Their outcry resounds as crocodile tears from the corridors of power paved by bad faith.

23   Moreover, many of the same conservative politicians who support the attack on gangsta rap also attack black women (from Lani Guinier to welfare mothers), affirmative action, and the redrawing of voting districts to achieve parity for black voters. The war on gangsta rap diverts attention away from the more substantive threat posed to women and blacks by many conservative politicians. Gangsta rap's critics are keenly aware of the harmful effects that genre's misogyny can have on black teens. Ironically, such critics appear oblivious to how their rhetoric of absolute opposition to gangsta rap has been used to justify political attacks on poor black teens.

24   That doesn't mean that gratuitous violence and virulent misogyny should not be opposed. They must be identified and destroyed. I am wholly sympathetic, for instance, to sharp criticism of gangsta rap's ruinous sexism and homophobia though neither Dole, Bennett, nor Tucker has made much of the latter plague. "Fags" and "dykes" are prominent in the genre's vocabulary of rage. Critics' failure to make this an issue only reinforces the inferior, invisible status of gay men and lesbians in mainstream and black cultural institutions: Homophobia is a vicious emotion and practice that links mainstream middle-class and black institutions to the vulgar expressions of gangsta rap. There seems to be an implicit agreement between gangsta rappers and political elites that gays, lesbians, and bisexuals basically deserve what they get.

25   But before we discard the genre, we should understand that gangsta rap often reaches higher than its ugliest, lowest common denominator. Misogyny, violence, materialism, and sexual transgression are not its exclusive domain. At its best, this music draws attention to complex dimensions of ghetto life ignored by many Americans. Of all the genres of hip-hop—from socially conscious rap to black nationalist expressions, from pop to hardcore—gangsta rap has most aggressively narrated the pains and possibilities, the fantasies and fears, of poor black urban youth. Gangsta rap is situated in the violent climes of postindustrial Los Angeles and its bordering cities. It draws its metaphoric capital in part from the mix of myth and murder that gave the Western frontier a dangerous appeal a century ago.

26   Gangsta rap is largely an indictment of mainstream and bourgeois black institutions by young people who do not find conventional methods of addressing personal and social calamity useful. The leaders of those institutions often castigate the excessive and romanticized violence of this music without trying to understand what precipitated its rise in the first place. In so doing, they drive a greater wedge between themselves and the youth they so desperately want to help.

27   If Americans really want to strike at the heart of sexism and misogyny in our communities, shouldn't we take a closer look at one crucial source of these blights—religious institutions, including the synagogue, the temple,

and the church? For instance, the central institution of black culture, the black church, which has given hope and inspiration to millions of blacks, has also given us an embarrassing legacy of sexism and misogyny. Despite the great good it has achieved through a heroic tradition of emancipatory leadership, the black church continues to practice and justify *ecclesiastical apartheid*. More than 70 percent of black church members are female, yet they are generally excluded from the church's central station of power, the pulpit. And rarely are the few ordained female ministers elected pastors.

28   Yet black leaders, many of them ministers, excoriate rappers for their verbal sexual misconduct. It is difficult to listen to civil rights veterans deplore the hostile depiction of women in gangsta rap without mentioning the vicious sexism of the movements for racial liberation of the 1960s. And of course the problem persists in many civil rights organizations today.

29   Attacking figures like Snoop Doggy Dogg or Tupac Shakur—or the companies that record or distribute them—is an easy out. It allows scapegoating without sophisticated moral analysis and action. While these young black males become whipping boys for sexism and misogyny, the places in our culture where these ancient traditions are nurtured and rationalized—including religious and educational institutions and the nuclear family—remain immune to forceful and just criticism.

30   Corporate capitalism, mindless materialism, and pop culture have surely helped unravel the moral fabric of our society. But the moral condition of our nation is equally affected by political policies that harm the vulnerable and poor. It would behoove Senator Dole to examine the glass house of politics he abides in before he decides to throw stones again. If he really wants to do something about violence, he should change his mind about the ban on assault weapons he seeks to repeal. That may not be as sexy or self-serving as attacking pop culture, but it might help save lives.

31   Gangsta rap's greatest "sin" may be that it tells the truth about practices and beliefs that rappers hold in common with the mainstream and with black elites. This music has embarrassed mainstream society and black bourgeois culture. It has forced us to confront the demands of racial representation that plague and provoke black artists. It has also exposed our polite sexism and our disregard for gay men and lesbians. We should not continue to blame gangsta rap for ills that existed long before hip-hop uttered its first syllable. Indeed, gangsta rap's in-your-face style may do more to force our nation to confront crucial social problems than countless sermons or political speeches. ∎

Sample Student Evaluation Argument

Rashaun Giddens
Professor Chen
English 1302
21 April 2009

Stop Loss or "Loss of Trust"

Looking back on my high school career, my social and extracurricular lives were filled with countless highs: hanging out with my friends, prom, and varsity track to name a few. My academic career, however, was a bit shakier. So busy with what I saw then as the important things in life, I often procrastinated or altogether avoided my schoolwork. My senior year, the recruiter from the U.S. Army Reserves spoke at a school assembly. He asked that we as seniors consider the prospect of becoming "weekend warriors." In the wake of September 11, we could help protect our country and simultaneously work toward paying for a college education, which seemed like a great idea to many students. For those who could not otherwise afford college, the prospect of receiving a higher education in return for patriotism and some good hard work sounded fair enough. My life, however, took a different turn. When I received my track scholarship, I decided to head off to college right away. Many of my friends, however, heeded the call to service. So far, their realities have been far from the lives that were pitched to them; rather, this was the beginning of a path to broken dreams and broken promises.

My cousin, moved to action by a charismatic recruiter, an Army announcement of fifteen-month active tours, and the prospect of a paid college education, chose to join the United States Army Reserves. The Army, suffering from a recruitment shortfall, had recently announced a policy that would allow recruits to serve in active duty for a mere fifteen months. For serving for just over a year, my cousin could do his national duty and put himself on a path to self-improvement. The recruiter did not, however, highlight the fine print to this new program. No one told my cousin that he could be called back to active duty for up to eight years under the government's "stop loss" policy. Further, no one told him that just one day after the Army announced the incentive program, an appeals court ruled that the Army could, under stop loss, compel soldiers to remain beyond the initial eight-year obligation (Wickham).

The stop loss policy forces thousands of soldiers to serve beyond their volunteer enlistment contracts. The all-volunteer army—on which the government prides itself—is slowly developing into a disgruntled mass of men and women being held against their will. These men and women wanted to serve their countries and their families, and they signed what they believed were binding agreements with a trustworthy employer—the United States government—only to find that their government didn't bargain in good faith.

As far back as the Civil War, the government needed incentives to retain its troops. (Although we all want freedom, few actually want to put our own lives on the line in the pursuit of that goal.) Both the Union and the Confederacy needed to make tough decisions to maintain strong armed forces when soldiers' contracts were expiring. The Union chose to offer financial incentives to keep its young men in uniform, while the Confederacy instituted a series of (not so) "voluntary" reenlistment policies (Robertson). During World War II all soldiers were forced to remain active until they reached a designated number of points. Vietnam saw the last stage of a mandatory draft, with soldiers serving one-year tours (Hockstader). Today's military relies on stop loss, making soldiers stay in the military after their commitment ends. Congress first gave the military the authority to retain soldiers after the Vietnam War when new volunteers were too few to replace departing soldiers. In November 2002, the Pentagon gave stop loss orders for Reserve and National Guard units activated to fight terrorism (Robertson).

This policy is neither forthcoming, safe, nor compassionate toward those most directly impacted—the soldiers and their families. As the United States became more and more entrenched in the conflict in Iraq, the military was stretched thinner and thinner. By 2004, approximately 40% of those serving in Iraq and Afghanistan came from the ranks of the part-time soldiers: the Reserves and the National Guard (Gerard). While these individuals did know that their countries could call if they enlisted, they continue to bear an inordinate burden of actual combat time, and this new policy continues to create situations further removed from the job for which they enlisted. Recruiters often pitch the military—including the Reserves and the Guard—to young, impressionable, and often underprivileged kids. I have experienced this pitch firsthand and have seen the eyes of my classmates as the recruiter promised them a better and richer tomorrow. Seeing a golden opportunity for self-respect and achievement, young men and women sign on the dotted line. Today, other young men and women are buying a bill of goods. These recruits—and those who came before them— deserve to have an honest relationship with the government they protect. As policymakers tout the all-volunteer Army, those who serve find their rights threatened. The military claims to teach soldiers respect and honor. Is misleading your employees honest?

Aside from being less than forthright, stop loss may be putting our soldiers in harm's way. The policy forces these soldiers to suffer the strain of combat for extended periods of time. Because of the way the policy works, troops may learn of tour extensions mere hours before they had planned to return stateside to lower-stress positions and their loved ones. These troops need to be ready, alert, and equipped with a morale which allows them to fight effectively. Stop loss instead forces these soldiers—often those trained for short stints—to work beyond their experience and training. This policy may prove to overextend, both emotionally and physically, our fighting men and women. As they repeatedly suffer disappointment because of changes in their orders and delays of departure, morale is likely to drop. Based on reports from families, this practice has been devastating to their soldiers. Nancy Durst, wife of United States Reservist Staff Sergeant Scott Durst, told *Talk of the Nation*'s Neal Conan that the military detained her husband's unit just thirty minutes before it was to board the bus scheduled to deliver it to a stateside flight. The unit was later informed that tours had been extended for another four months (Durst). War breeds stress, but how can soldiers be expected to function at an optimal level when forced to suffer disappointments at the hands of their own government?

Finally, this policy simply runs contrary to the current administration's stated interest in the preservation of family and the bolstering of small businesses. First (and most obviously), this less-than-forthright policy keeps families separated. Husbands, wives, and children find themselves separated for longer periods of time, left with uncertainty and ambiguity for comfort. How does this aid in preserving the family? Second, when the government deploys reservists, soldiers often take a severe pay cut. Forced to leave their regular jobs, soldiers—and their families—must survive on an often much smaller government wage. Stop loss extends tours of duty and consequently the economic struggles of the families in question. Third, the policy has proven detrimental to the small-business owner. Men and women have used their military experience, discipline, and training to further themselves economically. The United States prides itself on the power of the small businessman; however, individuals such as Chief Warrant Officer Ronald Eagle have been hurt by this policy. After twenty years of service, Eagle was set to retire from the Army and focus on his aircraft-maintenance business. Instead, the Army has indefinitely moved his retirement date. As a consequence, Eagle has taken a $45,000 pay cut and wonders whether his business will survive his hiatus (Hockstader). Is this the way the government and military fight to preserve the family—emotionally and economically?

Because American men and women risk their lives in the name of bettering those of Iraqis, the military should think about how their policy affects the lives of their soldiers and those back home. While the stop loss policy does allow the armed forces to build a larger active force without the public backlash (and political suicide) of instituting the draft, this policy comes at a cost. Those who have chosen to serve their country—whether for the training, educational possibilities, economic support, or expression of patriotism—are being bamboozled.

Watch the television commercials that, even now, tout training and part-time service. Read the stories of those serving and the families left behind. The sales pitch and the real picture do not match. The United States is undeniably one of the strongest nations in the world and a bastion of freedom. For these very reasons, the armed forces and the United States government, which represents all citizens, must find a way to lead this war (or conflict or crusade) honestly. If we have to pay soldiers double what they currently make in order to get them to reenlist, we should do so. Even a draft would at least be aboveboard and honest. But we cannot continue to trick people into risking their lives for our national security. Our country must show the honor and respect deserved by those who fight, and stop loss undeniably dishonors and shows disrespect to our soldiers. The military must take a cue from its own advertising and "be all they can be." Be honest.

Works Cited

Durst, Nancy. Interview by Neal Conan. *Talk of the Nation*. Natl. Public Radio. WNYC, New York. 19 Apr. 2004. Radio.

Gerard, Philip. "When the Cry Was 'Over the Hill in October.'" *Charleston Gazette* 16 May 2004: 1E. *LexisNexis Academic*. Web. 6 Apr. 2009.

Hockstader, Lee. "Army Stops Many Soldiers from Quitting; Orders Extend Enlistments to Curtail Troop Shortages." *Washington Post* 29 Dec. 2003: A01. *LexisNexis Academic*. Web. 8 Apr. 2009.

Robertson, John. "The Folly of Stop Loss." *Pittsburgh Post-Gazette* 19 Dec. 2004: J1. *LexisNexis Academic*. Web. 7 Apr. 2009.

Wickham, DeWayne. "A 15-Month Enlistment? Check Army's Fine Print." *USA Today* 17 May 2005: 13A. *LexisNexis Academic*. Web. 6 Apr. 2009.

Steps to Writing an Evaluation Argument

Step 1 Make a Claim

Make an evaluative claim based on criteria.

Template

- SOMETHING is good (bad, the best, the worst) if measured by certain criteria (practicality, aesthetics, ethics).

Examples

- A book or movie review.
- A defense of a particular kind of music or art.
- An evaluation of a controversial aspect of sports (e.g., the current system of determining who is champion in Division I college football by a system of bowls and polls) or a sports event (e.g., this year's WNBA playoffs) or a team.
- An evaluation of the effectiveness of an educational program (such as your high school honors program or your college's core curriculum requirement) or some other aspect of your campus.
- An evaluation of the effectiveness of a social policy or law such as legislating 21 as the legal drinking age, current gun control laws, or environmental regulation.

Step 2 Think About What's at Stake

- Does nearly everyone agree with you? Then your claim probably isn't interesting or important. If you can think of people who disagree, then something is at stake.
- Who argues the opposite of your claim?
- Why do they make a different evaluation?

Step 3 **List the Criteria**

- Which criteria make something either good or bad?
- Which criteria are the most important?
- Which criteria are fairly obvious, and which will you have to argue for?

Step 4 **Analyze Your Potential Readers**

- Who are your readers?
- How familiar will they be with what you are evaluating?
- What are they likely to know and not know?
- Which criteria are they most likely to accept with little explanation, and which will they disagree with?

Step 5 **Write a Draft**

Introduction

- Introduce the person, group, institution, event, or object that you are going to evaluate. You might want to announce your stance at this point or wait until the concluding section.
- Give the background that your intended readers will need.

Body

- Describe each criterion and then analyze how well what you are evaluating meets that criterion.
- If you are making an evaluation according to the effects someone or something produces, describe each effect in detail.
- Anticipate where readers might question either your criteria or how they apply to your subject.
- Address opposing viewpoints by acknowledging how their evaluations might differ and by showing why your evaluation is better.

Conclusion

- If you have not yet announced your stance, conclude that, on the basis of the criteria you set out or the effects you have analyzed, something is good (bad, the best, the worst).
- If you have made your stance clear from the beginning, end with a compelling example or analogy.

Step 6 Revise, Edit, Proofread

- For detailed instructions, see Chapter 4.
- For a checklist to use to evaluate your draft, see pages 61–62.

11

Narrative Arguments

The U.S. Postal Service has issued a stamp to honor the AMBER Alert program, a system created in response to the abduction and murder of nine-year-old Amber Hagerman. The system seemed to be effective at first, but the number of false alarms, including numerous cases where a parent seized a child in a custody dispute, has undermined its credibility. To what extent can a large-scale solution be built on one case, no matter how tragic?

In 1996, nine-year-old Amber Hagerman was kidnapped while riding her bicycle in Arlington, Texas, and brutally murdered. Local police had information that might have saved her life, but they lacked a way to broadcast that information. Shortly after the tragedy, Dallas-Fort Worth broadcasters teamed with local police to develop a system to notify the public when a child is abducted. The program, AMBER (America's Missing: Broadcast Emergency Response), began in Texas and spread to all 50 U.S. states with federal government support. The story of Amber Hagerman's death appealed to shared community values in ways that statistics did not. It vividly demonstrated that something was very wrong if children could not be protected from abduction and exploitation.

A single, detailed personal story sometimes makes a stronger case than large-scale statistical evidence. The Annenberg Public Policy Center reported that an estimated 1.6 million of 17 million U.S. college students gambled online in 2005, but it was the story of Greg Hogan that made the problem real for many Americans. Hogan, the son of a Baptist minister, was an extraordinarily talented musician, playing onstage twice at Carnegie Hall by age 13. He chose to attend Lehigh University in Pennsylvania, where he was a member of the orchestra and class president. At Lehigh he also acquired an addiction to online poker. He lost $7,500, much of which he borrowed from fraternity brothers. To pay them back, he robbed a bank, only to be arrested a few hours later. Eventually he received a prison sentence of 22 months to 10 years. Hogan's story helped to influence Congress to pass the Unlawful Internet Gambling Enforcement Act, which requires financial institutions to stop money transfers to gambling sites.

Ronald Reagan and Martin Luther King Jr. are acknowledged as masters in using narratives to make arguments. Reagan once said that facts are stupid things until we give them meaning, which he supplied by putting facts in stories. In "Letter from Birmingham Jail," King relates in one sentence the pettiness of segregation laws and their effect on children:

> ... when you suddenly find your tongue twisted and your speech stammering as you seek to explain to your six-year-old daughter why she can't go to the public amusement park that has just been advertised on television, and see tears welling up in her eyes when she is told that Funtown is closed to colored children, and see ominous clouds of inferiority beginning to form in her little mental sky, and see her beginning to distort her personality by developing an unconscious bitterness toward white people.

This tiny story drives home King's point.

Understand How Narrative Arguments Work

Successful narrative arguments typically don't have a thesis statement but instead tell a compelling story. From the experience of one individual, readers infer a claim and the reasons that support the claim.

A personal account illustrates the reasons that support a claim. Sometimes the reader must infer these reasons, as well as the claim.

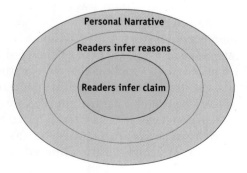

Journalist Bob Woodruff's detailed account of his arduous recovery from a head injury suffered during a roadside bomb attack in Iraq illustrates the need for the U.S. military to reassess its methods of treating troops with brain injuries.

Recognize Kinds of Narrative Arguments

Using narratives to advocate for change is nothing new. As far back as we have records, we find people telling stories and singing songs that argue for change. Folk songs have always given voice to political protest and have celebrated marginalized people. When workers in the United States began to organize in the 1880s, they adapted melodies that soldiers had sung in the Civil War. In the 1930s, performers and songwriters such as Paul Robeson, Woody Guthrie, Huddie Ledbetter (Leadbelly), and Aunt Molly Jackson relied on traditions of hymns, folk songs, and African American blues to protest social conditions. In the midst of the politically quiet 1950s, folk songs told stories that critiqued social conformity and the dangers of nuclear war. In the 1960s, the

Folk singer/songwriter Shawn Colvin is one of many contemporary folk and blues singers who continue the tradition of making narrative arguments in their songs. Can you think of a song that makes a narrative argument?

civil rights movement and the movement against the Vietnam War brought a strong resurgence of folk music. The history of folk music is a continuous recycling of old tunes, verses, and narratives to engage new political situations. What can be said for folk songs is also true for any popular narrative genre, be it the short story, novel, drama, movies, or even rap music.

Narrative arguments work differently from arguments that spell out their criteria and argue for explicit links. A narrative argument succeeds if the experience being described invokes the life experiences of readers or listeners. Anyone who has ever been around children knows that most kids love amusement parks. When Martin Luther King Jr. describes the tears in his young daughter's eyes when he tells her she cannot go to a public amusement park because of the color of her skin, he does not have to explain to his readers why going to an amusement park advertised on television is so important for his daughter.

Likewise, the story of Amber Hagerman was effective because even if you have not known a child who was abducted and murdered or exploited, you will probably agree that children should be protected against these crimes. Narrative arguments allow readers to fill in the good reasons. In the cases of King's argument

Finding Good Reasons
CAN A STORY MAKE AN ARGUMENT?

This aerial photograph, taken on September 1, 2005, shows an evacuation point on Interstate 10 where victims of Hurricane Katrina were stranded. In the excerpt below, paramedics Larry Bradshaw and Lorrie Beth Slonsky describe what happened on the fourth day after the storm as they were forced to leave the hotel they were staying in and find a way out of New Orleans. Officials told them and a group of evacuees waiting for transportation that they were "on their own." Bradshaw and Slonsky describe what happened next:

> Our little encampment began to blossom. Someone stole a water delivery truck and brought it up to us. . . . A mile or so down the freeway, an army truck lost a couple of pallets of C-rations on a tight turn. We ferried the food back to our camp in shopping carts. Now secure with the two necessities, food and water, cooperation, community and creativity flowered. We organized a clean up, and hung garbage bags from the rebar poles. We made beds from wood pallets and cardboard. We designated a storm drain as the bathroom and the kids built an elaborate enclosure for privacy out of plastic, broken umbrellas, and other scraps.

Write about it

1. What argument might the authors be making about the official response to Katrina? What details reveal their argument?

2. How does the authors' account of their experience differ from media reports that you heard or saw about the evacuation effort after Katrina? Does their account change your thinking about the experiences of New Orleans evacuees? Why or why not?

against segregation laws and AMBER Alert's effort to protect children, that's exactly what happened. Public outcry led to changes in laws and public opinion.

Narrative arguments can be representative anecdotes, as with the previous examples, or they can be longer accounts of particular events that express larger ideas. One such story is George Orwell's account of a hanging in Burma (the country that is now known as Myanmar) while he was a colonial administrator in the late 1920s. In "A Hanging," first published in 1931, Orwell narrates an execution of a nameless prisoner who was convicted of a nameless crime. Everyone quietly and dispassionately performs his job—the prison guards, the hangman, the superintendent, and even the prisoner, who offers no resistance when he is bound and led to the gallows. All is totally routine until a very small incident makes Orwell aware of what is happening:

> It was about forty yards to the gallows. I watched the bare brown back of the prisoner marching in front of me. He walked clumsily with his bound arms, but quite steadily, with that bobbing gait of the Indian who never straightens his knees. At each step his muscles slid neatly into place, the lock of hair on his scalp danced up and down, his feet printed themselves on the wet gravel. And once, in spite of the men who gripped him by each shoulder, he stepped lightly aside to avoid a puddle on the path.
>
> It is curious; but till that moment I had never realized what it means to destroy a healthy, conscious man. When I saw the prisoner step aside to avoid the puddle, I saw the mystery, the unspeakable wrongness, of cutting a life short when it is in full tide. This man was not dying, he was alive just as we are alive. All the organs of his body were working—bowels digesting food, skin renewing itself, nails growing, tissues forming—all toiling away in solemn foolery. His nails would still be growing when he stood on the drop, when he was falling through the air with a tenth-of-a-second to live. His eyes saw the yellow gravel and gray walls, and his brain still remembered, foresaw, reasoned—even about puddles. He and we were a party of men walking together, seeing, hearing, feeling, understanding the same world; and in two minutes, with a sudden snap, one of us would be gone—one mind less, one world less.

Orwell's narrative leads to a dramatic moment of recognition, which gives this story its lasting power.

Build a Narrative Argument

The biggest problem with narrative arguments is that anyone can tell a story. On the one hand, there are compelling stories that argue against capital punishment. For example, a mentally retarded man who was executed in Arkansas refused a piece of pie at his last meal. He asked the guards to save the pie for later. On the other hand, there are also many stories about the victims of murder and other crimes. Many families have Web sites on which they call for killing the people responsible for murdering their loved ones. They too have compelling stories to tell.

Violent deaths of all kinds make for especially vivid narrative arguments. In the past decade we have witnessed several tragedies in which schoolchildren used guns taken from the family home to kill other students. In 2007 a mentally disturbed student at Virginia Tech was able to buy handguns that he used to kill 32 students and faculty members. Stories of these tragedies provided strong arguments for gun control. Gun rights organizations, including the National Rifle Association (NRA), counters these stories by claiming that they are not truly representative. The NRA argues that over 99 percent of all guns will not be used to commit crimes in any given year.

There are two keys to making effective narrative arguments: establishing that the narrative is truthful and representative of more than one person's experience. First, writing from personal experience can give you a great deal of impact, but that impact vanishes if your readers doubt that you are telling the truth. Second, the story you tell may be true enough, but it is important that the incident be representative. We don't ban bananas because someone once slipped on a banana peel.

Narratives are often useful for illustrating how people are affected by particular issues or events, but narrative arguments are more effective if you have more evidence than just one incident. The abduction and murder of Amber Hagerman was a personal tragedy for her family and community, but the fact that an average of 2100 children are reported missing each day made Amber Hagerman's story representative of a national tragedy. Thus, it had power because people understood it to be representative of a much larger—and preventable—problem.

Leslie Marmon Silko

The Border Patrol State

Leslie Marmon Silko (1948–) was born in Albuquerque and graduated from the University of New Mexico. She now teaches at the University of Arizona. She has received much critical acclaim for her writings about Native Americans. Her first novel, Ceremony *(1977), describes the struggles of a veteran returning home after World War II to civilian life on a New Mexico reservation. Her incorporation of Indian storytelling techniques in* Ceremony *drew strong praise. One critic called her "the most accomplished Indian writer of her generation." She has since published two more novels,* Almanac of the Dead *(1991) and* Gardens in the Dunes *(1999); a collection of essays,* Yellow Woman and a Beauty of the Spirit: Essays on Native American Life Today *(1996); two volumes of poems and stories; and many shorter works. Silko's talents as a storyteller are evident in this essay, which first appeared in the magazine* The Nation *in 1994.*

I used to travel the highways of New Mexico and Arizona with a wonderful sensation of absolute freedom as I cruised down the open road and across the vast desert plateaus. On the Laguna Pueblo reservation, where I was raised, the people were patriotic despite the way the U.S. government had treated Native Americans. As proud citizens, we grew up believing the freedom to travel was our inalienable right, a right that some Native Americans had been denied in the early twentieth century. Our cousin, old Bill Pratt, used to ride his horse 300 miles overland from Laguna, New Mexico, to Prescott, Arizona, every summer to work as a fire lookout.

2   In school in the 1950s, we were taught that our right to travel from state to state without special papers or threat of detainment was a right that citizens under communist and totalitarian governments did not possess. That wide open highway told us we were U.S. citizens; we were free. . . .

3   Not so long ago, my companion Gus and I were driving south from Albuquerque, returning to Tucson after a book promotion for the paperback edition of my novel *Almanac of the Dead*. I had settled back and gone to sleep while Gus drove, but I was awakened when I felt the car slowing to a stop. It was nearly midnight on New Mexico State Road 26, a dark, lonely stretch of two-lane highway between Hatch and Deming. When I sat up, I saw the headlights and emergency flashers of six vehicles—Border Patrol cars and a van were blocking both lanes of the highway. Gus stopped the car and rolled down the window to ask what was wrong. But the closest Border Patrolman and his companion did not reply; instead, the first agent ordered us to "step out of the car." Gus asked why, but his question seemed to set them off. Two more Border Patrol agents immediately approached our car, and one of them snapped, "Are you looking for trouble?" as if he would relish it.

4   I will never forget that night beside the highway. There was an awful feeling of menace and violence straining to break loose. It was clear that the uniformed men would be only too happy to drag us out of the car if we did not speedily comply with their request (asking a question is tantamount to resistance, it seems). So we stepped out of the car and they motioned for us to stand on the shoulder of the road. The night was very dark, and no other traffic had come down the road since we had been stopped. All I could think about was a book I had read—*Nunca Mas*—the official report of a human rights commission that investigated and certified more than 12,000 "disappearances" during Argentina's "dirty war" in the late 1970s.

5   The weird anger of these Border Patrolmen made me think about descriptions in the report of Argentine police and military officers who became addicted to interrogation, torture and the murder that followed. When the military and police ran out of political suspects to torture and kill, they resorted to the random abduction of citizens off the streets. I thought how easy it would be for the Border Patrol to shoot us and leave our bodies and car beside the highway, like so many bodies found in these parts and ascribed to "drug runners."

6   Two other Border Patrolmen stood by the white van. The one who had asked if we were looking for trouble ordered his partner to "get the dog," and from the back of the van another patrolman brought a small female German shepherd on a leash. The dog apparently did not heel well enough

to suit him, and the handler jerked the leash. They opened the doors of our car and pulled the dog's head into it, but I saw immediately from the expression in her eyes that the dog hated them, and that she would not serve them. When she showed no interest in the inside of the car, they brought her around back to the trunk, near where we were standing. They half-dragged her up into the trunk, but still she did not indicate any stowed-away human beings or illegal drugs.

7   The mood got uglier; the officers seemed outraged that the dog could not find any contraband, and they dragged her over to us and commanded her to sniff our legs and feet. To my relief, the strange violence the Border Patrol agents had focused on us now seemed shifted to the dog. I no longer felt so strongly that we would be murdered. We exchanged looks—the dog and I. She was afraid of what they might do, just as I was. The dog's handler jerked the leash sharply as she sniffed us, as if to make her perform better, but the dog refused to accuse us: She had an innate dignity that did not permit her to serve the murderous impulses of those men. I can't forget the expression in the dog's eyes; it was as if she were embarrassed to be associated with them. I had a small amount of medicinal marijuana in my purse that night, but she refused to expose me. I am not partial to dogs, but I will always remember the small German shepherd that night.

8   Unfortunately, what happened to me is an everyday occurrence here now. Since the 1980s, on top of greatly expanding border checkpoints, the Immigration and Naturalization Service and the Border Patrol have implemented policies that interfere with the rights of U.S. citizens to travel freely within our borders. I.N.S. agents now patrol all interstate highways and roads that lead to or from the U.S.–Mexico border in Texas, New Mexico, Arizona and California. Now, when you drive east from Tucson on Interstate 10 toward El Paso, you encounter an I.N.S. check station outside Las Cruces, New Mexico. When you drive north from Las Cruces up Interstate 25, two miles north of the town of Truth or Consequences, the highway is blocked with orange emergency barriers, and all traffic is diverted into a two-lane Border Patrol checkpoint—ninety-five miles north of the U.S.–Mexico border.

9   I was detained once at Truth or Consequences, despite my and my companion's Arizona driver's licenses. Two men, both Chicanos, were detained at the same time, despite the fact that they too presented ID and spoke English without the thick Texas accents of the Border Patrol agents. While we were stopped, we watched as other vehicles—whose occupants were white—were waved through the checkpoint. White people traveling with brown people, however, can expect to be stopped on suspicion they work with the sanctuary movement, which shelters refugees. White people who appear to be clergy, those who wear ethnic clothing or jewelry and women with very long hair or very short hair (they could be nuns) are also frequently detained; white men with beards or men with long hair are likely to be detained, too, because Border Patrol agents have "profiles" of "those sorts" of white people who may help

political refugees. (Most of the political refugees from Guatemala and El Salvador are Native American or mestizo because the indigenous people of the Americas have continued to resist efforts by invaders to displace them from their ancestral lands.) Alleged increases in illegal immigration by people of Asian ancestry mean that the Border Patrol now routinely detains anyone who appears to be Asian or part Asian, as well.

10   Once your car is diverted from the Interstate Highway into the checkpoint area, you are under the control of the Border Patrol, which in practical terms exercises a power that no highway patrol or city patrolman possesses: They are willing to detain anyone, for no apparent reason. Other law-enforcement officers need a shred of probable cause in order to detain someone. On the books, so does the Border Patrol; but on the road, it's another matter. They'll order you to stop your car and step out; then they'll ask you to open the trunk. If you ask why or request a search warrant, you'll be told that they'll have to have a dog sniff the car before they can request a search warrant, and the dog might not get there for two or three hours. The search warrant might require an hour or two past that. They make it clear that if you force them to obtain a search warrant for the car, they will make you submit to a strip search as well.

11   Traveling in the open, though, the sense of violation can be even worse. Never mind high-profile cases like that of former Border Patrol agent Michael Elmer, acquitted of murder by claiming self-defense, despite admitting that as an officer he shot an "illegal" immigrant in the back and then hid the body, which remained undiscovered until another Border Patrolman reported the event. (Last month, Elmer was convicted of reckless endangerment in a separate incident, for shooting at least ten rounds from his M-16 too close to a group of immigrants as they were crossing illegally into Nogales in March 1992.) Or that in El Paso a high school football coach driving a vanload of players in full uniform was pulled over on the freeway and a Border Patrol agent put a cocked revolver to his head. (The football coach was Mexican-American, as were most of the players in his van; the incident eventually caused a federal judge to issue a restraining order against the Border Patrol.) We've a mountain of personal experiences like that which never make the newspapers. A history professor at U.C.L.A. told me she had been traveling by train from Los Angeles to Albuquerque twice a month doing research. On each of her trips, she had noticed that the Border Patrol agents were at the station in Albuquerque scrutinizing the passengers. Since she is six feet tall and of Irish and German ancestry, she was not particularly concerned. Then one day when she stepped off the train in Albuquerque, two Border Patrolmen accosted her, wanting to know what she was doing, and why she was traveling between Los Angeles and Albuquerque twice a month. She presented identification and an explanation deemed "suitable" by the agents, and was allowed to go about her business.

12   Just the other day, I mentioned to a friend that I was writing this article and he told me about his 73-year-old father, who is half Chinese and who had

set out alone by car from Tucson to Albuquerque the week before. His father had become confused by road construction and missed a turnoff from Interstate 10 to Interstate 25; when he turned around and circled back, he missed the turnoff a second time. But when he looped back for yet another try, Border Patrol agents stopped him and forced him to open his trunk. After they satisfied themselves that he was not smuggling Chinese immigrants, they sent him on his way. He was so rattled by the event that he had to be driven home by his daughter.

13   This is the police state that has developed in the southwestern United States since the 1980s. No person, no citizen, is free to travel without the scrutiny of the Border Patrol. In the city of South Tucson, where 80 percent of the respondents were Chicano or Mexicano, a joint research project by the University of Wisconsin and the University of Arizona recently concluded that one out of every five people there had been detained, mistreated verbally or nonverbally, or questioned by I.N.S. agents in the past two years.

14   Manifest Destiny may lack its old grandeur of theft and blood—"lock the door" is what it means now, with racism a trump card to be played again and again, shamelessly, by both major political parties. "Immigration," like "street crime" and "welfare fraud," is a political euphemism that refers to people of color. Politicians and media people talk about "illegal aliens" to dehumanize and demonize undocumented immigrants, who are for the most part people of color. Even in the days of Spanish and Mexican rule, no attempts were made to interfere with the flow of people and goods from south to north and north to south. It is the U.S. government that has continually attempted to sever contact between the tribal people north of the border and those to the south.

15   Now that the "Iron Curtain" is gone, it is ironic that the U.S. government and its Border Patrol are constructing a steel wall ten feet high to span sections of the border with Mexico. While politicians and multinational corporations extol the virtues of NAFTA and "free trade" (in goods, not flesh), the ominous curtain is already up in a six-mile section at the border crossing at Mexicali; two miles are being erected but are not yet finished at Naco; and at Nogales, sixty miles south of Tucson, the steel wall has been all rubber-stamped and awaits construction likely to begin in March. Like the pathetic multimillion-dollar "antidrug" border surveillance balloons that were continually deflated by high winds and made only a couple of meager interceptions before they blew away, the fence along the border is a theatrical prop, a bit of pork for contractors. Border entrepreneurs have already used blowtorches to cut passageways through the fence to collect "tolls," and are doing a brisk business. Back in Washington, the I.N.S. announces a $300 million computer contract to modernize its record-keeping and Congress passes a crime bill that shunts $255 million to the I.N.S. for 1995, $181 million earmarked for border control, which is to include 700 new partners for the men who stopped Gus and me in our travels, and the history professor, and my friend's father, and as many as they could from South Tucson.

16   It is no use; borders haven't worked, and they won't work, not now, as the indigenous people of the Americas reassert their kinship and solidarity with

one another. A mass migration is already under way; its roots are not simply economic. The Uto–Aztecan languages are spoken as far north as Taos Pueblo near the Colorado border, all the way south to Mexico City. Before the arrival of the Europeans, the indigenous communities throughout this region not only conducted commerce, the people shared cosmologies, and oral narratives about the Maize Mothers, the Twin Brothers and their Grandmother, Spider Woman, as well as Quetzalcoatl the benevolent snake. The great human migration within the Americas cannot be stopped; human beings are natural forces of the Earth, just as rivers and winds are natural forces.

17   Deep down the issue is simple: The so-called "Indian Wars" from the days of Sitting Bull and Red Cloud have never really ended in the Americas. The Indian people of southern Mexico, of Guatemala and those left in El Salvador, too, are still fighting for their lives and for their land against the "cavalry" patrols sent out by the governments of those lands. The Americas are Indian country, and the "Indian problem" is not about to go away.

18   One evening at sundown, we were stopped in traffic at a railroad crossing in downtown Tucson while a freight train passed us, slowly gaining speed as it headed north to Phoenix. In the twilight I saw the most amazing sight: Dozens of human beings, mostly young men, were riding the train; everywhere, on flat cars, inside open boxcars, perched on top of boxcars, hanging off ladders on tank cars and between boxcars. I couldn't count fast enough, but I saw fifty or sixty people headed north. They were dark young men, Indian and mestizo; they were smiling and a few of them waved at us in our cars. I was reminded of the ancient story of Aztlán, told by the Aztecs but known in other Uto–Aztecan communities as well. Aztlán is the beautiful land to the north, the origin place of the Aztec people. I don't remember how or why the people left Aztlán to journey farther south, but the old story says that one day, they will return. ■

Dagoberto Gilb

My Landlady's Yard

Dagoberto Gilb (1950-) was born in Los Angeles to a Mexican mother and a German father. After college, he worked as a journeyman carpenter in Los Angeles and El Paso, which allowed him to take off time to write between jobs. He published his first collection of stories, Winners on the Pass Line, *in 1985, and a second collection,* The Magic of Blood, *in 1992. Despite the success of his first collection, Gilb initially could not get New York publishers interested in his nonstereotypical depictions of Mexican-American life. Nonetheless,* The Magic of Blood *was critically acclaimed, and his next work,* Last Known Residence of Mickey Acuna, *published by Grove Press in 1994, brought Gilb national recognition as a major literary talent.*

Gilb's writing has appeared in The New Yorker, Harper's, *and other publications. "My Landlady's Yard" is taken from his first collection of essays,* Gritos *(2003). Many of the essays in* Gritos, *including the one below, portray the complicated cultural mixings and way of life in the borderlands of Texas.*

It's been a very dry season here. Not enough rain. And the sun's beginning to feel closer. Which, of course, explains why this is called the desert. Why the kinds of plants that do well enough in the region—creosote, mesquite, ocotillo, yucca—aren't what you'd consider lush, tropical blooms. All that's obvious, right? To you, I'm sure, it's obvious, and to me it is, too, but not to my landlady. My landlady doesn't think of this rock house I rent in central El Paso as being in the desert. To her, it's the big city. She's from the country, from a ranch probably just like the one she now calls home, a few miles up the paved highway in Chaparral, New Mexico, where the roads are graded dirt. She must still see the house as she did when she lived here as a young wife and mother, as part of the city's peaceful suburbs, which it certainly was thirty years ago. She probably planted the shrubs and evergreens that snuggle the walls of the house now, probably seeded the back- and front-yard grass herself. And she wants those Yankee plants and that imported grass to continue to thrive as they would in all other American, nondesert neighborhoods, even if these West Texas suburbs moved on to the east and west many years ago, even if the population has quadrupled and water is more scarce, and expensive, than back then.

2   So I go ahead and drag around a green hose despite my perception that *gold*, colorless and liquid, is pouring out onto this desert, an offering as unquenchable and ruthless as to any Aztec deity (don't water a couple of days and watch how fast it dries away). Superstitions, if you don't mind my calling them that, die hard, and property values are dependent on shared impressions. I'm not ready to rent and load another U-Haul truck.

3   With my thumb over the brass fitting and squeezed against the water, I use the digits on my other hand to pluck up loose garbage. You've heard, maybe, of West Texas wind. That explains why so much of it lands here on my front yard, but also a high school is my backyard: the school's rear exit is only a dirt alley and fence away from my garage, and teenagers pass by in the morning, during lunch, and when school lets out. I find the latest Salsa Rio brand of Doritos, Big Gulp Grande cups, paper (or plastic or both) bowls with the slimy remains of what goes for cheese on nachos from the smiley-faced Good Time Store two blocks away, used napkins, orange burger pouches, the new glossy-clean plastic soda containers, waxy candy wrappers from Mounds and Mars and Milky Way. Also beer cans and bottles, grocery-store bags both plastic and paper, and fragments from everything else (believe me) possible.

4   I'm betting you think I'm not too happy about accumulating such evidence. You're right. But I'm not mentioning it to complain. I want the image of all the trash, as well as the one of me spraying precious water onto this dusty alkaline soil, to get your attention. Because both stand for the odd way we live and think out here, a few hundred miles (at least) from everyplace else in the United States.

5   My green grass in the desert, for instance. My landlady wants thick, luxuriant grass because that's the way of this side of the border, and this side is

undeniably better, whatever misconception of place and history and natural resources the desire for that image depends on. It's not just her, and it's not just lawns. Take another example: a year ago about this time, police cars squealed onto the asphalt handball and basketball courts on the other side of the school fence to regain control of a hundred or so students lumped around a fight, most of them watching, some swinging baseball bats. What happened? According to the local newspaper, the fight broke out between a group of black students, all of them dependents of Fort Bliss military personnel (as their jargon has it), and a group of Hispanic students. "Hispanic" is the current media term for those of descent from South of the Border. Even around here. Which is the point: that even in this town—the other side of the concrete river considered the official land of Spanish-language history and culture—the latest minority-language terminology is used to describe its historic, multigenerational majority population. With the exception of one high school on the more affluent west side of town, Anglos are the overwhelming minority: at the high school behind my backyard the ratio must be ten to one. Though Mexico has been the mother of this region, and remains so, it's the language and understanding of The North that labels the account of the school incident: "Hispanic" students, black dependents of GIs.

6   If green grass is the aspiration, the realization of an American fantasy, then the trash is from the past, the husks of a frontier mentality that it took to be here, and stay, in the first place. Trash blowing by, snared by limbs and curbs and fences, is a display of what was the attitude of the West. The endlessness of its range. The ultimate principle of every man, woman, animal, and thing for itself. The meanness required to survive. The wild joy that could abandon rules. The immediacy of life. Or the stupidity of the non-Indian hunter eating one meal, then leaving behind the carcass. Except that vultures and coyotes and finally ants used to clean that mess up. The remains of the modernized hunt don't balance well in nature or its hybrid shrubs, do not biodegrade. And there are a lot more hunters than before.

7   Trash contradicts the well-tended lawn. And in my neighborhood, not all is Saint Augustine or Bermuda. Hardy weeds sprout and grow tall everywhere, gray-green century plants shoot stalks beside many homes. El Paso is still crossing cultures and times, the wind blows often, particularly this time of year, the sun will be getting bigger, but the pretty nights cool things off here on the desert. Let me admit this: I'd like it if grass grew well in my backyard. What I've got is patchy at best, and neglected, the brown dirt is a stronger color than the green. So the other day, I soaked that hard soil, dug it up, threw seed grown and packaged in Missouri, covered it with peat humus from Menard, Texas, and I'm waiting. ■

Steps to Writing a Narrative Argument

Step 1 Identify an Experience that Makes an Implicit Argument

Think about experiences that made you realize that something is wrong or that things need to be changed. The experience does not have to be one that leads to a moral lesson at the end, but it should be one that makes your readers think.

Examples

- Being accused of and perhaps even arrested and hauled to jail for something you didn't do or for standing up for something you believed in.
- Going through treatment for a serious medical condition, dealing with a complicated system of insurance and referrals, or having health care denied by an HMO.
- Moving from a well-financed suburban school to a much poorer rural or urban school in the same state.
- Experiencing stereotyping or prejudice in any way—for the way you look, the way you act, your age, your gender, your race, or your sexual orientation.

Step 2 List All the Details You Can Remember

- When did it happen?
- How old were you?
- Why were you there?
- Who else was there?
- Where did it happen? If the place is important, describe what it looked like.

Step 3 Examine the Significance of the Event

- How did you feel about the experience when it happened?
- How did it affect you then?
- How do you feel about the experience now?
- What long-term effects has it had on your life?

Step 4 Analyze Your Potential Readers

- Who are your readers?
- How much will your readers know about the background of the experience you are describing?
- Are they familiar with the place where it happened?
- Would anything similar ever likely have happened to them?
- How likely are they to agree with your feelings about the experience?

Step 5 Write a Draft

- You might need to give some background first, but if you have a compelling story, often it's best to launch right in.
- You might want to tell the story as it happened (chronological order), or you might want to begin with a striking incident and then go back to tell how it happened (flashback).
- You might want to reflect on your experience at the end, but you want your story to do most of the work. Avoid drawing a simple moral lesson. Your readers should share your feelings if you tell your story well.

Step 6 Revise, Edit, Proofread

- For detailed instructions, see Chapter 4.
- For a checklist to use to evaluate your draft, see pages 61–62.

12

Rebuttal Arguments

In May 2007, demonstrators in Lewes, Delaware, hung cloth strips with the names of dead soldiers to protest the Iraq War. Could their action be considered a rebuttal argument?

When you hear the word *rebuttal*, you might think of a debate team or the part of a trial when the attorney for the defense answers the plaintiff's accusations. Although rebuttal has those definitions, a rebuttal argument can be thought of in much larger terms. Indeed, much of what people know about the world today is the result of centuries of arguments of rebuttal.

In high school and college, you no doubt have taken many courses that required the memorization of facts, which you demonstrated by repeating these facts on tests. You probably didn't think much about how this knowledge came about. Once in a while, though, something happens that makes people think consciously about a fact they have learned. For example, in elementary school, you learned that the earth rotates on its axis once a day. Maybe you didn't think about it much at the time, but once, years later, you were outside on a clear night and noticed the Big Dipper in one part of the sky, and then you looked for it later and found it in another part of the sky. If you've ever spent a clear night out stargazing, you have observed that the North Star, called Polaris, stays in the same place. The stars near Polaris appear to move in a circle around it, and the stars farther away move from east to west until they sink below the horizon.

If you are lucky enough to live in a place where the night sky is often clear, you can see the same pattern repeated night after night. And if you stop to think about why you see the stars circling around Polaris, you remember what you were taught long ago—that you live on a rotating ball, so the stars appear to move across the sky, but in fact, stars are so distant from Earth that their actual movement is not visible to humans over a short period of time.

An alternative explanation for these facts is not only possible; it is the explanation that people believed from ancient times until about 500 years ago. People assumed that their position on Earth was fixed and that the entire sky rotated on an axis connecting Polaris and Earth. The flaw in this theory is the movement of the planets. If you watch the path of Mars over several nights, you will observe that it also moves across the sky from east to west, but it makes an anomalous backward movement during its journey and then goes forward again. The other planets also seem to wander back and forth as they cross the night sky. The ancient Greeks developed an explanation of the strange wanderings of the planets by theorizing that the planets move in small circles imposed on larger orbits. By graphing little circles on top of bigger circles, the courses of planets could be plotted and predicted. This theory culminated in the work of Ptolemy, who lived in Alexandria in the second century CE. Ptolemy proposed displaced centers for the small circles called epicycles, which provided a better fit for predicting the paths of planets.

Because Ptolemy's model of the universe was numerically accurate in its predictions, educated people assumed its validity for centuries, even though there was evidence to the contrary. For example, Aristarchus of Samos, who lived in the fourth century BCE, used the size of Earth's shadow cast on the Moon during a lunar eclipse to compute the sizes of the Moon and Sun and their distances from Earth. Even though his calculations were inaccurate, Aristarchus recognized that the Sun is much bigger than Earth, and he advanced the heliocentric hypothesis: that Earth orbits the Sun.

Many centuries passed, however, before educated people believed that the Sun, not Earth, was the center of the solar system. In the early sixteenth century, the Polish astronomer Nicolaus Copernicus recognized that Ptolemy's model could be greatly simplified if the Sun were at the center of the solar system. He kept his theory a secret for much of his life and saw the published account of his work only a few hours before his death in 1543. Even though Copernicus made a major breakthrough, he was not able to take full advantage of the heliocentric hypothesis because he followed the tradition that orbits are perfect circles: thus, he still needed circles on top of circles to explain the motion of the planets—but he needed far fewer circles than did Ptolemy.

The definitive rebuttal of Ptolemy's model came a century later with the work of the German astronomer Johannes Kepler. Kepler performed many tedious calculations, which were complicated by the fact that he first had to assume an orbit for Earth before he could compute orbits for the planets. Finally he made a stunning discovery: all the orbits of the planets could be described as an ellipse with the Sun at the center. The dominance of the Ptolemaic model of the universe was finally over.

Understand How Rebuttal Arguments Work

When you rebut the argument of someone else, you can do one of two things. You can refute the argument, or you can counterargue. In the first case, **refutation,** you emphasize the shortcomings of the argument that you wish to undermine without really making a positive case of your own. In the second case, **counterargument**, you emphasize not the shortcomings of the argument that you are rebutting but the strengths of the position you wish to support. Often there is considerable overlap between refutation and counterargument, and often both are present in a rebuttal.

Refutation: The opposing argument has serious shortcomings that undermine the claim.

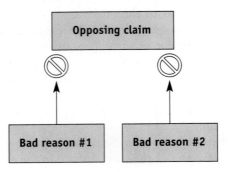

The great white shark gained a reputation as a "man eater" from the 1975 movie *Jaws*, but in fact attacks on humans are rare and most bites have been "test bites," which is a common shark behavior with unfamiliar objects.

Counterarguments: The opposing argument has some merit, but my argument is superior.

Those who argue for tariffs on goods from China claim that tariffs will protect American manufacturing jobs, but tariffs would increase prices on clothing, furniture, toys, and other consumer goods for everyone and would cause the loss of retailing jobs.

Finding Good Reasons

CAN THE WEB BE TRUSTED FOR RESEARCH?

Most Web users are familiar with the huge and immensely popular Wikipedia, the online encyclopedia. What makes Wikipedia so different from traditional, print encyclopedias is that entries can be contributed or edited by anyone.

In a recent edition of the *Wall Street Journal*, Jimmy Wales, president of Wikimedia and one of its founders, debated the legitimacy of Wikipedia with Dale Hoiberg, editor-in-chief of *Encyclopedia Britannica*. Hoiberg's main criticism of Wikipedia is that its structure—an open-source wiki without the formal editorial control that shapes traditional, print encyclopedias—allows for inaccurate entries.

In response, Wales argues that *Britannica* and newspapers also contain errors, but Wikipedia has the advantage that they are easily corrected. Furthermore, he asserts that Wikipedia's policy of using volunteer administrators to delete irrelevant entries and requiring authors of entries to cite reliable, published sources ensures quality. Nonetheless, some universities including UCLA and the University of Pennsylvania along with many instructors strongly discourage and even ban students from citing Wikipedia in their work. (Wikipedia also cautions against using its entries as a primary source for serious research.)

Write about it

1. If your college decided to ban the use of Wikipedia as a reference because it lacked the authority of a traditional encyclopedia, would you want to challenge it? Why or why not?

2. If you chose to challenge the college's policy, how would you do so? Would it be effective to refute the college's claims point by point, noting fallacies in logic and reasoning? Would it be effective to build a counterargument in which you examine the assumptions on which the college's claims are based? Which strategy would you choose, and why?

Recognize Kinds of Rebuttal Arguments

Refutation

There are two primary strategies for refutation arguments. First, you can challenge the assumptions on which a claim is based. Copernicus did not question Ptolemy's data concerning how the stars and planets appear in the sky to an observer on Earth. Instead, he questioned Ptolemy's central assumption that Earth is the center of the solar system.

Second, you can question the evidence supporting the claim. Sometimes the evidence presented is simply wrong. Sometimes the evidence is incomplete or unrepresentative, and sometimes counterevidence can be found. Often when you refute an argument, you make the case that your opponent has been guilty of one or more fallacies of arguments (see pages 27–28). A lively debate has developed in recent years over the impacts of Web 2.0, a term that has come to stand for a Web-based social phenomenon characterized by open communication and a decentralization of authority. Various new genre and software are associated with Web 2.0, including wikis, blogs, YouTube, MySpace, Facebook, eBay, craigslist, Second Life—anything that encourages participation and can exist only on the Internet.

From the beginning the Internet inspired grand visions of a better society through access to information and instant communication. The initial enthusiasm declined after the Web turned into a giant home-shopping network and the potential for dialog among different groups was lost in the proliferation of political and advocacy sites. But Web 2.0 rekindled that enthusiasm with the potential of connecting billions of human minds. Wikipedia is held up as a glorious example of the age of participation because it allows us to pool the collective wisdom of all our brains. Amateurism is celebrated. Anyone can publish writing, videos, songs, photographs, and other art for everyone else connected to the Internet to see and hear, and millions of people are doing just that.

One of Web 2.0's greatest proponents, Kevin Kelly, issued the manifesto "We Are the Web" in *Wired* magazine in August 2005, proclaiming the beginning of a new era of collective human consciousness (www.wired.com/wired/archive/13.08/tech_pr.html):

> There is only one time in the history of each planet when its inhabitants first wire up its innumerable parts to make one large Machine. Later that Machine may run faster, but there is only one time when it is born. You and I are alive at this moment. . . . Weaving nerves out of glass and radio waves, our species began wiring up all regions, all processes, all facts and notions into a grand network. From this embryonic neural net was born a collaborative interface for our civilization, a sensing, cognitive device with power that exceeded any previous invention. The Machine provided a new way of thinking (perfect search, total recall) and a new mind for an old species. It was the Beginning.

In case his readers miss the spiritual overtones, Kelly compares the present to the era of Jesus, Confucius, and the later Jewish prophets, when the world's great religions emerged.

Not surprisingly, the hype over Web 2.0 has drawn critics. In June 2007, Andrew Keen published *The Cult of the Amateur: How Today's Internet Is Killing Our Culture*, which upholds the authority of the expert against the thousands of amateurs who contribute to YouTube and Wikipedia. He challenges the assumptions of those who inflate the promise of Web 2.0:

> The Web 2.0 revolution has peddled the promise of bringing more truth to more people—more depth of information, more global perspective, more unbiased opinion from dispassionate observers. But this is all a smokescreen. What the Web 2.0 revolution is really delivering is superficial observations of the world around us rather than deep analysis, shrill opinion rather than considered judgment. The information business is being transformed by the Internet into the sheer noise of a hundred million bloggers all simultaneously talking about themselves. (16)

Keen repeats several of the frequent charges against the Internet: identity theft is made easy, pornographers and gamblers thrive, personal data is vulnerable, and political and corporate interests spread propaganda. What bothers him the most, however, is how all the "free information" will eventually destroy traditional media—magazines, newspapers, recording studios, and book publishers—with their resources of writers, editors, journalists, musicians, and reporters. Amateurs, according to Keen, do not have the resources to produce in-depth reporting or great music or great books, and even if they did, how could anyone find it? The sheer numbers of amateurs publishing on the Web makes it next to impossible to sort the good from the bad.

Keen begins by recalling the hypothetical example that if an infinite number of monkeys were given typewriters to pound, eventually one of them will type out a masterpiece. He writes, "today's amateur monkeys can use their networked computers to publish everything from uninformed political commentary, to unseemly home videos, to embarrassingly amateurish music, to unreadable poems, reviews, essays and novels" (3).

Keen's comparison of bloggers to millions of monkeys with typewriters drew the ire of bloggers even before the book appeared. Lawrence Lessig wrote in his blog (www.lessig.org/blog/) in May 2007 that Keen's book is no more reliable than the typical blog. Lessig goes after Keen's evidence:

> [W]hat is puzzling about this book is that it purports to be a book attacking the sloppiness, error and ignorance of the Internet, yet it itself is shot through with sloppiness, error and ignorance. It tells us that without institutions, and standards, to signal what we can trust (like the institution, Doubleday, that decided to print his book), we won't know what's true and what's false. But

the book itself is riddled with falsity—from simple errors of fact, to gross misreadings of arguments, to the most basic errors of economics.

If an edited book from a major publisher contains errors and misreadings, Lessig contends, it undermines Keen's claim that experts save us from these inaccuracies.

The Web 2.0 debate is a series of rebuttal arguments in which the debaters attempt to knock the evidence out from under the competing claims and thus to remove the good reasons.

Counterargument

Another way to rebut is to counterargue. In a counterargument, you do not really show the shortcomings of your opponent's point of view; you may not refer to the details of the other argument at all. Rather, you offer an argument of another point of view in the hope that it will outweigh the argument that is being rebutted. A counterarguer, in effect, says, "I hear your argument. But there is more to it than that. Now listen while I explain why another position is stronger."

The counterarguer depends on the wisdom of her or his audience members to hear all sides of an issue and to make up their minds about the merits of the case. In the following short poem, Wilfred Owen, a veteran of the horrors of World War I trench warfare, offers a counterargument to those who argue that war is noble, to those who believe along with the poet Horace that "dulce et decorum est pro patria mori"—that it is sweet and fitting to die for one's country. This poem gains in popularity whenever there is an unpopular war, for it rebuts the belief that it is noble to die for one's country in modern warfare.

Dulce Et Decorum Est

Bent double, like old beggars under sacks,
Knock-kneed, coughing like hags, we cursed through sludge,
Till on the haunting flares we turned our backs
And towards our distant rest began to trudge.
Men marched asleep. Many had lost their boots
But limped on, blood-shod. All went lame; all blind;
Drunk with fatigue; deaf even to the hoots
Of disappointed shells that dropped behind.

Gas! Gas! Quick, boys!—An ecstacy of fumbling,
Fitting the clumsy helmets just in time;
But someone still was yelling out and stumbling
And floundering like a man in fire or lime.—
Dim, through the misty panes and thick green light
As under a green sea, I saw him drowning.
In all my dreams, before my helpless sight,
He plunges at me, guttering, choking, drowning.

If in some smothering dreams you too could pace
Behind the wagon that we flung him in,
And watch the white eyes writhing in his face,
His hanging face, like a devil's sick of sin;
If you could hear, at every jolt, the blood
Come gargling from the froth-corrupted lungs,
Obscene as cancer, bitter as the cud
Of vile, incurable sores on innocent tongues,—
My friend, you would not tell with such high zest
To children ardent for some desperate glory,
The old Lie: Dulce et decorum est
Pro patria mori.

Owen does not summarize the argument in favor of being willing to die for one's country and then refute that argument premise by premise. Rather, his poem presents an opposing argument, supported by a narrative of the speaker's experience in a poison-gas attack, that he hopes will more than counterbalance what he calls "the old lie." Owen simply ignores the good reasons that people give for being willing to die for one's country and argues instead that there are also good reasons not to do so. And he hopes that the evidence that he summons for his countering position will outweigh for his audience ("My friend") the evidence in support of the other side.

This example shows that it can be artificial to oppose refutation and counterargument, particularly because all arguments, in a broad sense, are counterarguments. Rebuttal arguments frequently offer both refutation and counterargument. In short, people who write rebuttals work like attorneys do in a trial: they make their own cases with good reasons and hard evidence, but they also do what they can to undermine their opponent's argument. In the end the jury, the audience, decides.

Build a Rebuttal Argument

Rebuttal arguments begin with critical interrogations of the evidence underlying claims. In the era of the Internet, many writers use what turns up on the first page of a Google search. Google reports the most popular sites, however, not the most accurate ones. Mistakes and outright falsehoods are repeated because many writers on the Internet do not check their facts.

Look up a writer's sources to judge the quality of the evidence. Also, check if the writer is reporting sources accurately. Do your own fact checking. Having access to your library's databases gives you a great advantage because database sources are usually more reliable than the information you can find on the Internet.

Treat facts like a detective would. Sometimes there are alternative explanations. For example, arguments that schools are getting worse and students are

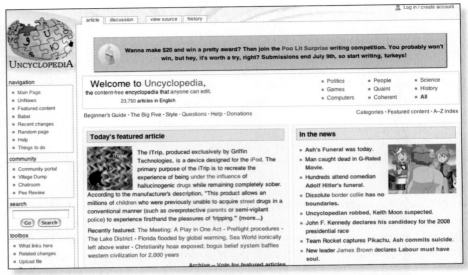

Uncyclopedia is a parody of Wikipedia that claims to be "an encyclopedia full of misinformation and utter lies." Is parody a rebuttal argument or something else?

getting dumber often use standardized test scores as evidence. On close inspection, however, you will find that writers often use these test scores selectively, quoting some scores and ignoring others that don't support their arguments. Furthermore, writers who quote test scores rarely take into account the population of test takers, which seldom remains constant from year to year.

When you write a counterargument with the goal of convincing readers that you have the stronger argument, your readers will appreciate your being fair about other arguments. Remember that you don't have to demolish the other person's argument, just establish that yours is better. Often you can be convincing by showing that you have thought about an issue in more depth and have taken into account more of its complexity.

Dan Stein

Crossing the Line

Dan Stein is president of the Federation for American Immigration Reform, a Washington D.C.-based nonprofit organization that seeks to stop illegal immigration. He frequently speaks and writes about immigration issues. He published "Crossing the Line" in the Los Angeles Business Journal *in February 2007.*

The timing could not have been worse for Bank of America to announce that it would begin issuing credit cards to illegal aliens in Los Angeles. News of Bank of America's decision was published in the *Wall Street Journal* on February 13, the same day that a new Harris Poll revealed that Americans perceive the two greatest threats to their security to be illegal immigration and the outsourcing of American jobs.

2   Even more than the prospect of the Iranians or the North Koreans with nukes, Americans believe that their security is threatened by millions of people pouring across our borders and by corporations that appear willing to sell out the interests of American workers. In one decision, Bank of America managed to pluck two raw nerves by appearing to encourage illegal immigration, while sending the message that it would not let any national interest stand in the way of it making a buck.

3   The Bank of America decision and the overwhelming negative public reaction to it illustrates the growing disconnect between the elite and everyone else in this country. To the elite—including the current occupant of the White House—the traditional idea of the nation has become a bothersome anachronism. To the extent that the entity known as the United States has any relevance at all to them, it is to secure their ability to conduct business and maximize their corporate bottom lines. Concepts of patriotism and loyalty are marketing tools and nothing more.

4   To Bank of America and other large corporations, illegal immigrants are a source of low wage labor and an untapped customer market. It matters not that illegal immigrants are breaking the laws of the United States, taking jobs from and driving down wages for middle class workers, burdening schools (not the ones the children of Bank of America executives attend, of course) and other vital public services. What matters to the banking industry is that the estimated 12 to 15 million illegal aliens living in the United States have purchasing power and that there is money to be made off of serving them.

5   It is true that Bank of America did not create the illegal immigration crisis in the United States, although banking industry decisions to allow illegal aliens to open bank accounts, take out home mortgages and now obtain credit cards has certainly added to the problem. But the fact that the federal government has done little to resolve the problem of illegal immigration does not mean that banks and other business interests have an unfettered right to profit from illegal immigration. Bank of America did not create the illegal drug problem in the United States, but that does not entitle it to market services to the drug cartels, even though it would be enormously profitable to do so.

Overtly discriminatory

The plan to issue credit cards to illegal aliens is also overtly discriminatory, giving a new meaning to their corporate slogan: "Bank of America, Higher Standards" (for some). While American citizens and legal U.S. residents are held to one standard in order to obtain credit, illegal aliens will be held to a lower standard. The plastic that any of us tote around in our wallets required us to open our entire lives to our creditors and to provide verification of our identities and credit-worthiness. In their hunger to make money off of illegal aliens Bank of America is prepared to accept easily counterfeited Mexican matricula cards as proof of identity, and maintaining a checking account for three months as a credit history.

7   Bank of America has obviously felt the sting of a public backlash, as evidenced by their sudden reluctance to discuss it in the media. Some people have gone so far as to pull their accounts out of Bank of America. But given the consolidation of the banking industry generally, and the fact that a handful of banks have corner on the credit card market, it will require government action to stop financial institutions from pursuing profits in blatant disregard of the law and the public interest.

8   Existing federal law clearly prohibits "encouraging or inducing unauthorized aliens to enter the United States, and engaging in a conspiracy or aiding and abetting" people who violate U.S. immigration laws. Products and services specifically marketed to illegal aliens, intended to make it easier to live and work in the U.S. illegally, violates the spirit if not the letter of the law.

9   To Bank of America, illegal aliens are just customers and the United States nothing more than a market. To the American people, illegal immigration and corporate greed are seen as serious threats to their security. Bank of America has provided the proof that both are inexorably intertwined. ■

Gregory Rodriguez

Illegal Immigrants—They're Money

Gregory Rodriguez is a Los Angeles-based Irvine Senior Fellow at the New America Foundation, a nonpartisan think tank in Washington, D.C. He has written widely about issues of national identity, social cohesion, assimilation, race relations, religion, immigration, demographics, and social and political trends. He published "Illegal Immigrants—They're Money," a rebuttal to Dan Stein's article about the Bank of America, as a column in the Los Angeles Times *on March 4, 2007.*

Dan Stein, the premier American nativist and president of the Federation for American Immigration Reform, is shocked, shocked. He's mad at Bank of America for issuing credit cards to illegal immigrants. He says that to Bank of America "and other large corporations, illegal immigrants are a source of low-wage labor and an untapped customer market." You bet they are, and that's the American way.

2   Sure, I'm proud to be a citizen of a nation that portrays itself as a refuge for the "tired," "the poor" and the "huddled masses yearning to breathe free." But let's face it, Emma Lazarus, the poet who wrote those

words, may have laid it on a bit thick. The truth, no less beautiful in its way, is a little more crass and self-serving. But it wouldn't have sounded nearly as poetic to say, "bring us your able-bodied, poor, hardworking masses yearning for a chance to climb out of poverty, establish a credit history and . . . ." We all love to rhapsodize about immigrants' embrace of the American dream, but it's more like a hard-nosed American deal — you come here, you work your tail off under grueling conditions, and you can try your damnedest to better your lot over time.

3   In their generational struggle for acceptance and security, from outsider to insider and, dare I say, from exploited to exploiter, immigrants could avail themselves of those inalienable rights that stand at the core of our national political philosophy—life, liberty and the pursuit of happiness.

4   But that, of course, was before the invention of illegal immigration.

5   Until the early 1900s, pretty much anybody who wasn't diseased, a criminal, a prostitute, a pauper, an anarchist or a Chinese laborer could gain entrance to the U.S. Between 1880 and 1914, only 1% of a total of 25 million European immigrants were excluded from this country. But after transatlantic crossings had already been halted by World War I, Congress buckled to anti-foreign sentiment and closed the proverbial Golden Door by passing a series of restrictionist laws in 1917, 1921 and 1924.

6   Yet even as the historical front door of the nation was being closed, business interests were busy prying open a new side-door. Only three months after the passage of the Immigration Act of 1917, which required all newcomers to pass a literacy test and pay a head tax, the U.S. Secretary of Commerce waived the regulations for Mexican workers. Thus began America's dishonorable relationship with Mexican immigrant labor.

7   For the next several decades, Mexican workers were brought in when the economy expanded and kicked out when times got bad. They were recruited in the 1920s, only to be deported in the 1930s. They were brought in again during the labor shortage in the 1940s. By the 1950s, one branch of the government recruited Mexican workers, under the illusion that they were "temporary," while another sought to keep them out.

8   The *piece de resistance* in the creation of the illegal immigrant is the Immigration Act of 1965. Although touted as a great piece of liberal legislation that ended discriminatory immigration barriers, it imposed an annual cap on migrants from the Western Hemisphere that was 40% less than the number that had been arriving yearly before 1965. A decade later, Congress placed a 20,000 limit per country in this hemisphere.

9   In other words, after importing millions of Mexicans over the decades, particularly during the bracero guest-worker program from 1942 to 1963, and establishing well-trod routes to employment north of the border, the U.S. drastically reduced the number of visas available to Mexicans. This reduction, of course, coincided with a rapid rise in Mexico's population. And guess what? When jobs were available on this side of the border, Mexicans just kept coming, whether they had papers or not.

10   Clearly, today as ever, mass migration to the U.S. is being driven by economic need—the immigrants' and our economy's. But the hard-nosed American deal has become unfair because, on top of the handicaps we have always imposed on new arrivals, we've added a rather brutal one—criminal status. Good luck with that pursuit of happiness as you engage in backbreaking labor when your place in society is summed up with that one cutting word, "illegal."

11   No, I'm not advocating open borders. Nor do I believe that immigrants should be guaranteed anything but a chance to achieve their end of the nation's cruel bargain. For hardworking illegal immigrants who've established roots here, we should uphold our end of the bargain and give them a chance to achieve their piece of the American dream. Bank of America is not wrong to give illegal immigrants the tools with which to compete legitimately in the marketplace. We as a nation are wrong for treating all these people as illegitimate. ■

Steps to Writing a Rebuttal Argument

Step 1 Identify an Argument to Argue Against as well as its Main Claim(s)

- What exactly are you arguing against?
- Are there secondary claims attached to the main claim?
- Include a fair summary of your opponent's position in your finished rebuttal.

Examples

- Arguing against raising taxes for the purpose of building a new sports stadium (examine how proponents claim that a new sports facility will benefit the local economy).
- Arguing for raising the minimum wage (examine how opponents claim that a higher minimum wage isn't necessary and negatively affects small-business owners).

Step 2 Examine the Facts on Which the Claim Is Based

- Are the facts accurate?
- Are the facts a truly representative sample?
- Are the facts current?
- Is there another body of facts that you can present as counterevidence?
- If the author uses statistics, is evidence for the validity of those statistics presented?
- Can the statistics be interpreted differently?
- If the author quotes from sources, how reliable are those sources?
- Are the sources treated fairly, or are quotations taken out of context?
- If the author cites outside authority, how much trust can you place in that authority?

Step 3 Examine the Assumptions on Which the Claim Is Based

- What is the primary assumption of the claim you are rejecting?
- What other assumptions support that claim?
- How are those assumptions flawed?
- If you are arguing against a specific piece of writing, how does the author fall short?
- Does the author resort to name calling, use faulty reasoning, or ignore key facts?
- What fallacies is the author guilty of committing?

Step 4 Analyze Your Potential Readers

- To what extent do your potential readers support the claim that you are rejecting?
- If they strongly support that claim, how might you appeal to them to change their minds?
- What common assumptions and beliefs do you share with them?

Step 5 Decide Whether to Write a Refutation, a Counterargument—or Both

- Make your aim clear in your thesis statement.

Examples

- For a refutation, your thesis statement might be as follows: Proponents of making the percentages of intercollegiate athletes proportionate to the number of male and female students ignore the facts that when participation is entirely voluntary, as in intramural sports, men participate at a far higher rate than women, and women participate at far higher rates in all activities but sports: student government, dance, band, orchestra, debate, and drama.

- For a counterargument, your thesis statement might be as follows: Critics of Title IX who focus only on the effects on men's sports neglect that women who play sports—especially minority women—make better grades, have higher self-esteem, are more likely to become community leaders, are less likely to smoke or to use drugs, and have higher graduation rates from high school and college than women who don't play sports.

Step 6 Write a Draft

Introduction

Identify the issue and the argument you are rejecting.

- Provide background if the issue is unfamiliar to most of your readers.
- Give a quick summary of the competing positions even if the issue is familiar to your readers.
- Remember that offering a fair and accurate summary is a good way to build credibility with your audience.

Body

Take on the argument that you are rejecting. Consider questioning the evidence that is used to support the argument by doing one or more of the following:

- Challenge the facts.
- Present counterevidence and countertestimony.
- Cast doubt on the representativeness of the sample or the currency and relevance of the examples.
- Challenge the credibility of any authorities cited.
- Question the way in which statistical evidence is presented and interpreted.
- Argue that quotations are taken out of context.

Conclusion

Conclude on a firm note by underscoring your objections.

- Consider closing with a counterargument or counterproposal.

Step 7 Revise, Edit, Proofread

- For detailed instructions, see Chapter 4.
- For a checklist to use to evaluate your draft, see pages 61–62.

13

Proposal Arguments

Manufactured goods from China move through the Panama Canal on their way to the United States. Do you agree or disagree with those who propose trade restrictions aimed at keeping manufacturing jobs in the U.S.?

At this moment, you might not think that you feel strongly enough about anything to write a proposal argument. But if you write a list of things that make you mad or at least a little annoyed, then you have a start toward writing a proposal argument. Some things on your list are not going to produce proposal arguments that many people would want to read. If your roommate is a slob, you might be able to write a proposal for that person to start cleaning up more, but who else would be interested? Similarly, it might be annoying to you that where you live is too far from the ocean, but it is hard to imagine making a serious proposal to move your city closer to the coast. Short of those extremes, however, are a lot of things that might make you think, "Why hasn't someone done something about this?" If you believe that others have something to gain if a problem is solved, or at least that the situation can be made a little better, then you might be able to develop a good proposal argument.

For instance, suppose you are living off campus, and you buy a student parking sticker when you register for courses so that you can park in the student lot. However, you quickly find out that there are too many cars and trucks for the number of available spaces, and unless you get to campus by 8:00 a.m., you aren't going to find a place to park in your assigned lot. The situation makes you angry because you believe that if you pay for a sticker, you should have a reasonable chance of finding a place to park. You see that there are unfilled lots reserved for faculty and staff next to the student parking lot, and you wonder why more spaces aren't allotted to students. You decide to write to the president of your college. You want her to direct parking and traffic services to give more spaces to students or else to build a parking garage that will accommodate more vehicles.

When you start talking to other students on campus, however, you begin to realize that the problem may be more complex than your first view of it. Your college has taken the position that if fewer students drive to campus, there will be less traffic on and around your campus. The administration wants more students to ride shuttle buses, to form car pools, or to bicycle to campus instead of driving alone. You also find out that faculty and staff members pay ten times as much as students for their parking permits, so they pay a very high premium for a guaranteed space—much too high for

209

most students. If the president of your college is your primary audience, you first have to argue that a problem really exists. You have to convince the president that many students have no choice but to drive if they are to attend classes. You, for example, are willing to ride the shuttle buses, but they don't run often enough for you to make your classes, get back to your car that you left at home, and then drive to your job.

Next, you have to argue that your solution will solve the problem. An eight-story parking garage might be adequate to park all the cars of students who want to drive, but parking garages are very expensive to build. Even if a parking garage is the best solution, the question remains: who is going to pay for it? Many problems in life could be solved if you had access to unlimited resources, but very few people—or organizations—have such resources at their command. It's not enough to propose a solution that can resolve the problem. You have to be able to argue for the feasibility of your solution. If you want to argue that a parking garage is the solution to the parking problem on your campus, then you must also propose how to finance the garage.

Understand How Proposal Arguments Work

Proposal arguments call for some action to be taken (or not to be taken). The challenge for writers is to convince readers that they should take action, which usually involves their commitment of effort or money. It's always easier to do nothing and wait for someone else to act. Thus, the key is using good reasons to convince readers that good things will result if some action is taken and bad things can be avoided. If readers are convinced that the proposal serves their interests, they will take action. Proposal arguments take this form:

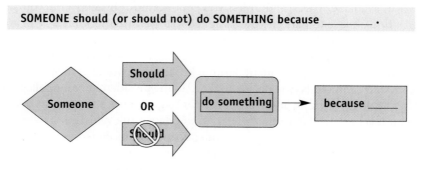

SOMEONE should (or should not) do SOMETHING because _____ .

Someone — Should OR Should — do something → because _____

We should convert existing train tracks in the downtown area to a light-rail system and build a new freight track around the city because we need to relieve traffic and parking congestion downtown.

Recognize Components of Proposal Arguments

Proposal arguments are often complex and involve the kinds of arguments that are discussed in Chapters 8 through 12. Successful proposals have four major components:

- **Identifying the problem.** Sometimes, problems are evident to your intended readers. If your city is constantly tearing up the streets and then leaving them for months without doing anything to repair them, then you shouldn't have much trouble convincing the citizens of your city that streets should be repaired more quickly. But if you raise a problem that will be unfamiliar to most of your readers, first you will have to argue that the problem exists. Recall that in Chapter 1, Rachel Carson had to use several kinds of arguments in *Silent Spring* to make people aware of the dangers of pesticides, including narrative arguments, definition arguments, evaluation arguments, and arguments of comparison. Often, you will have to do similar work to establish exactly what problem you are attempting to solve. You will have to define the scope of the problem. Some of the bad roads in your city might be the responsibility of the state, not the city, government.

- **Stating a proposed solution.** You need a clear, definite statement of exactly what you are proposing. You might want to place this statement near the beginning of your argument, or later, after you have considered and rejected other possible solutions.

- **Using good reasons to convince readers that the proposed solution is fair and will work.** When your readers agree that a problem exists and a solution should be found, your next task is to convince them that your solution is the best one to resolve the problem. If you're writing about the problem your city has in getting streets repaired promptly, then you need to analyze carefully the process that is involved in repairing streets. Sometimes there are mandatory delays so that competing bids can be solicited, and sometimes there are unexpected delays when tax revenue falls short of expectations. You should be able to put your finger on the problem in a detailed causal analysis. You should be able to make an evaluation argument that your solution is fair to all concerned. You should also be prepared to make arguments of rebuttal against other possible solutions.

- **Demonstrating that the solution is feasible.** Your solution not only has to work; it must be feasible to implement. Malaysia effectively ended its drug problem by imposing mandatory death sentences for anyone caught selling even small amounts of drugs. Foreign nationals, teenagers, and grandmothers have all been hanged under this law. Malaysia came up with a solution for its

Finding Good Reasons
WHO SHOULD MAKE DECISIONS ABOUT ECONOMIC DEVELOPMENT?

Northcross Mall in Austin, Texas, is a declining neighborhood shopping center with several empty stores. In 2006, Wal-Mart proposed taking over the site and building a Supercenter. Surrounding neighborhood associations rallied together and formed Responsible Growth for Northcross. They agreed that Northcross Mall should be re-developed, but they objected to Wal-Mart because of the traffic the Supercenter would generate and because the sprawling structure and large parking lot would not comply with the city's guidelines for redevelopment. Their opposition raises an important question: should surrounding neighborhoods have the right to decide on the kinds of businesses that are appropriate for their neighborhood on commercially zoned property?

Write about it

1. If you were the spokesperson for Wal-Mart, what reasons would you give to the Austin City Council to persuade them to allow Wal-Mart to build a Supercenter on the site?

2. If you were the spokesperson for Responsible Growth for Northcross, what good reasons would you give to convince the city council to deny Wal-Mart permission to build a Supercenter?

3. If you were a member of the Austin City Council, what reasons might you expect to hear from these two groups? Draft a proposal that would win your vote.

purposes, but this solution probably would not work in most countries because the punishment seems too extreme. If you want a parking garage built on your campus and you learn that no college funds can be used to construct it, then you have to be able to argue that the potential users of the garage will be willing to pay greatly increased fees for the convenience of parking on campus.

Build a Proposal Argument

Proposal arguments often grow out of long histories of debate. An issue with a much shorter history can also quickly pile up mountains of arguments if it gains wide public attention. In 1972, President Richard Nixon signed into law the Education Amendments Act, including Title IX, which prohibits gender discrimination at schools and colleges that receive federal aid. Few people at the time guessed that Title IX would have the far-reaching consequences that it has. When Title IX was passed, 31,000 women participated in intercollegiate athletics. In the academic year 2002–2003, over 160,000 women athletes participated in varsity college sports. The 2006 data show the highest-ever participation by women in intercollegiate athletics programs. Even more striking is the increase in girls' participation in high school sports. The number of boy athletes rose gradually from about 3.6 million in 1971 to approximately 4 million in 2003–2004, while the number of girl athletes increased tenfold—from 294,000 in 1971 to over 2.9 million in 2006.

The participation of women in intercollegiate athletics has stalled since 2000. The proportion of female undergraduates was 55.8 percent in 2004–2005, but the percentage of women athletes was only 41.7 percent. Do you think women should participate in intercollegiate athletics at a level equal to men?

Proponents of Title IX are justifiably proud of the increased level of participation of women in varsity athletics. But for all the good that Title IX has done to increase athletic opportunities for women, critics blame Title IX for decreasing athletic opportunities for college men. According to the U.S. General Accounting Office (GAO), more than three hundred men's teams have been eliminated in college athletics since 1993. In 2000 the University of Miami dropped its men's swimming team, which had produced many Olympians, including Greg Louganis, who won gold medals in both platform and springboard diving in two consecutive Olympics. In 2001 the University of Nebraska also discontinued its men's swimming team, which had been in place since 1922, and the University of Kansas dropped men's swimming and tennis.

Wrestling teams have been especially hard hit, dropping from 363 in 1981 to 192 in 1999. The effects were noticeable at the 2000 Olympics in Australia, where U.S. freestyle wrestlers failed to win any gold medals for the first time since 1968.

College and university administrators claim that they have no choice but to drop men's teams if more women's teams are added. Their position comes not from the original Title IX legislation, which does not mention athletics, but from a 1979 clarification by the Office of Civil Rights (OCR), the agency that enforces Title IX. OCR set out three options for schools to comply with Title IX:

1. Bring the proportion of women in varsity athletics roughly equal to the percentage of women students.
2. Prove a "history and continuing practice" of creating new opportunities for women.
3. Prove that the school has done everything to "effectively accommodate" the athletic interests of women students.

University administrators have argued that the first option, known as proportionality, is the only one that can be argued successfully in a courtroom if the school is sued.

Proportionality is difficult to achieve at schools with football programs. Universities that play NCAA Division I-A football offer 85 football scholarships to men. Since there is no equivalent sport for women, football throws the gender statistics way out of balance. Defenders of football ask that it be exempted from Title IX because it is the cash cow that pays most of the bills for both men's and women's sports. Only a handful of women's basketball programs make money. All other women's sports are money losers and, like men's "minor" sports, depend on men's football and basketball revenues and student fees to pay their bills. College officials maintain that if they cut the spending for football, football will bring in less revenue, and thus all sports will be harmed.

Those who criticize Title IX argue that it assumes that women's interest in athletics is identical to men's. They point out that male students participate at much higher rates in intramural sports, which have no limitations on who can play. In contrast, women participate at much higher rates in music, dance, theater, and other extracurricular activities, yet Title IX is not being applied to those activities.

Defenders of Title IX argue that women's interest in athletics cannot be determined until they have had equal opportunities to participate. They claim Title IX is being used as a scapegoat for college administrators who do not want to make tough decisions. They point out that in 2004–2005, women made up 55.8 percent of all college students but only 41.7 percent of all college athletes. Without Title IX, in their view, schools would have no incentive to increase opportunities for women. The battle over Title IX is not likely to go away soon.

Thomas Homer-Dixon and S. Julio Freidmann

Coal in a Nice Shade of Green

Thomas Homer-Dixon is the director of the Center for Peace and Conflict Studies at the University of Toronto. His award-winning works include The Ingenuity Gap, *which won the 2001 Governor-General's Non-fiction Award, and* Environment, Scarcity, and Violence, *which received the 2000 Lynton Caldwell Prize from the American Political Science Association. His latest work is* The Upside of Down: Catastrophe, Creativity, and the Renewal of Civilization *(2006). S. Julio Friedmann directs the carbon sequestration project at Lawrence Livermore National Laboratory in Livermore, California. In this article, which appeared in the March 25, 2005, edition of the* New York Times, *Homer-Dixon and Friedmann argue for gasification as a solution to our reliance on costly crude oil.*

W hen it comes to energy, we are trapped between a rock and several hard places. The world's soaring demand for oil is pushing against the limits of production, lifting the price of crude nearly 90 percent in the last 18 months. Congress's vote in favor of drilling in the Arctic National Wildlife Refuge won't make much difference because the amount of oil there, at best, is tiny relative to global or even American needs. And relief isn't likely to come anytime soon from drilling elsewhere: oil companies spent $8 billion on exploration in 2003, but discovered only $4 billion of commercially useful oil.

2   Sadly, most alternatives to conventional oil can't give us the immense amount of energy we need without damaging our environment, jeopardizing our national security or bankrupting us. The obvious alternatives are other fossil fuels: natural gas and oil products derived from tar sands, oil shale and even coal. But natural gas supplies are tightening, at least in North America.

3   And, of course, all fossil fuels have a major disadvantage: burning them releases carbon dioxide, a greenhouse gas that may contribute to climate change. This drawback is especially acute for tar sands, oil shale and coal, which, joule for joule, release far more carbon dioxide than either conventional oil or natural gas.

4   As for energy sources not based on carbon, it would be enormously hard to meet a major percentage of America's energy needs at a reasonable cost, at least in the near term. Take nuclear power—a source that produces no greenhouse emissions. Even assuming we can find a place to dispose of nuclear waste and deal with the security risks, to meet the expected growth in total American energy demand over the next 50 years would require building 1,200 new nuclear power plants in addition to the current 104—or one plant every two weeks until 2050.

5   Solar power? To satisfy its current electricity demand using today's technology, the United States would need 10 billion square meters of photovoltaic panels; this would cost $5 trillion, or nearly half the country's annual gross domestic product.

6   How about hydrogen? To replace just America's surface transportation with cars and trucks running on fuel cells powered by hydrogen, America would have to produce 230,000 tons of the gas—or enough to fill 13,000 Hindenburg dirigibles—every day. This could be generated by electrolyzing water, but to do so America would have to nearly double its electricity output, and generating this extra power with carbon-free renewable energy would mean covering an area the size of Massachusetts with solar panels or of New York State with windmills.

7   Of course technology is always improving, and down the road some or all of these technologies may become more feasible. But for the near term, there is no silver bullet. The scale and complexity of American energy consumption are such that the country needs to look at many different solutions simultaneously. On the demand side, this means huge investments in conservation and energy efficiency—two areas that policy makers and consumers have sadly neglected.

8   On the supply side, the important thing is to come up with so-called bridge technologies that can power our cities, factories and cars with fewer emissions than traditional fossil fuels while we move to clean energy like solar, wind and safe nuclear power. A prime example of a bridge technology—one that exists right now—is gasification.

9   Here's how it works: in a type of power plant called an integrated gasification combined-cycle facility, we change any fossil fuel, including coal, into a superhot gas that is rich in hydrogen—and in the process strip out pollutants like sulfur and mercury. As in a traditional combustion power plant, the heat generates large amounts of electricity; but in this case, the gas byproducts can be pure streams of hydrogen and carbon dioxide.

10   This matters for several reasons. The hydrogen produced could be used as a transportation fuel. Equally important, the harmful carbon dioxide waste is in a form that can be pumped deep underground and stored, theoretically for millions of years, in old oil and gas fields or saline aquifers. This process is called geologic storage, or carbon sequestration, and recent field demonstrations in Canada and Norway have shown it can work and work safely.

11   The marriage of gasified coal plants and geologic storage could allow us to build power plants that produce vast amounts of energy with virtually no carbon dioxide emissions in the air. The Department of Energy is pursuing plans to build such a zero-emission power plant and is encouraging energy companies to come up with proposals of their own. The United States, Britain, and Germany are also collaborating to build such plants in China and India as part of an effort by the Group of 8. Moreover, these plants are very flexible: although coal is the most obvious fuel source, they could burn almost any organic material, including waste cornhusks and woodchips.

12   This is an emerging technology, so inevitably there are hurdles. For example, we need a crash program of research to find out which geological formations best lock up the carbon dioxide for the longest time, followed by global geological surveys to locate these formations and determine their

capacity. Also, coal mining is dangerous and strip-mining, of course, devastates the environment; if we are to mine a lot more coal in the future we will want more environmentally friendly methods.

13   On balance, though, this combination of technologies is probably among the best ways to provide the energy needed by modern societies—including populous, energy-hungry and coal-rich societies like China and India—without wrecking the global climate.

14   Fossil fuels, especially petroleum, powered the industrialization of today's rich countries and they still drive the world economy. But within the lifetimes of our grandchildren, the age of petroleum will wane. The combination of gasified coal plants and geologic storage can be our bridge to the clean energy—derived from renewable resources like solar and wind power and perhaps nuclear fusion—of the 22nd century and beyond. ■

Sample Student Proposal Argument

Kim Lee
Professor Patel
RHE 306
31 March 2009

Let's Make It a Real Melting Pot with Presidential Hopes for All

The image the United States likes to advertise is a country that embraces diversity and creates a land of equal opportunity for all. As the Statue of Liberty cries out, "give me your tired, your poor, your huddled masses yearning to breathe free," American politicians gleefully evoke such images to frame the United States as a bastion for all things good, fair, and equal. As a proud American, however, I must nonetheless highlight one of the cracks in this façade of equality. Imagine that an infertile couple decides to adopt an orphaned child from China. They follow all of the legal processes deemed necessary by both countries. They fly abroad and bring home their (once parentless) six-month-old baby boy. They raise and nurture him, and while teaching him to embrace his ethnicity, they also teach him to love Captain Crunch, baseball, and *The Three Stooges*. He grows and eventually attends an ethnically diverse American public school. One day his fifth-grade teacher tells the class that anyone can grow up to be president. To clarify her point, she turns to the boy, knowing his background, and states, "No, you could not be president, Stu, but you could still be a senator. That's something to aspire to!" How do Stu's parents explain this rule to this American-raised child? This scenario will become increasingly common, yet as the Constitution currently reads, only "natural-born" citizens may run for the offices of president and vice president. Neither these children nor the thousands of hardworking Americans who chose to make America their official homeland may aspire to the highest political position in the land. While the huddled masses may enter, it appears they must retain a second-class citizen ranking.

The "natural-born" stipulation regarding the presidency stems from the self-same meeting of minds that brought the American people the Electoral College. During the Constitutional Convention of 1787, the Congress formulated the regulatory measures associated with the office of the president. A letter sent from John Jay to George Washington during this period reads as follows:

> "Permit me to hint," Jay wrote, "whether it would not be wise and seasonable to provide a strong check to the admission of foreigners into the administration of our national government; and to declare expressly that the Commander in Chief of the American army shall not be given to, nor devolve on, any but a natural-born citizen." (Mathews A1)

Shortly thereafter, Article II, Section I, Clause V, of the Constitution declared that "No Person except a natural born Citizen, or a Citizen of the United States at the time of the Adoption of this Constitution, shall be eligible to the Office of President." Jill A. Pryor states in the *Yale Law Journal* that "some writers have suggested that Jay was responding to rumors that foreign princes might be asked to assume the presidency" (881). Many cite disastrous examples of foreign rule in the eighteenth century as the impetus for the "natural-born" clause. For example, in 1772—only 15 years prior to the adoption of the statute—Poland had been divided up by Prussia, Russia, and Austria (Kasindorf). Perhaps an element of self-preservation and not ethnocentrism led to the questionable stipulation. Nonetheless, in the twenty-first century this clause reeks of xenophobia.

The 2003 election of action-film star Arnold Schwarzenegger as governor of California stirred up a movement to change this Constitutional statute. Politicians such as Senators Orrin Hatch (R-Utah) and Ted Kennedy (D-Massachusetts and Arnold's uncle by marriage) have created a buzz for ratifying a would-be twenty-eighth amendment. In addition, grassroots campaigns like Amend for Arnold are trying to rally popular support as they dream of the Terminator-cum-president's political slogans ("I'll be back . . . for four more years" or "Hasta la vista, baby, and hasta la vista to high taxes"). Schwarzenegger has become the face—and the bulked-up body—of the viable *naturalized* president.

We as a nation should follow the lead set by those enamored of the action star, but distance the fight from this one extremely wealthy actor. We must instead take a stand against the discriminatory practice applied to all foreign-born American citizens by this obsolete provision of the Constitution. Congress has made minor attempts to update this biased clause. The Fourteenth Amendment clarified the difference between "natural-born" and "native-born" citizens by spelling out the citizenship status of children born to American parents outside of the United States (Ginsberg 929). (Such a clause qualifies individuals such as Senator John McCain—born in Panama—for presidency.) This change is not enough. I propose that the United States abolish the natural-born clause and replace it with a stipulation that allows naturalized citizens to run for president. This amendment would state that a candidate must have been naturalized and must have lived in residence in the United States for a period of at least twenty-five years. The present time is ideal for this change. This amendment could simultaneously honor the spirit of the Constitution, protect and ensure the interests of the United States, promote an international image of inclusiveness, and grant heretofore-withheld rights to thousands of legal and loyal United States citizens.

In our push for change, we must make clear the importance of this amendment. It would not provide special rights for would-be terrorists. To the contrary, it would fulfill the longtime promises of the nation. The United States claims to allow all people to blend into the great stew of citizenship. It has already suffered embarrassment and international cries of ethnic bias as a result of political moves such as Japanese-American internment and the Guantanamo Bay detention center. This amendment can help mend the national image as every American takes one more step toward equality. Naturalized citizens have been contributing to the United States for centuries. Many nameless Mexican, Irish, and Asian Americans sweated and toiled to build the American railroads. The public has welcomed naturalized Americans such as Bob Hope, Albert Pujols, and Peter Jennings into their hearts and living rooms. Individuals such as German-born Henry Kissinger and Czechoslovakian-born Madeleine Albright have held high posts in the American government and have served as respected aides to its presidents. The amendment must make clear that it is not about one man's celebrity. Approximately seven hundred foreign-born Americans have won the Medal of Honor and over sixty thousand proudly serve in the United States military today (Siskind 5). The "natural-born" clause must be removed to provide each of these people—over half a million naturalized in 2003 alone—with equal footing to those who were born into citizenship rather than working for it (U.S. Census Bureau).

Since the passing of the Bill of Rights, only 17 amendments have been ratified. This process takes time and overwhelming congressional

Lee 4

and statewide support. To alter the Constitution, a proposed amendment must pass with a two-thirds "super-majority" in both the House of Representatives and the Senate. In addition, the proposal must find favor in two-thirds (38) of state legislatures. In short, this task will not be easy. In order for this change to occur, a grassroots campaign must work to dispel misinformation regarding naturalized citizens and to force the hands of senators and representatives wishing to retain their congressional seats. We must take this proposal to ethnicity-specific political groups from both sides of the aisle, business organizations, and community activist groups. We must convince representatives that this issue matters. Only through raising voices and casting votes can the people enact change. Only then can every American child see the possibility for limitless achievement and equality. Only then can everyone find the same sense of pride in the possibility for true American diversity in the highest office in the land.

Lee 5

Works Cited

Epstein, Edward. "Doubt about a Foreign-Born President." *San Francisco Chronicle* 6 Oct. 2004: A5. *LexisNexis Academic*. Web. 6 Mar. 2009.

Ginsberg, Gordon. "Citizenship: Expatriation: Distinction between Naturalized and Natural Born Citizens." *Michigan Law Review* 50 (1952): 926-29. *JSTOR*. Web. 6 Mar. 2009.

Kasindorf, Martin. "Should the Constitution Be Amended for Arnold?" *USA Today* 2 Dec. 2004. *LexisNexis Academic*. Web. 8 Mar. 2009.

Mathews, Joe. "Maybe Anyone Can Be President." *Los Angeles Times* 2 Feb. 2005: A1. *LexisNexis Academic*. Web. 6 Mar. 2009.

Pryor, Jill A. "The Natural Born Citizen Clause and Presidential Eligibility: An Approach for Resolving Two Hundred Years of Uncertainty." *Yale Law Journal* 97.5 (1988): 881-99. Print.

Siskind, Lawrence J. "Why Shouldn't Arnold Run?" *Recorder* 10 Dec. 2004: 5. *LexisNexis Academic*. Web. 10 Mar. 2009.

United States. Dept. of Commerce. Census Bureau. "The Fourth of July 2005." *Facts for Features*. US Dept. of Commerce, 27 June 2005. Web. 17 Mar. 2009.

Steps to Writing a Proposal Argument

Step 1 Make a Claim

Make a proposal claim advocating a specific change or course of action.

Template

- *We should (or should not) do SOMETHING.* In an essay of five or fewer pages, it's difficult to propose solutions to big problems such as persistent poverty. Proposals that address local problems are more manageable, and sometimes they get actual results.

Examples

- Redesigning the process of registering for courses, getting email, or making appointments to be more efficient.
- Creating bicycle lanes to make cycling safer and to reduce traffic.
- Building a pedestrian overpass over a busy street to improve safety for walkers.
- Streamlining the rules for recycling newspapers, bottles, and cans to encourage increased participation.

Step 2 Identify the Problem

- What exactly is the problem?
- Who is most affected by the problem?
- What causes the problem?
- Has anyone tried to do anything about it? If so, why haven't they succeeded?
- What is likely to happen in the future if the problem isn't solved?

Step 3 **Propose Your Solution**

State your solution as specifically as you can.

- What exactly do you want to achieve?
- How exactly will your solution work?
- Can it be accomplished quickly, or will it have to be phased in over a few years?
- Has anything like it been tried elsewhere? If so, what happened?
- Who will be involved?
- Can you think of any reasons why your solution might not work?
- How will you address those arguments?
- Can you think of any ways to strengthen your proposed solution in light of those possible criticisms?

Step 4 **Consider Other Solutions**

- What other solutions have been or might be proposed for this problem, including doing nothing?
- What are the advantages and disadvantages of those solutions?
- Why is your solution better?

Step 5 **Examine the Feasibility of Your Solution**

- How easy is your solution to implement?
- Will the people most affected by your solution be willing to go along with it? (For example, lots of things can be accomplished if enough people volunteer, but groups often have difficulty getting enough volunteers to work without pay.)
- If your solution costs money, how do you propose to pay for it?
- Who is most likely to reject your proposal because it is not practical enough?
- How can you convince your readers that your proposal can be achieved?

Step 6 Analyze Your Potential Readers

- Whom are you writing for?
- How interested will your readers be in this problem?
- How much does this problem affect them?
- How would your solution benefit them directly and indirectly?

Step 7 Write a Draft

Introduction

- Set out the issue or problem, perhaps by telling about your experience or the experience of someone you know.
- Argue for the seriousness of the problem.
- Give some background about the problem if necessary.

Body

- Present your solution. Consider setting out your solution first, explaining how it will work, discussing other possible solutions, and arguing that yours is better. Or consider discussing other possible solutions first, arguing that they don't solve the problem or are not feasible, and then presenting your solution.
- Make clear the goals of your solution. Many solutions cannot solve problems completely. If you are proposing a solution for juvenile crime in your neighborhood, for example, you cannot expect to eliminate all juvenile crime.
- Describe in detail the steps in implementing your solution and how they will solve the problem you have identified. You can impress your readers with the care with which you have thought through this problem.
- Explain the positive consequences that will follow from your proposal. What good things will happen, and what bad things will be avoided, if your advice is taken?
- Argue that your proposal is feasible and can be put into practice.
- If people have to change the ways they are doing things now, explain why they would want to change. If your proposal costs money, you need to identify exactly where the money would come from.

Conclusion

- Issue a call to action—if your readers agree with you, they will want to take action.
- Restate and emphasize exactly what readers need to do to solve the problem.

Step 8 Revise, Edit, Proofread

- For detailed instructions, see Chapter 4.
- For a checklist to use to evaluate your draft, see pages 61–62.

Designing and Presenting Arguments

14

Designing Arguments

Arguments do not communicate with words alone. Even written arguments that do not contain graphics or images have a look and feel that also communicate meaning. In daily life we infer a great deal from what we see. Designers are well aware that, like people, writing has a body language that often communicates a strong message. It all has to do with understanding how particular effects can be achieved for particular readers in particular situations. Becoming more attentive to design will make your arguments more effective.

Think About Your Readers

Imagine yourself in the shoes of your reader. As a reader of an argument, you expect to find reasons supported by evidence. But you also expect the writer to do the little things that make it easier to read and understand the argument.

Telling readers what you are writing about

An accurate and informative title is critical for readers to decide whether they want to read what you have written. Furthermore, the title is critical to allow readers to return to something they read earlier.

Some kinds of writing require abstracts, which are short summaries of the overall document. Abstracts are required for scholarly articles in the sciences and social sciences as well as dissertations. Business reports and other reports often have executive summaries, which are similar to abstracts but often briefer.

Making your organization visible

Most longer texts and many shorter ones include headings, which give readers an at-a-glance overview and make the text easier to follow and remember. Readers increasingly expect you to divide what you write into sections and to label those sections with headings. A system of consistent headings should map the overall organization.

Use different levels of headings to show the hierarchy of your ideas. Determine the level of importance of each heading by making an outline to see what subpoint fits under what main point. Then make the headings conform to the different levels by choosing a font size and an effect such as boldfacing for each level. The type, the size, and the effect should signal the level of importance.

Helping readers navigate your text

Do the little things that help readers. Remember to include page numbers, which word-processing software can create for you automatically. Make cross-references to other parts of your document when a subject is covered elsewhere. If you are citing sources, make sure they are all in your list of works cited.

A traditional way to add information to a text without interrupting the main text is to add footnotes to the bottoms of pages or to include endnotes at the end of a paper. Today writers often use boxes or sidebars to supply extra information. If you use boxes or sidebars, indicate them with a different design or a different color. The key is to make what *is* different *look* different.

Know When to Use Images and Graphics

Personal computers, digital cameras, scanners, printers, and the Web have made it easy to include images and graphics in writing. But these technologies don't tell you if, when, or how images and graphics should be used.

Thinking about what an image or graphic communicates

- **What are your readers' expectations for the medium you are using?** Most essays don't include images; however, most Web sites and brochures do.

- **What is the purpose for an image or graphic?** Does it illustrate a concept? Does it highlight an important point? Does it show something that is hard to explain with words alone? If you don't know the purpose, you may not need the image.

- **Where should an image or graphic be placed in your text?** Images should be as close as possible to the relevant point in your text.

- **What will readers focus on when they see the image?** Will they focus on the part that matters? If not, you may need to crop the image.

- **What explanation do readers need in order to understand the image?** Provide informative captions for the images and graphics you use, and refer to them in your text.

Formatting images for the medium you are using

Images that you want to print need to be of higher quality than those intended for the Web or the screen. Pay attention to the settings on your camera or scanner.

- **Digital cameras** frequently make images with 72 dpi (dots per inch), which is the maximum you can display on the screen. Most printers use a resolution from 300 to 600 dpi. Use the high-quality setting on your camera for images you intend to print.

- **Scanners** typically offer a range of resolution from 72 to 1600 dpi. The higher the number, the finer the image, but the larger the file size. Images on the Web or a screen display at 72 dpi, so higher resolutions do not improve the quality but do make the image slow to load.

Compose and Edit Images

Photographs often provide evidence in arguments, especially involving local issues. For example, if you are proposing that your city should devote more money to park maintenance, photographs showing neglect help to document your case. Inexpensive digital cameras now can take high-quality photographs. Keeping a few principles in mind can give your photos more impact.

Taking better photographs

- **Nonessential elements:** Most people include too much in their photographs. Decide what is essential and concentrate on getting those elements in the frame.

- **Framing:** If you are taking a portrait, usually the closer you can get to your subject, the better. If your camera has a zoom lens, use it.

The boredom of waiting is expressed in the boys' faces.

Editing photographs

If you own a digital camera, you likely have an image-editing program that came with your camera. Image editors are now standard software on most new computers.

Decide what you want in a frame. If your goal is to show the habitat of sea lions, you'll need a wide shot. But if you want a portrait of a sea lion, get in tight.

■ **Cropping:** Most images can be trimmed to improve visual focus and file size. To crop an image, select the rectangle tool, draw the rectangle over the area you want to keep, and select the Crop or Trim command. The part of the image outside the rectangle will be discarded.

Cropping improves your photos by eliminating unnecessary elements and by allowing them to load faster on a computer.

- **Rotating:** Often you'll find that you held your camera at a slight angle when taking pictures, especially if your subjects were moving. You can make small adjustments by using the Rotate Image command. You can also rotate images 90 degrees to give them a vertical orientation.
- **Resizing:** Photo-editing programs will tell you the height and width of an image. You can resize images to fit in a particular area of a Web page or printed page. You can also change the resolution in the dpi window.
- **Adjusting color:** You can adjust color using controls for brightness, contrast, and saturation that are similar to those on your color TV. Be aware that colors look different on different monitors, and what you print may not look like the colors on your screen.

Create Tables, Charts, and Graphs

Tables are useful for presenting evidence in arguments if you have an array of statistical data that you want readers to take in at a glance. Charts and graphs are useful for visually representing statistical trends and for making comparisons.

Tables

Population Change for the Ten Largest U.S. Cities, 1990 to 2000

City and State	April 1, 2000	April 1, 1990	Number	Percentage
New York, NY	8,008,278	7,322,564	685,714	9.4
Los Angeles, CA	3,694,820	3,485,398	209,422	6.0
Chicago, IL	2,896,016	2,783,726	112,290	4.0
Houston, TX	1,953,631	1,630,553	323,078	19.8
Philadelphia, PA	1,517,550	1,585,577	−68,027	−4.3
Phoenix, AZ	1,321,045	983,403	337,642	34.3
San Diego, CA	1,223,400	1,110,549	112,851	10.2
Dallas, TX	1,188,580	1,006,877	181,703	18.0
San Antonio, TX	1,144,646	935,933	208,713	22.3
Detroit, MI	951,270	1,027,974	−76,704	−7.5

Source: U.S. Census Bureau, *Census 2000*; 1990 Census, Population and Housing Unit Counts, United States (1990 CPH-2-1).

A table is used to display numerical data and similar types of information. It usually includes several items as well as variables for each item.

Bar graphs

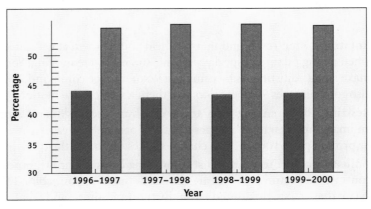

A bar graph compares the values of two or more items.

Line graphs

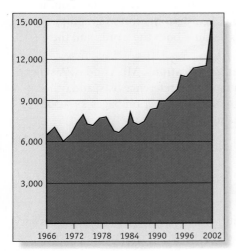

A line graph shows change over time.

Pie charts

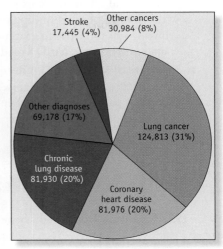

A pie chart shows the parts making up a whole.

Design Pages for Print

Word-processing programs design pages for you through default settings for margins, paragraph indentions, bullets, justification, and so on. Even if you use the default settings, you still have a range of options for designing a page that is appropriate to your assignment. Thinking about design will lead to a more effective presentation of your argument.

- **Choose the orientation, size of your page, and number of columns.** You can usually use the defaults on your word-processing program for academic essays (remember to select double-spacing for line spacing if the default is single-spaced). For other kinds of texts you may want a horizontal rather than a vertical orientation, a size other than a standard sheet of paper, and two or more columns rather than one.
- **Divide your text into units.** The paragraph is the basic unit of extended writing, but also think about when to use lists. This list is a bulleted list. You can also use a numbered list.
- **Use left-aligned text with a ragged-right margin.** Fully justified text aligns the right margin, which gives a more formal look but can also leave unsightly rivers of extra white space running through the middle of your text. Ragged-right text is easier to read.

- **Be conscious of white space.** White space can make your text more readable and set off more important elements. Headings stand out more with white space surrounding them. Leave room around graphics. Don't crowd words too close to graphics because both the words and the visuals will become hard to read.
- **Be aware of MLA and APA design specifications.** MLA and APA styles have specifications for margins, indentions, reference lists, and other aspects of paper formatting. See the sample paper on pages 297–303 for guidelines on designing a paper using MLA style.

Design Pages for the Web

If your argument calls for or might benefit from a Web site, a handsome, easy-to-read site is most likely to convince your readers that your argument is valid.

Creating a visual theme

A Web site does not need a loud background, an attention-grabbing image, or flashy animation to achieve a visual theme. Instead, a consistent look that supports the content and a simple set of colors for the text, headings, links, and background often work much better to create a unified visual theme. Similar graphics and images should be the same size, and often their placement can be repeated from page to page.

Keeping visuals simple

An uncomplicated site with simple elements is usually more friendly to readers because it loads faster, and if it is well designed, it can be elegant. Too many icons, bullets, horizontal rules, and other embellishments clutter the page. A simple, consistent design is always effective for pages that contain text.

Making text readable

Long stretches of text on the Web tend not to get read. You can make your text more readable on the Web if you do the following:

- **Divide your information into chunks.** If your information runs longer than a page, consider placing it on two Web pages.

- **Use shorter paragraphs when possible.** Long paragraphs are harder to read on screen than in print.
- **Use a sans serif typeface.** Consider using Arial, Helvetica, or Verdana, which are easier to read on screen. You can specify typefaces using the Font command on your Web-editing software.
- **Use white space to separate elements and to provide visual relief.**
- **Avoid dark backgrounds.** Dark backgrounds make your text hard to read.

Making navigation easy

People typically scan a Web site quickly and move around a lot. They are likely to click on links as they follow their interests. If you put content on more than one page, provide a navigation bar so readers can navigate easily. A navigation bar can be a simple text bar or icons that are easy to create with image-editing software.

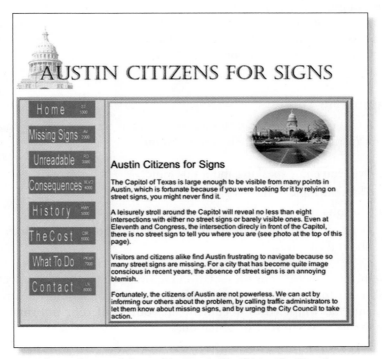

Kat Schwegel created the multi-page *Austin Citizens for Signs* for a proposal-argument assignment to address the problem of missing street signs. Her use of signs as navigation icons supports the visual theme of her site.

15

Presenting Arguments

Becoming effective in oral communication is just as important as in written communication. You likely will give many oral presentations in later life and perhaps in your college career. In the workplace and in public life, arguments are often both written and presented, and one is developed from the other using the same visuals.

Plan in Advance

A successful presentation, like successful writing, requires careful planning. Look closely at what you are being asked to present and how much time you will have to deliver your presentation. Decide early what kind of presentation you will give and what visuals you will incorporate.

Selecting your topic

Choosing and researching a topic for a presentation is similar to choosing and researching a written argument. Ask these questions:

- Will you enjoy speaking about this topic?
- Does the topic fit the assignment?
- Do you know enough to speak about this topic?
- If you do not know enough, are you willing to do research to learn more about the topic?

Remember that if your presentation requires you to do any research, then you will need to develop a written bibliography as you would for a research assignment. You will need to document the sources of your information and provide those sources in your presentation.

Thinking about your audience

Unlike writing, when you give a speech, you have your audience directly before you. They will give you concrete feedback during your presentation by smiling or frowning, by paying attention or losing interest, by asking questions or sitting passively. Ask these questions:

- Will your audience likely be interested in your topic?
- Are there ways you can get them more interested?
- What is your audience likely to know or believe about your topic?
- What does your audience probably not know about your topic?
- What key terms will you have to define or explain?
- Where is your audience most likely to disagree with you?
- What questions are they likely to ask?

Organizing your presentation

The steps for writing various kinds of arguments, listed at the ends of Chapters 8–13, can be used to organize an oral presentation. Decide first the best way to order your main points. Then begin building your presentation.

Support your argument

Look at your research notes and think about how best to incorporate the information you found. Consider using one or more of these strategies.

- **Facts:** Speakers who know their facts build credibility.
- **Statistics:** Good use of statistics gives the impression that the speaker has done his or her homework. Statistics also can indicate that a particular example is representative. One tragic car accident doesn't mean a road is dangerous, but an especially high accident rate relative to other nearby roads does make the case.
- **Statements by authorities:** Quotations from credible experts are another common way of supporting key points.
- **Narratives:** Narratives are small stories that can illustrate key points. Narratives are a good way of keeping the attention of the audience. Keep them short so they don't distract from your major points.
- **Humor:** In most situations audiences appreciate humor. Humor is a good way to convince an audience that you have common beliefs and experiences, and that your argument may be one they can agree with.

Plan your introduction

No part of your presentation is more critical than the introduction. You have to get the audience's attention, introduce your topic, convince the audience that the topic is important to them, present your thesis, and give your audience either an overview of your presentation or a sense of your direction. Accomplishing all this in a short time is a tall order, but if you lose your audience in the first two minutes, you won't recover their attention. You might begin with a compelling example or anecdote that both introduces your topic and indicates your stance.

Plan your conclusion

The next most important part of your speech is your conclusion. You want to end on a strong note. First, you need to signal that you are entering the conclusion. You can announce that you are concluding, but you also can give signals in other ways. Touching on your main points again will help your audience to remember them. Simply summarizing is a dull way to close, however. Think of an example or an idea that your audience can take away with them. If your argument is a proposal, end with a call for action.

Design Effective Visuals

Visual elements can both support and reinforce your major points. They give you another means of reaching your audience and keeping them stimulated. Visuals should communicate content and not just be eye candy. Some of the easier visuals to create are outlines, statistical charts, flow charts, photographs, and maps. Presentation software, such as Microsoft PowerPoint, allows you to import charts and other graphics that you have created in other programs, and it gives you several options for presentation, including printed handouts and Web pages.

At a minimum, consider putting an outline of your talk on a transparency or on a PowerPoint slide. An outline allows an audience to keep track of where you are in your talk and when you are moving to your next point.

Creating visuals

Follow these guidelines to create better visuals.

- **Keep the text short.** You don't want your audience straining to read long passages on the screen and neglecting what you have to say. Except for quotations, use short words and phrases on transparencies and slides.

- **Use dark text on a white or light-colored background.** Light text on a dark background is hard to read.
- **Use graphics that reproduce well.** Some graphics do not show up well on the screen, often because there isn't enough contrast.
- **Avoid getting carried away with special effects.** Presentations with many special effects such as fade-ins, fade-outs, and sound effects often come off as heavy on style and light on substance. They also can be time-consuming to produce.
- **Plan your timing when using visuals.** Usually you can leave a slide on the screen for one to two minutes, which allows your audience time to read the slide and connect its points to what you are saying.
- **Always proofread.** Typos and misspelled words make you look careless and can distract the audience from your point.

Making an argument with slides

The organization of a presentation with visuals should be evident in the titles of the slides. Each title should give the main point of the slide and advance the story line of the presentation. If a slide has a box at the bottom with text, called a "take-away" box, it should either draw an implication from the body of the slide that isn't obvious or make the transition to the next slide.

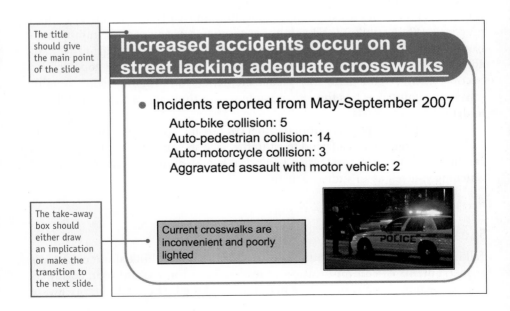

Generic titles like "Overview," "Problem," and "Solution" force readers to find the main point of the slide. Specific titles convey the story of the presentation. If you use a generic title, be sure to include a specific subtitle.

Overview: The success of First Thursday has created a major safety problem on South Congress Avenue
Problem: Increased accidents occur on a street lacking adequate crosswalks
Solution: Create temporary crosswalks with flashers

Focus on Your Delivery

The best speakers draw their inspiration from their audience, and they maintain contact with their audience by communicating with body language and presentation style in addition to content. Audience members leave feeling like they've had a conversation with the speaker even if they have been silent through the presentation.

The importance of practice

There is no substitute for rehearsing your speech several times in advance. You will become more confident and have more control over the content. The best way to overcome nervousness about speaking in front of others is to be well prepared. When you know what you are going to say, you can pay more attention to your audience, make eye contact, and watch body language for signals about how well you are making your points. When you rehearse you can also become comfortable with any visual elements you will be using. Finally, rehearsing your speech is the only reliable way to find out how long it will take to deliver.

Practice your speech in front of others. If possible, go to the room where you will be speaking and ask a friend to sit in the back so you can learn how well you can be heard. You can also learn a great deal by videotaping your rehearsal and watching yourself as an audience member.

Speaking effectively

Talking is so much a part of our daily lives that we rarely think about our voices as instruments of communication unless we have some training in acting or public speaking. You can become better at speaking by becoming more aware of your delivery. Pay attention to your breathing as you practice your speech. When you breathe at your normal rate, you will not rush your speech. Plan where you will pause during your speech. Pauses allow you to take a sip of water and give your audience a chance to sum up mentally what you have said. And don't be afraid to repeat key points. Repetition is one of the easiest strategies for achieving emphasis.

Most of the time nervousness is invisible. You can feel nervous and still impress your audience by appearing calm and confident. If you make mistakes while speaking, know that the audience understands and will be forgiving. Stage fright is normal; sometimes it can be helpful in raising the energy level of a presentation.

Nonverbal communication

While you are speaking, you are also communicating with your presence. Stand up unless you are required to sit. Move around instead of standing behind the podium. Use gestures to emphasize main points, and only main points; if you gesture continually, you may appear nervous.

Maintaining eye contact is crucial. Begin your speech by looking at the people directly in front of you and then move your eyes around the room, looking to both sides. Attempting to look at each person during a speech may seem unnatural, but it is the best way to convince all the members of your audience that you are speaking directly to them.

Handling questions

Your presentation doesn't end when you finish your planned talk. Speakers are usually expected to answer questions afterward. How you handle questions is also critical to your success. Speakers who are evasive or fail to acknowledge questions sometimes lose all the credibility they have built in their speech. But speakers who listen carefully to questions and answer them honestly build their credibility further. Have some strategies in mind for handling questions:

- **Repeat the question so that the entire audience can hear it and to confirm you understood it.**
- **Take a minute to reflect on the question.** If you do not understand the question, ask the questioner to restate it.
- **Avoid getting into a debate with audience members who make a small speech instead of asking a question.** Acknowledge their point of view and move on.

- **If you cannot answer a question, don't bluff and don't apologize.** You can offer to research the question or you can ask the audience if they know the answer.

- **If you are asked a question during your speech, answer it if it is a short, factual question or one of clarification.** Postpone questions that require long answers until the end to avoid losing the momentum of your speech.

PART 5

Researching Arguments

16

Planning Research

You do research every day. If you compare prices online before you buy an airline ticket, look up a detailed course description before registering for a class, or want to settle an argument about the first African American to win an Olympic gold medal, you need to do research. In college, research means both investigating existing knowledge that is stored on computers and in libraries, and creating new knowledge through original analysis, surveys, experiments, and theorizing. When you start a research task in a college course, you need to understand the different kinds of possible research and to plan your strategy in advance.

Analyze the Research Task

If you have an assignment that requires research, look closely at what you are being asked to do. The assignment may ask you to define, evaluate, analyze causes, rebut another's argument, or propose a course of action. You may be writing for experts, for students like yourself, or for the general public. The purpose of your research and your potential audience will help guide your strategies for research.

The key is understanding what is expected of you. You are being asked to do the following.

1. Find a subject.
2. Ask a question about the subject.
3. Find out what has been said about this subject.
4. Make a contribution to the discussion about this subject.

Find a Subject

Asking Questions

To find a subject that interests you, begin by asking meaningful questions about something that matters to you. Your courses may give you some ideas about questions to ask, such as are manufacturing jobs in the United States being lost primarily to outsourcing to other countries or to more efficient production?

STRATEGIES FOR RESEARCH

Find a subject that interests you. Research is more enjoyable if you are finding out new things rather than just confirming what you already know. The most exciting part of doing research is making small discoveries.

Make sure that you can do a thorough job of research. If you select a subject that is too broad, such as proposing how to end poverty, you will not be able to do an adequate job.

Develop a strategy for your research early on. If you are researching a campus issue such as a parking problem, then you probably will rely most on interviews, observations, and possibly a survey. But if you find out that one of the earliest baseball stadiums, Lakefront Park in Chicago (built in 1883), had the equivalent of today's luxury boxes and you want to make an argument that the trend toward building stadiums with luxury boxes is not a new development, then you will have to do library research.

Give yourself enough time to do a thorough job. As you conduct your research, expect to focus better on your subject, to find a few dead ends, and to spend more time on the project than you initially thought. Remember the first principle of doing research: things take longer than you think they will.

Personal experience is also often a good source of questions related to your research subject: What was the cause of something that happened to you? Was your experience typical or atypical? How can you solve a problem you have? What do experts think about the issues that concern you? Working with a subject that has already aroused your curiosity makes it more likely that your findings will interest others.

Browsing a subject directory

Another good way to begin exploring a research subject is by browsing, either in your library or on the Web. Browsing may lead you to subjects you hadn't yet considered; it may also show you a wide range of issues surrounding a potential subject. Subject directories can show you many different aspects of a single subject.

Browsing a general or specialized encyclopedia

Other ways to generate interesting subjects include consulting a general encyclopedia such as *Columbia Encyclopedia* (www.bartleby.com), Britannica Online (available on your library's Web site), or Wikipedia (en.wikipedia.org), or a specialized encyclopedia such as the *Encyclopedia of Crime and Justice*. The reference section of your library's Web site lists specialized encyclopedias and other specialized reference sources by subject.

Ask a Research Question

Often you'll be surprised by the amount of information your initial browsing uncovers. Your next task will be to identify a question for your research project within that mass of information. This **researchable question** will be the focus of the remainder of your research and ultimately of your research project or paper. Browsing on the subject of organic foods, for example, might lead you to one of the following researchable questions.

- How do farmers benefit from growing organic produce?
- Why are organic products more expensive than non-organic products?
- Are Americans being persuaded to buy more organic products?

Once you have formulated a research question, you should begin thinking about what kind of research you will need to do to address the question.

Gather Information About the Subject

Most researchers rely partly or exclusively on the work of others as sources of information. Research based on the work of others is called **secondary research**. In the past this information was contained almost exclusively in collections of print materials housed in libraries, but today enormous amounts of information are available through library databases and on the Web (see Chapter 17).

Much of the research done at a university creates new information through **primary research**—experiments, examination of historical documents—and **field research**, including data-gathering surveys, interviews, and detailed observations, described below.

Conducting field research

Sometimes you may be researching a question that requires you to gather first-hand information with field research. For example, if you are researching a campus issue such as the impact of a new library fee on students' budgets, you may need to conduct interviews, make observations, and give a survey.

Interviews

College campuses are a rich source of experts in many areas, including people on the faculty and in the surrounding community. Interviewing experts on your research subject can help build your knowledge base. You can use interviews to discover what the people most affected by a particular issue are thinking, such as why students object to some fees and not others.

Arrange interviews

Before you contact anyone, think carefully about your goals. Knowing what you want to find out through your interviews will help you determine whom you need to interview and what questions you need to ask. Use these guidelines to prepare for an interview.

- Decide what you want or need to know and who best can provide that for you.
- Schedule each interview in advance, and let the person know why you are conducting the interview. Estimate how long your interview will take, and tell your subject how much of her or his time you will need.
- Choose a location that is convenient for your subject but not too chaotic or loud. An office or study room is better than a noisy cafeteria.
- Plan your questions in advance. Write down a few questions and have a few more in mind.
- If you want to record the interview, ask for permission in advance. A recording device sometimes can intimidate the person you are interviewing.

Conduct interviews

- Come prepared with your questions, a notebook, and a pen or pencil.
- If you plan to record the interview (with your subject's permission), make sure whatever recording device you use has an adequate power supply and will not run out of tape, disk space, or memory.
- Listen carefully so you can follow up on key points. Make notes when important questions are raised or answered, but don't attempt to transcribe every word the person is saying.

- When you are finished, thank your subject, and ask his or her permission to get in touch again if you have additional questions.

Surveys

Extensive surveys that can be projected to large populations, like the ones used in political polls, require the effort of many people. Small surveys, however, often can provide insight on local issues, such as what percentage of students might be affected if library hours were reduced.

Plan surveys

What information do you need for your research question? Decide what exactly you want to know and design a survey that will provide that information. Likely you will want both close-ended questions (multiple choice, yes or no, rating scale) and open-ended questions that allow detailed responses. To create a survey, follow these guidelines.

- Write a few specific, unambiguous questions. People will fill out your survey quickly, and if the questions are confusing, the results will be meaningless.
- Include one or two open-ended questions, such as "What do you like about X?" or "What don't you like about X?" Open-ended questions can be difficult to interpret, but sometimes they turn up information you had not anticipated.
- Test the questions on a few people before you conduct the survey.
- Think about how you will interpret your survey. Multiple-choice formats make data easy to tabulate, but often they miss key information. Open-ended questions will require you to figure out a way to sort responses into categories.

Administer surveys

- Decide on who you need to survey and how many respondents your survey will require. For example, if you want to claim that the results of your survey represent the views of residents of your dormitory, your method of selecting respondents should give all residents an equal chance to be selected. Don't select only your friends.
- Decide how you will contact participants in your survey. If you are conducting your survey on private property, you will need permission from the property owner. Likewise, email lists and lists of mailing addresses are usually guarded closely to preserve privacy. You will need to secure permission from the appropriate parties if you want to contact people via an email list.

- If you mail or email your survey, include a statement about what the survey is for.

Observations

Observing can be a valuable source of data. For example, if you are researching why a particular office on your campus does not operate efficiently, observe what happens when students enter and how the staff responds to their presence.

Make observations

- Choose a place where you can observe with the least intrusion. The less people wonder about what you are doing, the better.
- Carry a notebook and write extensive field notes. Record as much information as you can, and worry about analyzing it later.
- Record the date, exactly where you were, exactly when you arrived and left, and important details like the number of people present.
- Write on one side of your notebook so you can use the facing page to note key observations and analyze your data later.

Analyze observations

You must interpret your observations so they make sense in the context of your argument. Ask yourself the following questions:

- What patterns of behavior did you observe?
- How was the situation you observed unique? How might it be similar to other locations?
- What constituted "normal" activity during the time when you were observing? Did anything out of the ordinary happen?
- Why were the people there? What can you determine about the purposes of the activities you observed?

Draft a Working Thesis

Once you have done some preliminary research into your question, you can begin to craft a working thesis. Perhaps you have found a lot of interesting material about the increasing popularity of organic products, including meat, dairy products, and produce. You have discovered that due to this trend, large corporations such as Wal-Mart are beginning to offer organic products in their stores. However, the enormous demand for organic products that this creates is endangering smaller organic farmers and producers. As you research the question of why small farmers and producers in the United States are endangered and what small farmers and producers in other countries have done to protect themselves, a working thesis begins to emerge.

Write your subject, research question, and working thesis on a note card or sheet of paper. Keep your working thesis handy. You may need to revise it several times until the wording is precise. As you research, ask yourself, does this information tend to support my thesis? Information that does not support your thesis is still important! It may lead you to adjust your thesis or even to abandon it altogether. You may need to find another source or reason that shows your thesis is still valid.

SUBJECT: Increased demand for organic products endangering smaller farmers and producers

RESEARCH QUESTION: How can smaller organic farms and producers protect themselves from becoming extinct?

WORKING THESIS: In order to meet the increasing demand for organic products that has been created by larger corporations such as Wal-Mart, smaller organic farmers and producers should form regional co-ops. These co-ops will work together to supply regional chains, much as co-ops of small farmers and dairies in Europe work together, thereby cutting transportation and labor costs and ensuring their survival in a much-expanded market.

17

Finding Sources

Newspapers

The distinction between doing research online and in the library is blurring as more and more libraries put their collections online. Many colleges and universities have made most of the major resources in their reference rooms available online. Still, your library is usually the best place to begin any research project because it contains some materials that are not available anywhere else. Moreover, professional librarians will help you locate sources quickly so you get the most out of your research time.

You will have a hard time finding the information you need if you don't know what you're looking for. To guide you in your library research, think about these questions.

Who are the parties involved in the issue?	Who are the experts? Who else is talking about it? Who is affected by the issue?
What is at stake?	How or why does this issue matter? What stands to be gained or lost? Who is likely to benefit or suffer?
What kinds of arguments are being made about the issue?	Are people making proposals? Are they trying to define terms? What kinds of reasons do they offer? What kinds of evidence do they present? What arguments are people *not* making that they could be making?
Who are the audiences for this debate?	Do people already have strong opinions? Are they still trying to make up their minds? How well informed are people about the issue?
What is your role?	What do you think? What else do you need to know? What do you think should be done?

Your answers to these questions will provide you with keywords and phrases to use as you begin your search for information.

Search with Keywords

For most research projects, you will begin with a subject search using one or more **keywords** or search terms that describe the subject.

Finding keywords

Entries for subjects in your library's online catalog and in databases will help you find keywords. If you find a book or article that is about your exact topic, use the subject terms to locate additional items. The sample below, for a book from an online catalog, shows the keywords under *subjects*. Try entering the subject terms individually and in combination in new subject searches to find more items similar to this one.

AUTHOR:

Solove, Daniel J., 1972-

TITLE:

The digital person: technology and privacy in the information age / Daniel J. Solove.

PUBLISHED:

New York: New York University Press, c2004.

SUBJECTS:

Data protection–Law and legislation–United States.

Electronic records–Access control–United States.

Public records–Law and legislation–United States.

Government information–United States.

Privacy, Right of–United States.

Single and multiple keyword searches

The simplest keyword searches return the most results, but often they are not the results you need. For example, imagine typing the word *capitalism* into the keyword search window on your library's online catalog and getting several thousand results, including subjects such as radicals and capitalism, global capitalism, American capitalism, new capitalism, women and capitalism, socialism and capitalism, slavery and capitalism, ethics and capitalism, and so on.

If you want to focus on how capitalism affects the natural world, however, then you can narrow your search using two or more keywords. For example, if you use the terms *capitalism* and *ecology* in the search window, you would likely receive a more manageable 25 or so results. You could then read through the titles and perhaps the brief abstracts provided and decide that a book such as *Wild Capitalism: Environmental Activists and Post-Socialist Political Ecology in Hungary* may not be as useful to you as a book titled *Ecology Against Capitalism*.

You can further limit your search by specifying what you don't want by using NOT. For example, if you are interested in air pollution control policies, but not those used in California, you would type *air pollution control policies* NOT *California*.

Find Books

Nearly all college libraries shelve books according to the Library of Congress Classification System, which uses a combination of letters and numbers to indicate the book's unique location in the library. The Library of Congress call number begins with a letter or letters that represent the broad subject area into which the book is classified.

The Library of Congress system groups books by subject, and you can often find other items relevant to your search shelved close to the particular one you are looking for. You can search the extensive Library of Congress online catalog (catalog. loc. gov) to find out how your subject might be indexed, or you can go straight to your own library's catalog and conduct a subject search. The call number will enable you to find the item in the stacks. You will need to consult the locations guide for your library to find the book on the shelves.

When you find a book in your library catalog, take time to notice the subject headings under which it is indexed. For example, if you locate Jeff Hawkins's *On Intelligence*, you will probably find it cross-listed under several subject categories, including the following.

Brain

Intellect

Artificial intelligence

Neural networks (Computer science)

Browsing within these categories, or using some of their keywords in a new search, may lead you to more useful sources.

Find Journal Articles

Searching for articles in scholarly journals and magazines works much the same way as searching for books. The starting point is your library's Web site. You should find a link to databases, which are listed by subject and by the name of the database.

Using databases

Databases are fully searchable by author, title, subject, or keywords. Many databases contain the full text of articles, allowing you to copy the contents onto your computer or email the article to yourself. To use databases effectively, make a list of keywords (see pages 255–256). For example, if you are researching the effects of hunting on deer populations, you could begin with the words *deer*, *hunting*, and *population*. If you are researching obesity in children, you might begin with *obesity*, *children*, and one more word such as *trend* or *United States* or *fast food*, depending on your focus.

Your next decision is to choose a database to begin your research. Newspapers might include stories on local deer populations and changes in hunting policy. Popular journals such as *Field and Stream* might have articles about national trends in deer hunting, and they might also summarize scholarly research about the subject. Scholarly journals, perhaps in the field of wildlife biology, would contain articles about formal research into the effects of deer hunting on population density, average size and weight of animals, range, and other factors.

To find newspaper stories, begin with LexisNexis Academic. To find popular and scholarly journal articles, go to Academic OneFile, Academic Search Premier or Academic Search Complete, InfoTrac OneFile, or MasterFILE Premier. If you have difficulty finding the right database, ask a librarian to help you.

Scholarly versus popular journals

Knowing what kinds of articles you want to look for—scholarly or popular—will help you select the right database. Many databases include more than one type of journal. Although the difference among journals is not always obvious, you should be able to judge whether a journal is scholarly or popular by its characteristics. Some instructors frown on using popular journals as sources in a research paper, but these journals can be valuable for researching current opinion on a particular topic. They cannot, however, be substituted for serious research articles written by accredited scholars.

Scholarly journals

Scholarly journals are excellent sources for research. They

- contain long articles typically written by scholars in the field, usually affiliated with a university or research center.
- usually include articles that report original research and have footnotes or a list of works cited at the end.
- are reviewed by other scholars in the field.
- assume that readers are also experts in the field.
- display few advertisements or illustrations.
- usually are published quarterly or biannually.

COMMON DATABASES

Academic OneFile	Indexes periodicals from the arts, humanities, sciences, social sciences, and general news, with full-text articles and images. (Formerly Expanded Academic ASAP.)
Academic Search Premier or **Academic Search Complete**	Provides full-text articles for thousands of scholarly publications, including social sciences, humanities, education, computer sciences, engineering, language and linguistics, literature, medical sciences, and ethnic-studies journals.
ArticleFirst	Indexes journals in business, the humanities, medicine, science, and social sciences.
EBSCOhost Research Databases	Gateway to a large collection of EBSCO databases, including Academic Search Premier, Academic Search Complete, and MasterFILE Premier.
Factiva	Provides full-text articles on business topics, including articles from *The Wall Street Journal*.
FirstSearch	Offers millions of full-text articles from many databases.
Google Scholar	Searches scholarly literature according to criteria of relevance.
InfoTrac OneFile	Contains millions of full-text articles about a wide range of academic and general-interest topics.
JSTOR	Provides scanned copies of scholarly journals.
LexisNexis Academic	Provides full text of a wide range of newspapers, magazines, government and legal documents, and company profiles from around the world.
MasterFILE Premier	Provides indexes and abstracts for business, consumer health, general science, and multicultural periodicals with many full-text articles.

Examples of scholarly journals include *American Journal of Mathematics, College English, JAMA: Journal of the American Medical Association, PMLA: Publication of the Modern Language Association*, and *Psychological Reports*.

Popular journals

Popular journals are found primarily on newsstands. They

- publish short articles aimed at the general public.
- contain many advertisements and photos.
- seldom include footnotes or the source of information.
- are published weekly or monthly.

Examples of popular journals include *Cosmopolitan*, *GQ*, *Rolling Stone*, *Sports Illustrated*, and *Time*.

Find Web Sources

You likely use the Web regularly to find information about products, restaurants, stores, services, jobs, people, maps, hobbies, music, films, and other entertainment. But researching an academic paper on the Web is different from such everyday tasks. The Web can be a powerful tool for research, but it also has many traps for the unwary.

Because anyone can publish on the Web, there is no overall quality control and there are no systems of organization as there are in a library. Nevertheless, the Web offers you some resources for current topics that would be difficult to find in a library. The keys to success are knowing where you are most likely to find current and accurate information about the particular question you are researching, and knowing how to access that information.

Using search engines

Search engines designed for the Web work in ways similar to library databases and your library's online catalog, but with one major difference. Databases typically do some screening of the items they list, but search engines potentially take you to every Web site that isn't password protected—millions of pages in all. Consequently, you have to work harder to limit searches on the Web or you can be deluged with tens of thousands of items.

Kinds of search engines

A search engine is a set of programs that sort through millions of items at incredible speed. There are four basic kinds of search engines.

- **Keyword search engines,** such as Ask.com, Answers.com, and Google, give unique results because they assign different weights to the information they find.
- **Web directories,** such as Yahoo! Directory, classify Web sites into categories and are the closest equivalent to the cataloging system used by libraries.

- **Metasearch agents,** such as Dogpile, Metacrawler, and WebCrawler, allow you to use several search engines simultaneously. While the concept is sound, metasearch agents are limited by the number of hits they can return and their inability to handle advanced searches.
- **Specialized search engines,** such as Froogle (shopping), Google Scholar (academic), Monster.com (jobs), Pubmed (medicine), Thomasnet (business), and WebMD (medicine), search specific subjects.

Advanced searches

Search engines often produce too many hits and are therefore not always useful. If you look only at the first few items, you may miss what is most valuable. The alternative is to refine your search. Most search engines offer you the option of an advanced search, which gives you the opportunity to limit numbers.

The advanced searches on Google and Yahoo! give you the options of using a string of words to search for sites that contain all the words, the exact phrase, or any of the words, or that exclude certain words. They also allow you to specify the language of the site, the date range, the file format, and the domain. For example, government statistics on crime are considered the most reliable, so if you want to find statistics on murder rates, you can specify the domain as *.gov* in an advanced search.

An advanced search on Google for government (.gov) sites only.

Finding discussion forums, groups, blogs, wikis, podcasts, and online video

Discussion forums and **discussion groups** are Internet sites for people to discuss thousands of specific topics. The Groups section of Google (groups.google.com) has an archive of several hundred million messages that can be searched. Much of the conversation on these sites is undocumented and highly opinionated, but you can still gather important information about people's attitudes and get tips about other sources, which you can verify later.

Web logs, better known as **blogs,** also are sources of public opinion. Several tools have been developed recently to search blogs: Blogdigger, Bloglines, Feedster, Google Blog Search, PubSub, Technorati, and IceRocket. Blogs are not screened and are not considered authoritative sources, but blogs can sometimes lead you to quality sources.

Wikis are web applications designed to let multiple authors write, edit, and review content. The best-known wiki is Wikipedia (en.wikipedia.org), a controversial online encyclopedia where any visitor can change an entry. Wikipedia can provide a useful introduction to many popular-culture topics, but do not rely on Wikipedia to be accurate. Many individual professors and teachers, as well as some colleges and universities, forbid the use of Wikipedia as a source in academic papers. If you include a Wikipedia entry in your works-cited list, prepare to be laughed at.

Podcasts are digital media files available on the Internet for playback on portable media players (such as the iPod). Many of these files are news, opinion, and entertainment broadcasts from major media outlets such as NPR (www.npr .org/rss/podcast/podcast_directory.php). Individuals can also create and distribute files for podcasts. Information from these podcasts should be treated with the same critical eye (and ear!) you use for blogs and personal Web pages.

Similarly, sites that offer **streaming video** such as YouTube (www.youtube .com) and Google Video (www.videogoogle.com) can be used to access videos from reputable sources, such as interviews and newscasts as well as eyewitness footage of events or situations around the world. Most videos on these sites, however, were created by a wide population of individuals—ranging from artists and video professionals to teenagers—strictly for entertainment purposes. Again, these video sites are not scholarly, but they can serve as examples or anecdotes if you are dealing with public opinion or popular-culture topics. Keep in mind also that videos originating from major media outlets appearing on these video sites are possibly there illegally.

Finding visual sources

You can find images published on the Web using Google and other search engines that allow you to specify searches for images. For example, if you are writing a research paper about invasive plant species, you might want to include an image of kudzu, an invasive vine common in the American South. In Google, choose Images and type *kudzu* in the search box. You'll find a selection of images of the plant, including several from the National Park Service.

Some search engines, such as Ditto (www.ditto.com), are designed specifically to find images. Yahoo! Picture Gallery has over 400,000 images that can be searched by subject (gallery.yahoo.com). In addition to images, you can find statistical data represented in charts and graphs on government Web sites. The Statistical Abstract of the United States is especially useful for finding charts and graphs of population statistics (www.census.gov/statab/www/). You can also find thousands of maps on the Web. (See www.lib.utexas.edu/maps/map_sites/map_sites.html for a directory of map sites.)

Kudzu

Pueraria montana var. *lobata* (Willd.) Maesen & S. Almeida
Pea family (Fabaceae)

NATIVE RANGE: Asia

DESCRIPTION: Kudzu ia a climbing, semi-woody, perennial vine in the pea family. Deciduous leaves are alternate and compound, with three broad leaflets up to 4 inches across. Leaflets may be entire or deeply 2-3 lobed with hairy margins. Individual flowers, about 1/2 inch long, are purple, highly fragrant and borne in long hanging clusters. Flowering occurs in late summer and is soon followed by production of brown, hairy, flattened, seed pods, each of which contains three to ten hard seeds.

Kudzu was planted widely in the South to reduce soil erosion but has itself become a major pest, smothering native trees and plants.

Just because images are easy to download from the Web does not mean that you are free to use every image you find. Look for the image creator's copyright notice and suggested credit line. This notice will tell you if you can reproduce the image. For example, the Cascades Volcano Observatory makes its images available to all: "The maps, graphics, images, and text found on our website, unless stated otherwise, are within the Public Domain. You may download and use them. Credit back to the USGS/Cascades Volcano Observatory is appreciated." Most images on government Web sites can be reproduced, but check the copyright restrictions. You should acknowledge the source of any image you use.

In many cases you will find a copyright notice that reads something like this: "Any use or re-transmission of text or images in this website without written consent of the copyright owner constitutes copyright infringement and is prohibited." You must write to the creator to ask permission to use an image from a site that is not in the public domain, even if you cannot find a copyright notice.

18

Evaluating and Recording Sources

A successful search for sources will turn up many more items than you can use in your final product. You have to make decisions about what is important and relevant. Return to your research question and working thesis (see Chapter 16) to determine which items are relevant and useful to your project.

Evaluate Print Sources

How reliable are your sources? Books are expensive to print and distribute, so book publishers generally protect their investment by providing some level of editorial oversight. Print sources in libraries have an additional layer of oversight because someone has decided that a book or journal is worth purchasing and cataloging. Web sites, in contrast, can be put up and changed quickly, so information can be—and often is—posted thoughtlessly.

But print sources contain their share of biased, inaccurate, and misleading information. Over the years librarians have developed a set of criteria for evaluating print sources. These criteria are summarized in the box below.

EVALUATING PRINT SOURCES	
Source	Who published the book or article? Scholarly books and articles in scholarly journals are reviewed by experts in the field before they are published. They are generally more reliable than popular magazines and books, which tend to emphasize what is entertaining at the expense of comprehensiveness.
Author	Who wrote the book or article? What are the author's qualifications?

(continued)

EVALUATING PRINT SOURCES *(continued)*

Timeliness	How current is the source? If you are researching a fast-developing subject such as vaccines for Asian bird flu, then currency is very important. Currency might not be as important for a historical subject, but even historical figures and events are often reinterpreted.
Evidence	Where does the evidence come from—facts, interviews, observations, surveys, or experiments? Is the evidence adequate to support the author's claims?
Biases	Can you detect particular biases of the author? How do the author's biases affect the interpretation offered?
Advertising	Is advertising a prominent part of the journal or newspaper? How might the ads affect what gets printed?

Find Information to Cite Print Sources

Recording the full bibliographic information for all of the articles, books, Web sites, and other materials you might want to use in your project will save you a great deal of time and trouble later. Determine which documentation style you should use (ask your instructor if you don't know). Two major documentation styles—Modern Language Association (MLA) and American Psychological Association (APA)—are explained in detail in Chapters 20 and 21 of this book.

For books you will need, at minimum, the following information. This information can typically be found on the front and back of the title page:

- Author's name
- Title of the book
- Place of publication
- Name of publisher
- Date of publication
- Medium of publication (Print)

You will also need the page numbers if you are quoting directly or referring to a specific passage, as well as the title and author of the individual chapter if your source is an edited book with contributions by several people. Add the call numbers for the book or journal so you can find it easily in the future. You can compile this information in a computer file, a notebook or on note cards.

HQ
799.7
K36
2006

Kamenetz, Anya. *Generation Debt: Why Now Is a Terrible
Time to Be Young.* New York: Penguin, 2006. Print.

For help with citing books, see pages 281–282 and 287–290 (MLA style) and 305 and 309–310 (APA style).

For journals you will need the following information:

■ Author's name
■ Title of the article
■ Title of the journal
■ Volume and issue of the journal
■ Date of the issue
■ Page numbers of the article
■ Medium of publication (Print)

Brazina, Paul R. "On the Trail: How Financial Audits Mark
the Path for Forensic Teams." *Pennsylvania CPA
Journal* 77 (2006): 13–16. Print.

For help with citing journals, see pages 282 and 291–293 (MLA style) and 306 and 310–311 (APA style).

Evaluate Database Sources

Databases collect print sources and put them in digital formats. Evaluate database sources the same way you evaluate print sources, asking the questions above in addition to those below.

Source: Is the source a scholarly or popular journal?

Author: What are the author's qualifications?

Timeliness: How current is the source?

Evidence: Where does the evidence come from?

Biases: Can you detect particular biases?

Advertising: Is advertising prominent?

Find Information to Cite a Database Source

To cite a source from a database, you will need the following information:

- Author if listed
- Title of article
- Name of periodical
- Date of publication (and edition for newspapers)
- Section and page number
- Name of database
- Medium of publication (Web)
- Date of access (the day you found the article in the database)

Often you have to look carefully to distinguish the name of the vendor from the name of the database. In the screen shot on the facing page, the vendor's name (EBSCO) is at the top of the screen, making it look like the name of the database (Academic Search Premier). EBSCO the company that sells access to Academic Search Premier and many other databases.

Do not include the database URL or (for a library-based subscription) information about the library system. For help with citing database sources, see pages 282–283 and 293 (MLA style) and 311 (APA style).

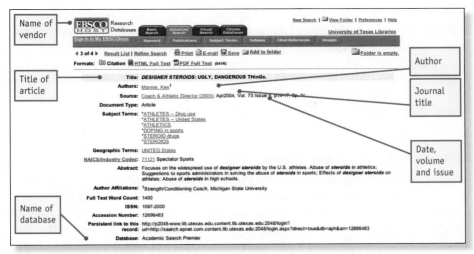

Citing a database article from Academic Search Premier.

Evaluate Web Sources

All electronic search tools share a common problem: They often give you too many sources. Web search engines pull up thousands of hits, and these hits may vary dramatically in quality. No one regulates or checks most information put on the Web, and it's no surprise that much of what is on the Web is highly opinionated or false.

Misleading Web sites

Some Web sites are put up as jokes. Other Web sites are deliberately misleading. Many prominent Web sites draw imitators who want to cash in on the commercial visibility. The Web site for the Campaign for Tobacco-Free Kids (www. tobaccofreekids.org), for example, has an imitator (www.smokefreekids.com) that sells software for antismoking education. The *.com* URL is often a tip-off that a site's main motive is profit.

Biased Web sites

Always approach Web sites with an eye toward evaluating their content. For example, Web sites with *.com* URLs that offer medical information often contain strong biases in addition to the motive to make money. The creators of the Web site Thinktwice.com, sponsored by the Global Vaccine Institute, oppose the vaccination of children. On the site you can find claims that the polio vaccine administered to millions of people in the United States causes cancer because it was contaminated with Simian Virus 40.

Always look for additional sources for verification. The U.S. Centers for Disease Control publishes fact sheets with the latest information about diseases and their prevention, including one on the polio vaccine and Simian Virus 40 (www.cdc.gov/od/science/iso/concerns/archive/polio_and_cancer.htm).

Criteria for evaluating Web sources

The criteria for evaluating print sources can be applied to Web sources if you keep in mind the special circumstances of the Web. For example, when you find a Web page by using a search engine, often you go deep into a complex site without having any sense of the context for that page. To evaluate the credibility of the site, you need to examine the home page, not just the first page you saw.

EVALUATING WEB SOURCES

Source	Look for the site's ownership in the Web address. If a Web site doesn't indicate ownership, attempt to discover who put it up and why. The domain can offer clues: *.gov* is used by government bodies and *.edu* is used by colleges and universities. In general, *.edu* sites are more reliable than *.com* sites.
Author	Often Web sites give no information about their authors other than an email address, if that. In such cases it is difficult or impossible to determine the author's qualifications. Look up the author on Google. If qualifications are listed, is the author an expert in the field? Some sites, such as Wikipedia, allow anyone to add or delete information. An entry on Wikipedia can (and often does) change from day to day, depending on who has edited the entry most recently.
Timeliness	Many Web pages do not list when they were last updated; thus you cannot determine their currency. Furthermore, there are thousands of deserted ghost sites on the Web—sites that the owners have abandoned but that search engines still turn up.
Evidence	The accuracy of any evidence found on the Web is often hard to verify. The most reliable information on the Web stands up to the tests of print evaluation, with clear indication of the sponsoring organization. Any factual information should be supported by indicating its source. Reliable Web sites list their sources.

(continued)

EVALUATING WEB SOURCES *(continued)*

Biases   Many Web sites announce their viewpoint on controversial issues, but others conceal their attitude with a reasonable tone and seemingly factual evidence such as statistics. Citations and bibliographies do not ensure that a site is reliable. Look carefully at the links and sources cited. Are the sources reliable?

Advertising Many Web sites are infomercials aimed at getting you to buy a product or service. While they might contain useful information, they are no more trustworthy than other forms of advertising.

Other Internet sources

Other Internet sources, such as online newsgroups, blogs, podcasts, wikis, and online videos, can give you useful ideas but are generally not considered authoritative. The use of Wikipedia for research is banned at some schools and by some instructors because many entries contain inaccuracies. If you do find facts on Wikipedia, be sure to confirm them with another source. Email communication from an expert in the field might be considered an authoritative source, but personal emails are generally not considered worthy of inclusion in a research paper. Remember that a key reason to cite sources is to allow other researchers to read and evaluate the sources you used.

Find Information to Cite a Web Source

To cite a Web site you will need the following information.

- Author (if listed)
- Title of the Web page
- Date the site was posted
- Sponsoring organization (if listed)
- Date you visited
- Complete URL

For help with citing Web sources, see pages 283–284 and 293–295 (MLA style) and 306–307 and 311–312 (APA style).

19

Writing the Research Paper

If you have chosen a subject you're interested in, asked questions about it, and researched it thoroughly, you have a wealth of ideas and information to communicate to your audience.

Review Your Goals and Thesis

Before you begin writing a research paper, review the assignment to remind you of the purpose of your argument, your potential readers, and the requested length.

By now you should have formulated a working thesis, which will be the focus of your paper. You also should have located, read, evaluated, and taken notes on enough source material to write your paper, and perhaps have conducted field research. At this stage in the writing process, your working thesis may be rough and may change as you write your draft, but having a working thesis will help keep your paper focused.

Determine Your Contribution

A convincing and compelling source-based argument does not make claims based solely on the word of you, the writer. To be persuasive, it must draw on the expertise and reputations of others as well. However, you must also demonstrate that you have thought about and synthesized the evidence you have gathered from your sources, and you must show your readers which elements of your paper represent your original thinking.

Determine exactly what you are adding to the larger conversation about your subject by answering these questions.

- Whom do you agree with?
- Whom do you disagree with?
- Whom do you agree with but have something else to add?
- What original analysis or theorizing do you have to offer?

See pages 42-44 for examples of how to identify your contribution in relation to your sources.

Determine Your Main Points

Look back over your notes on your sources and determine how to group the ideas you researched. Decide what your major points will be and how those points support your thesis. Group your research findings so that they match up with your major points.

Now it is time to create a working outline. Always include your thesis at the top of your outline as a guiding light. Some writers create formal outlines with roman numerals and the like; others compose the headings for the paragraphs of their paper and use them to guide their draft; still others may start writing and then determine how they will organize their draft when they have a few paragraphs written. Experiment and decide which method works best for you.

Avoid Plagiarism

Copying someone else's paper word for word or taking an article off the Internet and turning it in as yours is plagiarism. That's plain stealing, and people who take that risk should know that the punishment can be severe. But plagiarism also means using the ideas, melodies, or images of someone else without acknowledging them, and it is important to understand exactly what defines plagiarism.

What you don't have to document

Fortunately, common sense governs issues of academic plagiarism. The standards of documentation are not so strict that the source of every fact you cite must be acknowledged. Suppose you are writing about the causes of maritime disasters, and you want to know how many people drowned when the *Titanic* sank on the early morning of April 15, 1912. You check the Britannica Online and find that the death toll was around 1500. Since this fact is available in many other reference works, you would not need to cite Britannica Online as the source.

But let's say you want to challenge the version of the ship's sinking offered in the 1998 movie *Titanic*, which repeats the usual explanation that the *Titanic* sideswiped an iceberg, ripping a long gash along the hull that caused the ship to go down. Suppose that, in your reading, you discover that a September 1985 exploration of the wreck by an unmanned submersible did not find the long gash previously thought to have sunk the ship. The evidence instead suggested that the force of the collision with the iceberg broke the seams in the hull, allowing water to flood the ship's watertight compartments. You would need to cite the source of your information for this alternative version of the *Titanic*'s demise.

What you do have to document

For facts that are not easily found in general reference works, statements of opinion, and arguable claims, you should cite the source. You should also cite the sources of statistics, research findings, examples, graphs, charts, and illustrations. For example, if you state that the percentage of obese children aged 6 to 11 in the United States rose from 4 percent in 1974 to 15 percent in 2000, you need to cite the source.

As a reader you should be skeptical about statistics and research findings when the source is not mentioned. When a writer does not cite the sources of statistics and research findings, there is no way of knowing how reliable the sources are or whether the writer is making them up.

From the writer's perspective, careful citing of sources lends credibility. If you take your statistics from a generally trusted source, your readers are more likely to trust whatever conclusions or arguments you are presenting. When in doubt, always document the source.

Using caution with online source material

The best way to avoid unintentional plagiarism is to take care to distinguish source words from your own words.

- **Don't mix words from the source with your own words.** If you copy anything from a source when taking notes, place those words in quotation marks and note the page number(s) where those words appear.
- **Write down all the information you need for each source for a list of works cited or a list of references.** See Chapters 20 and 21.
- **If you copy words from an online source, take special care to note the source.** You could easily copy online material and later not be able to find where it came from.
- **Photocopy printed sources and print out online sources.** Having printed copies of sources allows you to double-check later that you haven't used words from the source by mistake and that any words you quote are accurate.

Quote Sources without Plagiarizing

Effective research writing builds on the work of others. You can summarize or paraphrase the work of others, but often it is best to let the authors speak in your text by quoting their exact words. Indicate the words of others by placing them inside quotation marks.

Most people who get into plagiarism trouble lift words from a source and use them without quotation marks. Where the line is drawn is easiest to illustrate with an example. In the following passage, Steven Johnson takes sharp issue with the metaphor of surfing applied to the Web:

> The concept of "surfing" does a terrible injustice to what it means to navigate around the Web. . . . What makes the idea of cybersurf so infuriating is the implicit connection drawn to television. Web surfing, after all, is a derivation of channel surfing—the term thrust upon the world by the rise of remote controls and cable panoply in the mid-eighties. . . . Applied to the boob tube, of course, the term was not altogether inappropriate. Surfing at least implied that channel-hopping was more dynamic, more involved, than the old routine of passive consumption. Just as a real-world surfer's enjoyment depended on the waves delivered up by the ocean, the channel surfer was at the mercy of the programmers and network executives. The analogy took off because it worked well in the one-to-many system of cable TV, where your navigational options were limited to the available channels.
>
> But when the term crossed over to the bustling new world of the Web, it lost a great deal of precision. . . . Web surfing and channel surfing are genuinely different pursuits; to imagine them as equivalents is to ignore the defining characteristics of each medium. Or at least that's what happens in theory. In practice, the Web takes on the greater burden. The television imagery casts the online surfer in the random, anesthetic shadow of TV programming, roaming from site to site like a CD player set on shuffle play. But what makes the online world so revolutionary is the fact that there *are* connections between each stop on a Web itinerant's journey. The links that join those various destinations are links of association, not randomness. A channel surfer hops back and forth between different channels because she's bored. A Web surfer clicks on a link because she's interested.
>
> —Steven Johnson. *Interface Culture: How New Technology Transforms the Way We Create and Communicate.* New York: Harper, 1997. 107–09.

If you were writing a paper or putting up a Web site that concerns Web surfing, you might want to mention the distinction that Johnson makes between channel surfing and surfing on the Web.

Quoting directly

If you quote directly, you must place quotation marks around all words you take from the original:

> One observer marks this contrast: "A channel surfer hops back and forth between different channels because she's bored. A Web surfer clicks on a link because she's interested" (Johnson 109).

Notice that the quotation is introduced and not just dropped in. This example follows MLA style, where the citation—(Johnson 109)—goes outside the quotation marks but before the final period. In MLA style, source references are made according to the author's last name, which refers you to the full citation in the list of works cited at the end. Following the author's name is the page number where the quotation can be located. (Notice that there is no comma after the name.)

Attributing every quotation

If the author's name appears in the sentence, cite only the page number, in parentheses:

> According to Steven Johnson, "A channel surfer hops back and forth between different channels because she's bored. A Web surfer clicks on a link because she's interested" (109).

Quoting words that are quoted in your source

Use single quotation marks to quote material that is already quoted in your source:

> Steven Johnson uses the metaphor of a Gothic cathedral to describe a computer interface: "'The principle of the Gothic architecture,' Coleridge once said, 'is infinity made imaginable.' The same could be said for the modern interface" (42).

Summarize and Paraphrase Sources without Plagiarizing

Summarizing

When you summarize, you state the major ideas of an entire source or part of a source in a paragraph or perhaps even a sentence. The key is to put the summary in your own words. If you use words from the source, you must put those words within quotation marks.

Plagiarized

Steven Johnson argues in *Interface Culture* that the concept of "surfing" is misapplied to the Internet because channel surfers hop back and forth between different channels because they're bored, but Web surfers click on links because they're interested. [Most of the words are lifted directly from the original; see page 273.]

Acceptable summary

Steven Johnson argues in *Interface Culture* that the concept of "surfing" is misapplied to the Internet because users of the Web consciously choose to link to other sites while television viewers mindlessly flip through the channels until something catches their attention.

Paraphrasing

When you paraphrase, you represent the idea of the source in your own words at about the same length as the original. You still need to include the reference to the source of the idea. The following example illustrates an unacceptable paraphrase.

Plagiarized

Steven Johnson argues that the concept of "surfing" does a terrible injustice to what it means to navigate around the Web. What makes the idea of Web surfing infuriating is the association with television. Surfing is not a bad metaphor for channel hopping, but it doesn't fit what people do on the Web. Web surfing and channel surfing are truly different activities; to imagine them as the same is to ignore their defining characteristics. A channel surfer skips around because she's bored while a Web surfer clicks on a link because she's interested (107-09).

Even though the source is listed, this paraphrase is unacceptable. Too many of the words in the original are used directly here, including much or all of entire sentences. When a string of words is lifted from a source and inserted without quotation marks, the passage is plagiarized. Changing a few words in a sentence is not a paraphrase. Compare these two sentences:

Source

Web surfing and channel surfing are genuinely different pursuits; to imagine them as equivalents is to ignore the defining characteristics of each medium.

Unacceptable paraphrase

Web surfing and channel surfing are truly different activities; to imagine them as the same is to ignore their defining characteristics.

The paraphrase takes the structure of the original sentence and substitutes a few words. It is much too similar to the original.

> **A true paraphrase represents an entire rewriting of the idea from the source.**

Acceptable paraphrase

Steven Johnson argues that "surfing" is a misleading term for describing how people navigate on the Web. He allows that "surfing" is appropriate for clicking across television channels because the viewer has to interact with what the networks and cable companies provide, just as the surfer has to interact with what the ocean provides. Web surfing, according to Johnson, operates at much greater depth and with much more consciousness of purpose. Web surfers actively follow links to make connections (107-09).

Even though this paraphrase contains a few words from the original, such as *navigate* and *connections*, these sentences are original in structure and wording while accurately conveying the meaning of the source.

Incorporate Quotations

Quotations are a frequent problem area in research papers. Review every quotation to ensure that each is used effectively and correctly, and follow these guidelines.

- **Limit the use of long quotations.** If you have more than one blocked quotation on a page, look closely to see if one or more can be paraphrased or summarized.

- **Check that each quotation supports your major points rather than making major points for you.** If the ideas rather than the original wording are what's important, paraphrase the quotation and cite the source.

- **Check that each quotation is introduced and attributed.** Each quotation should be introduced and the author or title named. Check for verbs that signal a quotation: *Smith claims, Jones argues, Brown states.* (See page 277 for a list of verbs that introduce quotations and paraphrases.)

- **Check that each quotation is properly formatted and punctuated.** Prose quotations longer than four lines (MLA) or forty words (APA) should be indented ten spaces in MLA style or five spaces in APA style. Shorter quotations should be enclosed within quotation marks.
- **Check that you cite the source for each quotation.** You are required to cite the sources of all direct quotations, paraphrases, and summaries.
- **Check the accuracy of each quotation.** It's easy to leave out words or to mistype a quotation. Compare what is in your paper to the original source. If you need to add words to make the quotation grammatical, make sure the added words are in brackets.
- **Read your paper aloud to a classmate or a friend.** Each quotation should flow smoothly when you read your paper aloud. Put a check beside rough spots as you read aloud so you can revise later.

VERBS THAT INTRODUCE QUOTATIONS AND PARAPHRASES

acknowledge	concede	interpret
add	conclude	maintain
admit	contend	note
advise	criticize	object
agree	declare	observe
allow	describe	offer
analyze	disagree	point out
answer	discuss	refute
argue	dispute	reject
ask	emphasize	remark
assert	explain	reply
believe	express	report
charge	find	respond
claim	grant	show
comment	illustrate	state
compare	imply	suggest
complain	insist	write

Quoting directly vs. paraphrasing

Use direct quotations when the original wording is important.

Direct quotation

Smith notes that

> Although the public grew to accept film as a teaching tool, it was not always aware of all it was being taught. That was because a second type of film was also being produced during these years, the "attitude-building" film, whose primary purpose was to motivate, not instruct. Carefully chosen visuals were combined with dramatic story lines, music, editing, and sharply drawn characters to create powerful instruments of mass manipulation. (21)

Paraphrase

Smith points out that a second kind of mental-hygiene film, the attitude-building film, was introduced during the 1940s. It attempted to motivate viewers, whereas earlier films explicitly tried to teach something. The attitude-building films were intended to manipulate their audiences to feel a certain way (21).

Here, the original wording provides stronger description of the attitude-building films. The direct quotation is a better choice.

Often, you can paraphrase the main idea of a lengthy passage and quote only the most striking phrase or sentence.

Paraphrase combined with quotation

In his analysis of the rise of fascism in twentieth-century Europe, George Mosse notes that the fascist movement was built on pre-existing ideas like individualism and sacrifice. It "scavenged" other ideologies and made use of them. "Fascism was a new political movement but not a movement which invented anything new," Mosse explains (xvii).

Incorporate Visuals

Here are a few guidelines to keep in mind for incorporating visual sources into your research paper.

- **Use visuals for examples and supporting evidence, not for decoration.** For example, if the subject of your research is Internet crime in San Francisco, including a picture of the Golden Gate Bridge is irrelevant and will detract from your paper.

- ■ **Refer to images and other graphics in the body of your research paper.** Explain the significance of any images or graphics in the body of your paper. The relevance of the visual should not be left to the reader to guess.

- ■ **Respect the copyright of visual sources.** You may need to request permission to use a visual from the Web. Use your own photographs or public domain material whenever possible.

- ■ **Get complete citation information.** You are required to cite visual sources in your list of works cited just as you are for other sources.

- ■ **Describe the content of the image or graphic in the caption.**

20

Documenting Sources in MLA Style

The two styles of documentation used most frequently are APA style and MLA style. APA stands for American Psychological Association, which publishes a style manual used widely in the social sciences and education (see Chapter 21). MLA stands for the Modern Language Association, and its style is the norm for the humanities and fine arts, including English and rhetoric and composition. If you have questions that this chapter does not address, consult the *MLA Handbook for Writers of Research Papers*, Seventh Edition (2009), and the *MLA Style Manual and Guide to Scholarly Publishing*, Third Edition (2008).

Elements of MLA Documentation

Citing a source in your paper

Citing sources is a two-part process. When readers find a reference to a source (called an in-text or parenthetical citation) in the body of your paper, they can turn to the works-cited list at the end and find the full publication information. Place the author's last name and the page number inside parentheses at the end of the sentence.

Anticipating the impact of Google's project of digitally scanning books in major research libraries, one observer predicts that "the real magic will come in the second act, as each word in each book is cross-linked, clustered, cited, extracted, indexed, analyzed, annotated, remixed, reassembled and woven deeper into the culture than ever before" (Kelly 43).

> Author not mentioned in text

If you mention the author's name in the sentence, you do not have to put the name in the parenthetical reference at the end. Just cite the page number.

Anticipating the impact of Google's project of digitally scanning books in major research libraries, Kevin Kelly predicts that "the real magic will come in the second act, as each word in each book is cross-linked, clustered, cited, extracted, indexed, analyzed, annotated, remixed, reassembled and woven deeper into the culture than ever before" (43).

> Author mentioned in the text

The corresponding entry in the work-cited list at the end of your paper would be as follows.

Works Cited

> Kelly, Kevin. "Scan This Book!" *New York Times* 14 May 2006, late ed., | Entry in the works-cited list
> sec 6: 43+. Print.

Citing an entire work, a Web site, or another electronic source

If you wish to cite an entire work (a book, a film, a performance, and so on), a Web site, or an electronic source that has no page numbers or paragraph numbers, MLA style instructs that you mention the name of the person (for example, the author or director) in the text with a corresponding entry in the works-cited list. You do not need to include the author's name in parentheses. If you cannot identify the author, mention the title in your text.

Author mentioned in the text | Joel Waldfogel discusses the implications of a study of alumni donations to colleges and universities, observing that parents give generously to top-rated colleges in the hope that their children chances for admission will improve.

Works Cited

> Waldfogel, Joel. "The Old College Try." *Slate*. Washington Post Newsweek
> Interactive, 6 July 2007. Web. 27 Jan. 2009.

MLA style now requires the medium of publication (print, Web, performance, etc.) to be included in each citation.

Creating an MLA-style works-cited list

To create your works-cited list, go through your paper and find every reference to the sources you consulted during your research. Each in-text reference must have an entry in your works-cited list.

Organize your works-cited list alphabetically by authors' last names or, if no author is listed, the first word in the title other than *a*, *an*, or *the*. (See pages 302–303 for a sample works-cited list.) MLA style uses four basic forms for entries in the works-cited list: books, periodicals (scholarly journals, newspapers, magazines), online library database sources, and other online sources (Web sites, discussion forums, blogs, online newspapers, online magazines, online government documents, and email messages).

Works-cited entries for books

Entries for books have three main elements.

> Poster, Mark. *Information Please: Culture and Politics in the Age of Digital
> Machines*. Durham: Duke UP, 2006. Print.

1. **Author's name.**
   - List the author's name with the last name first, followed by a period.

2. ***Title of book.***
   - Find the exact title on the title page, not the cover.
   - Separate the title and subtitle with a colon.
   - Italicize the title and put a period at the end.

3. **Publication information.**
   - Give the place (usually the city) of publication and a colon.
   - Give the name of the publisher, using accepted abbreviations, and a comma.
   - Give the date of publication, followed by a period.
   - Give the medium of publication (Print), followed by a period.

Works-cited entries for periodicals

Entries for periodicals (scholarly journals, newspapers, magazines) have three main elements.

MacDonald, Susan Peck. "The Erasure of Language." *College Composition and Communication* 58 (2007): 585-625. Print.

1. **Author's name.**
   - List the author's name with the last name first, followed by a period.

2. **"Title of article."**
   - Place the title of the article inside quotation marks.
   - Insert a period before the closing quotation mark.

3. **Publication information.**
   - Italicize the title of the journal.
   - Give the volume number.
   - List the date of publication, in parentheses, followed by a colon.
   - List the page numbers, followed by a period.
   - Give the medium of publication (Print), followed by a period.

Works-cited entries for library database sources

Basic entries for library database sources have four main elements. See pages 266–267 for where to find this information.

Hede, Jesper. "Jews and Muslims in Dante's Vision." *European Review* 16.1 (2008): 101-14. *Academic Search Premier*. Web. 14 Apr. 2009.

1. Author's name.
■ List the author's name with the last name first, followed by a period.

2. "Title of article."
■ Place the title of the article inside quotation marks.
■ Insert a period before the closing quotation mark.

3. Print publication information.
■ Give the print publication information in standard format, in this case for a periodical (see page 282).

4. Database information.
■ Italicize the name of the database, followed by a period.
■ List the medium of publication, followed by a period. For all database sources, the medium of publication is *Web*.
■ List the date you accessed the source (day, month, and year), followed by a period.

Works-cited entries for other online sources

Basic entries for online sources (Web sites, discussion forums, blogs, online newspapers, online magazines, online government documents, and email messages) have three main elements. Sometimes information such as the author's name or the date of publication is missing from the online source. Include the information you are able to locate.

There are many formats for the different kinds of electronic publications. Here is the format of an entry for an online article.

Broudy, Oliver. "Air Head." *Salon.com*. Salon, 7 July 2007. Web. 6 Apr. 2009.

1. **Author's name.**
   - List the author's name with the last name first, followed by a period.

2. **"Title of work"; *Title of the overall Web site.***
   - Place the title of the work inside quotation marks if it is part of a larger Web site.
   - Italicize name of overall site if different from title of the work.
   - Some Web sites are updated periodically, so list the version if you find it (e.g., 2009 edition).

3. **Publication information.**
   - List the publisher or sponsor of the site, followed by a comma. If not available, use *N.p.* (for *no publisher*).
   - List the date of publication if available; if not, use *n.d.*
   - List the medium of publication (*Web*).
   - List the date you accessed the source (day, month, and year).

MLA In-Text Citations

1. **Author named in your text**
   Put the author's name in a signal phrase in your sentence.

   Sociologist Daniel Bell called this emerging U.S. economy the "postindustrial society" (3).

2. **Author not named in your text**
   Put the author's last name and the page number inside parentheses at the end of the sentence.

   In 1997, the Gallup poll reported that 55% of adults in the United States think secondhand smoke is "very harmful," compared to only 36% in 1994 (Saad 4).

3. **Work by a single author**
   The author's last name comes first, followed by the page number. There is no comma.

   (Bell 3)

4. **Work by two or three authors**
   The authors' last names follow the order of the title page. If there are two authors, join the names with *and*. If there are three authors, use a comma between the first two names and a comma with *and* before the last name.

   (Francisco, Vaughn, and Lynn 7)

5. Work by four or more authors

You may use the phrase *et al.* (meaning "and others") for all names but the first, or you may write out all the names. Make sure you use the same method for both the in-text citations and the works-cited list.

> (Abrams et al. 1653)

6. Work by an unnamed author

Use a shortened version of the title that includes at least the first important word. Your reader will use the shortened title to find the full title in the works-cited list.

> A review in the *New Yorker* of Ryan Adams's new album focuses on the artist's age ("Pure" 25).

Notice that "Pure" is in quotation marks because it is the shortened title of an article. If it were a book, the short title would be underlined.

7. Work by a group or organization

Treat the group or organization as the author, but try to identify the group author in the text and place only the page number in parentheses. Shorten terms that are commonly abbreviated.

> According to the *Irish Free State Handbook*, published by the Ministry for Industry and Finance, the population of Ireland in 1929 was approximately 4,192,000 (23).

8. Quotations longer than four lines

When using indented (block) quotations of more than four lines, place the period *before* the parentheses enclosing the page number.

> In her article "Art for Everybody," Susan Orlean attempts to explain the popularity of painter Thomas Kinkade:
>> People like to own things they think are valuable. . . . The high price of limited editions is part of their appeal: it implies that they are choice and exclusive, and that only a certain class of people will be able to afford them. (128)
>
> This same statement could possibly also explain the popularity of phenomena like PBS's *Antiques Road Show*.

If the source is longer than one page, provide the page number for each quotation, paraphrase, and summary.

9. Web sources including Web pages, blogs, podcasts, wikis, videos, and other multimedia sources

Give the author in the text instead of putting the author's name in parentheses.

> Andrew Keen ironically used his own blog to claim that "blogs are boring to write (yawn), boring to read (yawn) and boring to discuss (yawn)."

If you cannot identify the author, mention the title in your text.

> The podcast "Catalina's Cubs" describes the excitement on Catalina Island when the Chicago Cubs went there for spring training in the 1940s.

10. Work in an anthology

Cite the name of the author of the work within an anthology, not the name of the editor of the collection. Alphabetize the entry in the list of works cited by the author, not the editor.

> In "Beard," Melissa Jane Hardie explores the role assumed by Elizabeth Taylor as the celebrity companion of gay actors including Rock Hudson and Montgomery Cliff (278-79).

11. Two or more works by the same author

When an author has two or more items in the works-cited list, distinguish which work you are citing by using the author's last name and then a shortened version of the title of each source.

> The majority of books written about coauthorship focus on partners of the same sex (Laird, *Women* 351).

Note that *Women* is underlined because it is the name of a book; if an article were named, quotation marks would be used.

12. Different authors with the same last name

If your list of works cited contains items by two or more different authors with the same last name, include the initial of the first name in the parenthetical reference.

> Web surfing requires more mental involvement than channel surfing (S. Johnson 107).

Note that a period follows the initial.

13. Two or more sources within the same sentence
Place each citation directly after the statement it supports.

> In the 1990s, many sweeping pronouncements were made that the Internet is the best opportunity to improve education since the printing press (Ellsworth xxii) or even in the history of the world (Dyrli and Kinnaman 79).

14. Two or more sources within the same citation
If two sources support a single point, separate them with a semicolon.

> (McKibbin 39; Gore 92)

15. Work quoted in another source
When you do not have access to the original source of the material you wish to use, put the abbreviation *qtd. in* (quoted in) before the information about the indirect source.

> National governments have become increasingly what Ulrich Beck, in a 1999 interview, calls "zombie institutions"—institutions that are "dead and still alive" (qtd. in Bauman 6).

16. Literary works
To supply a reference to a literary work, you sometimes need more than a page number from a specific edition. Readers should be able to locate a quotation in any edition of the book. Give the page number from the edition that you are using, then a semicolon and other identifying information.

> "Marriage is a house" is one of the most memorable lines in *Don Quixote* (546; pt. 2, bk. 3, ch. 19).

MLA Works-Cited List: Books

One author

17. Book by one author
The author's last name comes first, followed by a comma, the first name, and a period.

> Doctorow, E. L. *The March*. New York: Random, 2005. Print.

18. Two or more books by the same author

In the entry for the first book, include the author's name. In the second entry, substitute three hyphens and a period for the author's name. List the titles of books by the same author in alphabetical order.

> Grimsley, Jim. *Boulevard*. Chapel Hill: Algonquin, 2002. Print.
>
> ---. *Dream Boy*. New York: Simon, 1995. Print.

Multiple authors

19. Book by two or three authors

Second and subsequent authors' names appear first name first. A comma separates the authors' names.

> Chapkis, Wendy, and Richard J. Webb. *Dying to Get High: Marijuana as Medicine*. New York: New York UP, 2008. Print

20. Book by four or more authors

You may use the phrase *et al.* (meaning "and others") for all authors but the first, or you may write out all the names. Use the same method in the in-text citation as you do in the works-cited list.

> Zukin, Cliff, et al. *A New Engagement? Political Participation, Civic Life, and the Changing American Citizen*. New York: Oxford UP, 2006. Print.

Anonymous and group authors

21. Book by an unknown author

Begin the entry with the title.

> *Encyclopedia of Americana*. New York: Somerset, 2001. Print.

22. Book by a group or organization

Treat the group as the author of the work.

> United Nations. *The Charter of the United Nations: A Commentary*. New York: Oxford UP, 2000. Print.

23. Religious texts

Do not underline the title of a sacred text, including the Bible, unless you are citing a specific edition.

> *Holy Bible. King James Text: Modern Phrased Version*. New York:
> Oxford UP, 1980. Print.

Imprints, reprints, and undated books

24. Book with no publication date

If no year of publication is given, but can be approximated, put a *c.* ("circa") and the approximate date in brackets: [c. 1999]. Otherwise, put *n.d.* ("no date").

> O'Sullivan, Colin. *Traditions and Novelties of the Irish Country Folk*.
> Dublin, [c. 1793]. Print.

> James, Franklin. *In the Valley of the King*. Cambridge: Harvard UP, n.d. Print.

25. Reprinted works

For works of fiction that have been printed in many different editions or reprints, give the original publication date after the title.

> Wilde, Oscar. *The Picture of Dorian Gray*. 1890. New York: Norton, 2001. Print.

Parts of books

26. Introduction, foreword, preface, or afterword

Give the author and then the name of the specific part being cited. Next, name the book. Then, if the author for the whole work is different, put that author's name after the word *By*. Place inclusive page numbers at the end.

> Benstock, Sheri. Introduction. *The House of Mirth*. By Edith Wharton.
> Boston: Bedford-St. Martin's, 2002. 3-24. Print.

27. Single chapter written by same author as the book

> Ardis, Ann L. "Mapping the Middlebrow in Edwardian England." *Modernism
> and Cultural Conflict: 1880-1922*. Cambridge: Cambridge UP, 2002.
> 114-42. Print.

28. Selection from an anthology or edited collection

> Sedaris, David. "Full House." *The Best American Nonrequired Reading 2004.*
> Ed. Dave Eggers. Boston: Houghton, 2004. 350-58. Print.

29. Article in a reference work

You can omit the names of editors and most publishing information for an article from a familiar reference work. Identify the edition by date. There is no need to give the page numbers when a work is arranged alphabetically. Give the author's name, if known.

> "Utilitarianism." *The Columbia Encyclopedia.* 6th ed. 2001. Print.

Editions and translations

30. Book with an editor

List an edited book under the editor's name if your focus is on the editor. Otherwise, cite an edited book under the author's name as shown in the second example.

> Lewis, Gifford, ed. *The Big House of Inver.* By Edith Somerville and Martin
> Ross. Dublin: Farmar, 2000. Print.

> Somerville, Edith, and Martin Ross. *The Big House of Inver.* Ed. Gifford Lewis.
> Dublin: Farmar, 2000. Print.

31. Book with a translator

> Benjamin, Walter. *The Arcades Project.* Trans. Howard Eiland and Kevin
> McLaughlin. Cambridge: Harvard UP, 1999. Print.

32. Second or subsequent edition of a book

> Hawthorn, Jeremy, ed. *A Concise Glossary of Contemporary Literary Theory.*
> 3rd ed. London: Arnold, 2001. Print.

Multivolume works

33. Multivolume work

Identify both the volume you have used and the total number of volumes in the set.

> Samuel, Raphael. *Theatres of Memory.* Vol. 1. London: Verso, 1999. 2 vols.
> Print.

If you refer to more than one volume, identify the specific volume in your in-text citations, and list the total number of volumes in your list of works cited.

> Samuel, Raphael. *Theatres of Memory*. 2 vols. London: Verso, 1999. Print.

MLA Works-Cited List: Periodicals

Journal articles

34. Article by one author

> Mallory, Anne. "Burke, Boredom, and the Theater of Counterrevolution."
> *PMLA* 119 (2003): 329-43. Print.

35. Article by two or three authors

> Miller, Thomas P., and Brian Jackson. "What Are English Majors For?"
> *College Composition and Communication* 58 (2007): 825-31. Print.

36. Article by four or more authors

You may use the phrase *et al.* (meaning "and others") for all authors but the first, or you may write out all the names.

> Breece, Katherine E., et al. "Patterns of mtDNA Diversity in Northwestern
> North America." *Human Biology* 76 (2004): 33-54. Print.

Pagination in journals

37. Article in a scholarly journal
List the volume and issue number after the name of the journal.

> Duncan, Mike. "Whatever Happened to the Paragraph?" *College English* 69.5
> (2007): 470-95. Print.

38. Article in a scholarly journal that uses only issue numbers
List the issue number after the name of the journal.

> McCall, Sophie. "Double Vision Reading." *Canadian Literature* 194 (2007):
> 95-97. Print.

Magazines

39. Monthly or seasonal magazines
Use the month (or season) and year in place of the volume. Abbreviate the names of all months except May, June, and July.

> Barlow, John Perry. "Africa Rising: Everything You Know about Africa Is
> Wrong." *Wired* Jan. 1998: 142-58. Print.

40. Weekly or biweekly magazines
Give both the day and the month of publication, as listed on the issue.

> Brody, Richard. "A Clash of Symbols." *New Yorker* 25 June 2007: 16. Print.

Newspapers

41. Newspaper article by one author
The author's last name comes first, followed by a comma and the first name.

> Marriott, Michel. "Arts and Crafts for the Digital Age." *New York Times*
> 8 June 2006, late ed.: C13. Print.

42. Article by two or three authors
The second and subsequent authors' names are printed in regular order, first name first:

> Schwirtz, Michael, and Joshua Yaffa. "A Clash of Cultures at a Square in
> Moscow." *New York Times* 11 July 2007, late ed.: A9. Print.

43. Newspaper article by an unknown author
Begin the entry with the title.

> "The Dotted Line." *Washington Post* 8 June 2006, final ed.: E2. Print.

Reviews, editorials, letters to the editor

44. Review
If there is no title, just name the work reviewed.

> Mendelsohn, Daniel. "The Two Oscar Wildes." Rev. of *The Importance of
> Being Earnest*, dir. Oliver Parker. *The New York Review of Books*
> 10 Oct. 2002: 23-24. Print.

45. Editorial

"Hush-hush, Sweet Liberty." Editorial. *Los Angeles Times* 7 July 2007: A18. Print.

46. Letter to the editor

Doyle, Joe. Letter. *Direct* 1 July 2007: 48. Print.

MLA Works-Cited List: Library Database Sources

47. Work from a library database
Begin with the print publication information, then the name of the database (italicized), the medium of publication (*Web*), and the date of access.

Snider, Michael. "Wired to Another World." *Maclean's* 3 Mar. 2003: 23-24. *Academic Search Premier*. Web. 14 Jan. 2007.

MLA Works-Cited List: Online Sources

Web publications

When do you list a URL?
MLA style no longer requires including URLs of Web sources. URLs are of limited value because they change frequently and they can be specific to an individual search. Include the URL as supplementary information only when your readers probably cannot locate the source without the URL.

48. Publication by a known author

Boerner, Steve. "Leopold Mozart." *The Mozart Project: Biography*. The Mozart Project, 21 Mar. 1998. Web. 30 Oct. 2008.

49. Publication by a group or organization
If a work has no author's or editor's name listed, begin the entry with the title.

"State of the Birds." *Audubon*. National Audubon Society, 2008. Web. 19 Aug. 2008.

50. Article in a scholarly journal on the Web

Some scholarly journals are published on the Web only. List articles by author, title, name of journal in italics, volume and issue number, and year of publication. If the journal does not have page numbers, use *n. pag.* in place of page numbers. Then list the medium of publication (*Web*) and the date of access (day, month, and year).

> Fleckenstein, Kristie. "Who's Writing? Aristotelian Ethos and the Author Position in Digital Poetics." *Kairos* 11.3 (2007): n. pag. Web. 6 Apr. 2008.

51. Article in a newspaper on the Web

The first date is the date of publication; the second is the date of access.

> Brown, Patricia Leigh. "Australia in Sonoma." *New York Times*. New York Times, 5 July 2008. Web. 3 Aug. 2009.

52. Article in a magazine on the Web

> Brown, Patricia Leigh. "The Wild Horse Is Us." *Newsweek*. Newsweek, 1 July 2008. Web. 12 Dec. 2008.

53. Book on the Web

> Prebish, Charles S., and Kenneth K. Tanaka. *The Faces of Buddhism in America*. Berkeley: U of California P, 2003. *eScholarship Editions*. Web. 2 May 2009.

Other online sources

54. Blog entry

If there is no sponsor or publisher for the blog, use *N.p.*

> Arrington, Michael. "Think Before You Voicemail." *TechCrunch*. N.p., 5 July 2008. Web. 10 Sept. 2008.

55. E-mail

Give the name of the writer, the subject line, a description of the message, the date, and the medium of delivery (*E-mail*).

> Ballmer, Steve. "A New Era of Business Productivity and Innovation." Message
>   to Microsoft Executive E-mail. 30 Nov. 2006. E-mail.

56. Video on the Web

Video on the Web often lacks a creator and a date. Begin the entry with a title if you cannot find a creator. Use *n.d.* if you cannot find a date.

> Wesch, Michael. *A Vision of Students Today. YouTube.* YouTube, 2007. Web. 28
>   May 2008.

57. Personal home page

List *Home page* without quotation marks in place of the title. If no date is listed, use *n.d.*

> Graff, Harvey J. Home page. Dept. of English, Ohio State U, n.d. Web. 15 Nov.
>   2008.

58. Wiki entry

A wiki is a collaborative writing and editing tool. Although some topic-specific wikis are written and carefully edited by recognized scholars, the more popular wiki sites—such as *Wikipedia*—are often considered unreliable sources for academic papers.

> "Snowboard." *Wikipedia.* Wikimedia Foundation, 2009. Web. 30 Jan. 2009.

59. Podcast

> Sussingham, Robin. "All Things Autumn." No. 2. *HighLifeUtah.* N.p., 20 Nov.
>   2006. Web. 28 Feb. 2009.

60. PDFs and digital files

PDFs and other digital files can often be downloaded through links. Determine the kind of work you are citing, include the appropriate information for the particular kind of work, and list the type of file.

> Glaser, Edward L., and Albert Saiz. "The Rise of the Skilled City." Discussion Paper No. 2025. Harvard Institute of Economic Research. Cambridge: Harvard U, 2003. PDF file.

MLA Works-Cited List: Other Sources

61. Sound recording

> McCoury, Del, perf. "1952 Vincent Black Lightning." By Richard Thompson. *Del and the Boys*. Ceili, 2001. CD.

62. Film

Begin with the title in italics. List the director, the distributor, the date, and the medium. Other data, such as the names of the screenwriters and performers, is optional.

> *Wanted*. Dir. Timur Bekmambetov. Perf. James McAvoy, Angelina Jolie, and Morgan Freeman. Universal, 2008. Film.

63. DVD

> *No Country for Old Men*. Dir. Joel Coen and Ethan Coen. Perf. Tommy Lee Jones, Javier Bardem, and Josh Brolin. Paramount, 2007. DVD.

64. Television or radio program

> "Kaisha." *The Sopranos*. Perf. James Gandolfini, Lorraine Bracco, and Edie Falco. HBO. 4 June 2006. Television.

Sample MLA paper

Brian Witkowski
Professor Mendelsohn
RHE 309K
2 May 2009

Need a Cure for Tribe Fever?
How About a Dip in the Lake?

Everyone is familiar with the Cleveland Indians' Chief Wahoo logo—and I do mean everyone, not just Clevelanders. Across America one can see individuals sporting the smiling mascot on traditional Indians caps and jerseys, and recent trends in sports merchandise have popularized new groovy multicolored Indians sportswear. In fact, Indians merchandise recently was ranked just behind the New York Yankees' merchandise in terms of sales (Adams). Because of lucrative merchandising contracts between Major League Baseball and Little League, youth teams all over the country don Cleveland's famous (or infamous) smiling Indian each season as fresh-faced kids scamper onto the diamonds looking like mini major leaguers ("MLBP"). Various incarnations of the famous Chief Wahoo—described by sportswriter Rick Telander as "the red-faced, big-nosed, grinning, drywall-toothed moron who graces the peak of every Cleveland Indians cap"—have been around since the 1940s (qtd. in Eitzen). Now redder and even more cartoonish than the original hook-nosed, beige Indian with a devilish grin, Wahoo often passes as a cheerful baseball buddy like the San Diego Chicken or the St. Louis Cardinals' Fredbird. (See Fig. 1.)

Though defined by its distinctive logo, Cleveland baseball far preceded its famous mascot. The team changed from the Forest Citys to the Spiders to the Bluebirds/Blues to the Broncos to the Naps and finally to the Indians. Dubbed the Naps in 1903 in honor of its star player and manager Napoleon Lajoie, the team finally arrived at their current appellation in 1915. After Lajoie was traded, the team's president challenged sportswriters to devise a suitable "temporary" label for the floundering club. Publicity material has it that the writers decided on the Indians to celebrate Louis Sockalexis, a Penobscot Indian who played for the team from 1897 to 1899. With a heck of a

MLA style does not require a title page. Ask your instructor whether you need one.

Double-space everything.

Cite sources without a named author by title.

Indent each paragraph five spaces (1/2 inch on the ruler in your word-processing program).

Include your last name and the page number as your page header, beginning with the first page, 1/2 inch from the top.

Center your title. Do not put the title inside quotation marks or type it in all capital letters.

Witkowski 2

batting average and the notability of being the first Native American in professional baseball, Sockalexis was immortalized by the new Cleveland label (Schneider 10-23). (Contrary to popular lore, some cite alternative—and less reverent—motivations behind the team's naming and point to a lack of Sockalexis publicity in period newspaper articles discussing the team's naming process [Staurowsky 95-97].) Almost ninety years later, the "temporary" name continues to raise eyebrows, in both its marketability and its ideological questionability.

> Cite sources by the author's last name, if possible.

Fig. 1.   Many youth baseball and softball teams use the Chief Wahoo logo, including teams with American Indian players.

Today the logo is more than a little embarrassing. Since the high-profile actions of the American Indian Movement (AIM) in the 1970s, sports teams around the country—including the Indians—have been criticized and cajoled over their less than racially sensitive mascots. Native American groups question the sensitivity of such caricatured displays—not just because of grossly stereotyped mascots, but also because of what visual displays of team support say about Native American culture. Across the country, professional sporting teams, as well as high schools and colleges, perform faux rituals in the name of team spirit. As Tim Giago, publisher of the *Lakota Times*, a weekly South Dakotan Native American newspaper, has noted, "The sham rituals, such as the wearing of feathers, smoking of so-called peace pipes, beating of tomtoms, fake dances, horrendous attempts at singing Indian songs, the so-called war whoops, and the painted faces, address more than the issues of racism. They are direct attacks upon the spirituality of the Indian people" (qtd. in Wulf).

Since 1969, when Oklahoma disavowed its "Little Red" mascot, more than 600 school and minor league teams have followed a more ethnically sensitive trend and ditched their "tribal" mascots for ones less publicly explosive (Price). High-profile teams such as Berkeley, St. Johns University, and Miami (Ohio) University have buckled to public pressure, changing their team names from the Indians to the Cardinals (1972), the Redmen to the Red Storm (1993), and the Redskins to the Redhawks (1996), respectively. While many people see such controversies as mere bowing to the pressures of the late twentieth and early twenty-first centuries, others see the mascot issue as a topic well worthy of debate.

Cleveland's own Chief Wahoo has far from avoided controversy. Protests regarding the controversial figure have plagued the city. Multiple conflicts between Wahoo devotees and dissenters have arisen around the baseball season. At the opening game of 1995, fifty Native Americans and supporters took stations around Jacobs Field to demonstrate against the use of the cartoonish smiling crimson mascot. While protestors saw the event as a triumph for First Amendment rights and a strike against negative stereotyping, one befuddled fan stated, "I never thought of [Chief Wahoo] that way. It's all how you think of it" (Kropk). Arrests were made in 1998 when demonstrators from the United Church of Christ burned a three-foot Chief Wahoo doll in effigy ("Judge"). Wedded to their memorabilia, fans proudly stand behind their Indian as others lobby vociferously for its removal. Splitting government officials, fans, and social and religious groups, this issue draws hostility from both sides of the argument.

In 2000 Cleveland mayor Michael White came out publicly against the team mascot, joining an already established group of religious leaders, laypersons, and civil rights activists who had demanded Wahoo's retirement. African-American religious and civic leaders such as Rev. Gregory A. Jacobs had been speaking out throughout the 1990s and highlighting the absurdity of minority groups who embrace the Wahoo symbol. "Each of us has had to fight its [sic] own battle, quite frankly," Jacobs stated. "We cannot continue to live in this kind of hypocrisy that says, Yes, we are in solidarity with my [sic] brothers and sisters, yet we continue to exploit them" (qtd. in Briggs). These words clash with those of individuals such as former Indians owner Dick Jacobs, who said amidst protest that the Wahoo logo would remain as long as he was principal owner of the club (Bauman 1) and a delegate of the East Ohio Conference of the United Methodist Church, who quipped, "I would cease being a United Methodist before I would cease wearing my Chief Wahoo clothing" (Briggs).

This controversy also swirls outside of the greater Cleveland area. Individual newspapers in Nebraska, Kansas, Minnesota, and Oregon have banned the printing of Native American sports symbols and team names such as the Braves, Indians, or Redmen (Wulf), while the *Seattle Times* went so far as to digitally remove the Wahoo symbol from images of the Cleveland baseball cap ("Newspaper"). As other teams make ethnically sensitive and image-conscious choices to change their mascots, Cleveland stands firm in its resolve to retain the chief. Despite internal division and public ridicule fueled by the team icon, the city refuses to budge. Clevelanders consequently appear as insensitive and backward as those who continue to support the Redmen, Redskins, or Illini.

As the city of Cleveland continues to enjoy its recent improved image and downtown revitalization, must the plague of the Wahoo controversy continue? As a native of Cleveland, I understand the power of "Tribe Fever" and the unabashed pride one feels when wearing Wahoo garb during a winning (or losing) season. Often it is not until we leave northeastern Ohio that we realize the negative image that Wahoo projects. What then can Cleveland do to simultaneously save face and bolster its burgeoning positive city image? I propose that the team finally change the "temporary" Indians label. In a city so proud of its diverse ethnic heritage—African American, Italian American, and Eastern European American to name a few examples—why stand as a bearer of retrograde ethnic politics? Cleveland should take this opportunity to link its positive Midwestern image to the team of which it is so proud. Why not take the advice of the 1915 Cleveland management and change the team's "temporary" name? I propose a shift to the Cleveland Lakers.

The city's revival in the last twenty years has embraced the geographic and aesthetic grandeur of Lake Erie. Disavowing its "mistake on the lake" moniker of the late 1970s, Cleveland has traded aquatic pollution fires for a booming lakeside business district. Attractions such as the Great Lakes Science Center, the Rock and Roll Hall of Fame, and the new Cleveland Browns Stadium take advantage of the beauty of the landscape and take back the lake. Why not continue this trend through one of the city's biggest and highest-profile moneymakers: professional baseball? By changing the team's name to the Lakers, the city would gain national advertisement for one of its major selling points, while simultaneously announcing a new ethnically inclusive image that is appropriate to our wonderfully diverse city. It would be a public relations triumph for the city.

Of course this call will be met with many objections. Why do we have to buckle to pressure? Do we not live in a free country? What fans and citizens alike need to keep in mind is that ideological pressures would not be the sole motivation for this move. Yes, retiring Chief Wahoo would take Cleveland off AIM's hit list. Yes, such a move would promote a kinder and gentler Cleveland. At the same time, however, such a gesture would work toward uniting the community. So much civic division exists over this issue that a renaming could help start to heal these old wounds.

Additionally, this type of change could bring added economic prosperity to the city. First, a change in name will bring a new wave of team merchandise. Licensed sports apparel generates more than a 10-billion-dollar annual retail business in the United States, and teams have proven repeatedly that new uniforms and logos can provide new capital. After all, a new logo for the Seattle Mariners bolstered severely slumping merchandise sales (Lefton). Wahoo devotees need not panic; the booming vintage uniform business will keep him alive, as is demonstrated by the current ability to purchase replica 1940s jerseys with the old Indians logo. Also, good press created by this change will hopefully help increase tourism in Cleveland. If the goodwill created by the Cleveland Lakers can prove half as profitable as the Rock and Roll Hall of Fame, then local businesses will be humming a happy tune. Finally, if history repeats itself, a change to a more culturally inclusive logo could, in and of itself, prove to be a cash cow. When Miami University changed from the Redskins to the Redhawks, it saw alumni donations skyrocket to an unprecedented 25 million dollars (Price). Perhaps a less divisive mascot would prove lucrative to the ball club, the city, and the players themselves. (Sluggers with inoffensive logos make excellent spokesmen.)

Perhaps this proposal sounds far-fetched: Los Angeles may seem to have cornered the market on Lakers. But where is their lake? (The Lakers were formerly the Minneapolis Lakers, where the name makes sense in the "Land of 10,000 Lakes.") Various professional and collegiate sports teams—such as baseball's San Francisco Giants and football's New York Giants—share a team name, so licensing should not be an issue. If Los Angeles has qualms about sharing the name, perhaps Cleveland could persuade Los Angeles to become the Surfers or the Stars—after all, Los Angeles players seem to spend as much time on the big and small screens as on the court.

Now is the perfect time for Cleveland to make this jump. Sportscasters continue to tout the revitalized young Cleveland team as an up-and-coming contender. Perhaps a new look will help usher in a new era of Cleveland baseball. Like expansion teams such as the Florida Marlins and the Arizona Diamondbacks, Cleveland's new look could bring with it a vital sense of civic pride and a World Series ring to boot. Through various dry spells, the Cleveland Indians institution has symbolically turned to the descendants of Sockalexis, asking for goodwill or a latter-generation Penobscot slugger (Fleitz 3). Perhaps the best way to win goodwill, fortunes, and the team's first World Series title since 1948 would be to eschew a grinning life-size Chief Wahoo for the new and improved Cleveland Laker, an oversized furry monster sporting water wings, cleats, and a catcher's mask. His seventh-inning-stretch show could include an air-guitar solo with a baseball bat as he quietly reminds everyone that the Rock Hall is just down the street. Go Lakers and go Cleveland!

Works Cited ●

Adams, David. "Cleveland Indians Investors Watch Case on Native American Names." *Akron Beacon Journal* 6 Apr. 1999. *LexisNexis Academic*. Web. 20 Apr. 2009.

Center "Works Cited" on a new page.

Bauman, Michael. "Indians Logo, Mascot Are the Real Mistakes."
    Milwaukee Journal Sentinel 23 Oct. 1997: Sports 1. Print.

Briggs, David. "Churches Go to Bat Against Chief Wahoo." *Cleveland
    Plain Dealer* 25 Aug. 2000: 1A. Print.

Eitzen, D. Stanley, and Maxine Baca Zinn. "The Dark Side of Sports
    Symbols." *USA Today Magazine* Jan. 2001: 48. Print.

Fleitz, David L. *Louis Sockalexis: The First Cleveland Indian*. Jefferson:
    McFarland, 2002. Print.

"Judge Dismisses Charges Against City in Wahoo Protest." *Associated
    Press* 6 Aug. 2001. *LexisNexis Academic*. Web. 19 Apr. 2009.

Kropk, M. R. "Chief Wahoo Protestors Largely Ignored by Fans." *Austin
    American Statesman* 6 May 1995: D4. Print.

Lefton, Terry. "Looks Are Everything: For New Franchises, Licensing
    Battles Must Be Won Long before the Team Even Takes the Field."
    Sport 89 (May 1998): 32. Print.

"MLBP Reaches Youth League Apparel Agreements with Majestic
    Athletic, Outdoor Cap." *MLB.com*. Major League Baseball, 25 June
    2004. Web. 28 Apr. 2009.

"Newspaper Edits Cleveland Indian Logo from Cap Photo." *Associated
    Press* 31 Mar. 1997. *LexisNexis Academic*. Web. 17 Apr. 2009.

Price, S. L. "The Indian Wars." *Sports Illustrated* 4 Mar. 2002: 66+.
    Academic OneFile. Web. 20 Apr. 2009.

Schneider, Russell. *The Cleveland Indians Encyclopedia*. Philadelphia:
    Temple UP, 1996. Print.

Staurowsky, Ellen J. "Sockalexis and the Making of the Myth at the Core
    of the Cleveland's 'Indian' Image." *Team Spirits: The Native
    American Mascots Controversy*. Ed. C. Richard King and Charles
    Fruehling Springwood. Lincoln: U of Nebraska P, 2001. 82-106.
    Print.

Wulf, Steve. "A Brave Move." *Sports Illustrated* 24 Feb. 1992: 7. Print.

Alphabetize entries by the last names of the authors or by the first important word in the title if no author is listed.

Italicize the titles of books and periodicals.

Check to make sure all the sources you have cited in your text are in the list of works cited.

Double-space all entries. Indent all but the first line in each entry five spaces.

Documenting Sources in APA Style

Papers written for the social sciences, including government, linguistics, psychology, sociology, and education, frequently use the APA documentation style. For a detailed treatment of APA style, consult the *Publication Manual of the American Psychological Association*, fifth edition (2001), and the *APA Style Guide to Electronic References* (2007), available online.

Elements of APA Documentation

Citing a source in your paper

APA style emphasizes the date of publication. When you cite an author's name in the body of your paper, always include the date of publication. Notice too that APA style includes the abbreviation for page "(p.)" in front of the page number. A comma separates each element of the citation.

> Zukin (2004) observes that teens today begin to shop for themselves at age 13 or 14, "the same age when lower-class children, in the past, became apprentices or went to work in factories" (p. 50).

If the author's name is not mentioned in the sentence, cite the author, date, and page number inside parentheses.

> One sociologist notes that teens today begin to shop for themselves at age 13 or 14, "the same age when lower-class children, in the past, became apprentices or went to work in factories" (Zukin, 2004, p. 50).

The corresponding entry in the references list would be as follows.

> Zukin, S. (2004). *Point of purchase: How shopping changed American culture.* New York: Routledge.

Creating an APA-style references list

To create your references list, go through your paper and find every reference to the sources you consulted during your research. Each in-text citation must have an entry in your references list.

Organize your references list alphabetically by authors' last names or, if no author is listed, the first word in the title other than *a, an,* or *the.* APA style uses three basic forms for entries in the references list: books, periodicals (scholarly journals, newspapers, magazines), and online sources (online library database sources, Web sites, blogs, online newspapers, online magazines, and online government documents).

References entries for books

Orum, A. M. & Chen, X. (2003). *The world of cities: Places in comparative and historical perspective.* Malden, MA: Blackwell.

1. Author's or editor's name.
- List the author's name with the last name first, followed by a comma and the author's initials.
- Join two authors' names with an ampersand.
- If an editor, put "(Ed.)" after the name: Kavanaugh, P. (Ed.).

2. (Year of publication).
- Give the year of publication in parentheses. If no year of publication is given, write *(n.d.)* ("no date") : Smith, S. (n.d.).
- If it is a multivolume edited work, published over a period of more than one year, put the time span in parentheses: Smith, S. (1999–2001).

3. *Title of book.*
- Italicize the title.
- Capitalize only the first word, proper nouns, and the first word after a colon.
- If the title is in a foreign language, copy it exactly as it appears on the title page.

4. Publication information.
- List the city without a state abbreviation or country for major cities known for publishing (New York, Boston), but add the state abbreviation or country for other cities (as in this example). If the publisher is a university named for a state, omit the state abbreviation. If more than one city is given on the title page (as in this example), list only the first.
- Do not shorten or abbreviate words like *University* or *Press.* Omit words such as *Co., Inc.,* and *Publishers.*

References entries for periodicals

Lee, E. (2007). Wired for gender: Experientiality and gender-stereotyping in computer-mediated communication. *Media Psychology, 10, 182–210*.

1. Author's name.
- List the author's name, last name first, followed by the author's initials.
- Join two authors' names with a comma and an ampersand.

2. (Year of publication).
- Give the year the work was published in parentheses.

3. Title of article.
- Do not use quotation marks. If there is a book title in the article title, italicize it.
- Capitalize only the first word of the title, the first word of the subtitle, and any proper nouns in the title.

4. Publication information.
- Italicize the journal name.
- Capitalize all nouns, verbs, and pronouns, and the first word of the journal name. Do not capitalize any article, preposition, or coordinating conjunction unless it is the first word of the title or subtitle.
- Put a comma after the journal name.
- Italicize the volume number and follow it with a comma.
- Give page numbers of the article (see sample references 19 and 20 for more on pagination).

References entries for online sources

Department of Justice. Federal Bureau of Investigation. (2004). Hate crime statistics 2004: Report summary. Retrieved from http://www.fbi.gov/ucr/hc2004/openpage. htm

1. Author's name, associated institution, or organization.
- List the author's name, if given, with the last name first, followed by the author's initials.
- If the only authority you find is a group or organization (as in this example), list its name as the author.

- If the author or organization is not identified, begin the reference with the title of the document.

2. (Date of publication).
- List the date the site was produced, last revised, or copyrighted.

3. Title of page or article.
- If you are citing a page or article that has a title, treat the title like an article in a periodical. If you are citing an entire Web site, treat the name like a book.
- If the Web site has no title, list it by author or creator.

4. Retrieval date and URL
- List the date of retrieval if the content may change or be updated. For published books and scholarly articles, do not list the date of retrieval.
- Do not place angle brackets around the URL or end with a period.

APA In-Text Citations

1. Author named in your text

Influential sociologist Daniel Bell (1973) noted a shift in the United States to the "postindustrial society" (p. 3).

2. Author not named in your text

In 1997, the Gallup poll reported that 55% of adults in the United States think secondhand smoke is "very harmful," compared to only 36% in 1994 (Saad, 1997, p. 4).

3. Work by a single author

(Bell, 1973, p. 3)

4. Work by two authors
Notice that APA uses an ampersand (&) with multiple authors' names rather than *and*.

(Suzuki & Irabu, 2002, p. 404)

5. Work by three to five authors
The authors' last names follow the order of the title page.

(Francisco, Vaughn, & Romano, 2001, p. 7)

Subsequent references can use the first name and *et al.*

(Francisco et al., 2001, p. 17)

6. Work by six or more authors
Use the first author's last name and *et al.* for all in-text references.

(Swallit et al., 2004, p. 49)

7. Work by a group or organization
Identify the group author in the text and place only the page number in parentheses.

The National Organization for Women (2001) observed that this "generational shift in attitudes towards marriage and childrearing" will have profound consequences (p. 325).

8. Work by an unknown author
Use a shortened version of the title (or the full title if it is short) in place of the author's name. Capitalize all key words in the title. If it is an article title, place it in quotation marks.

("Derailing the Peace Process," 2003, p. 44)

9. Quotations of 40 words or longer
Indent long quotations five spaces and omit quotation marks. Note that the period appears before the parentheses in an indented block quote.

Orlean (2001) has attempted to explain the popularity of the painter Thomas Kinkade:

> People like to own things they think are valuable. . . . The high price of limited editions is part of their appeal; it implies that they are choice and exclusive, and that only a certain class of people will be able to afford them. (p. 128)

APA References List: Books

10. Book by one author

The author's last name comes first, followed by a comma and the author's initials.

> Ball, E. (2000). *Slaves in the family*. New York: Ballantine Books.

If an editor, put "(Ed.)" in parentheses after the name.

> Kavanagh, P. (Ed.). (1969). *Lapped furrows*. New York: Hand Press.

11. Book by two authors

Join two authors' names with a comma and ampersand.

> Hardt, M., & Negri, A. (2000). *Empire*. Cambridge, MA: Harvard University Press.

If editors, use "(Eds.)" after the names.

> McClelland, D., & Eismann, K. (Eds).

12. Book by three or more authors

Write out all of the authors' names up to six. The seventh and subsequent authors can be abbreviated to "et al."

> Anders, K., Child, H., Davis, K., Logan, O., Petersen, J., Tymes, J., et al.

13. Chapter in an edited collection

Add "In" after the selection title and before the names of the editor(s).

> Howard, A. (1997). Labor, history, and sweatshops in the new global economy. In A. Ross (Ed.), *No sweat: Fashion, free trade, and the rights of garment workers* (pp. 151–72). New York: Verso.

14. Published dissertation or thesis

If the dissertation you are citing is published by University Microfilms International (UMI), provide the order number as the last item in the entry.

> Price, J. J. (1998). Flight maps: Encounters with nature in modern American culture. *Dissertation Abstracts International, 59*(5), 1635. (UMI No. 9835237)

15. Government document

When the author and publisher are identical, use "Author" as the name of the publisher.

> U.S. Environmental Protection Agency. (2002). *Respiratory health effects of passive smoking: Lung cancer and other disorders.* (EPA Publication No. 600/6-90/006 F). Washington, DC: Author.

APA References List: Periodicals

16. Article by one author

> Kellogg, R. T. (2001). Competition for working memory among writing processes. *American Journal of Psychology, 114,* 175–192.

17. Article by multiple authors

Write out all of the authors' names, up to six authors. The seventh and subsequent authors can be abbreviated to "et al."

> Blades, J., & Rowe-Finkbeiner, K. (2006). The motherhood manifesto. *The Nation, 282*(20) 11–16.

18. Article by a group or organization

> National Organization for Women (2002). Where to find feminists in Austin. *The NOW guide for Austin women.* Austin, TX: Chapter Press.

19. Article in a journal with continuous pagination

Include the volume number and the year, but not the issue number.

> Engen, R., & Steen, S. (2000). The power to punish: Discretion and sentencing reform in the war on drugs. *American Journal of Sociology, 105,* 1357–1395.

20. Article in a journal paginated by issue

List the issue number in parentheses (not italicized) after the volume number. For a popular magazine that does not commonly use volume numbers, use the season or date of publication.

> McGinn, D. (2006, June 5). Marriage by the numbers. *Newsweek,* 40–48.

21. Monthly publication

> Barlow, J. P. (1998, January). Africa rising: Everything you know about Africa
> is wrong. *Wired,* 142–158.

22. Newspaper article

> Hagenbaugh, B. (2005, April 25). Grads welcome an uptick in hiring. *USA
> Today,* p. A1.

APA References List: Library Database Sources

23. Document from a library database

Increasingly, articles are accessed online. Because URLs frequently change, many scholarly publishers have begun to use a Digital Object Identifier (DOI), a unique alphanumeric string that is permanent. If a DOI is available, use the DOI.

APA no longer requires listing the names of well-known databases. The article below was retrieved from the PsychARTICLES database, but there is no need to list the database, the retrieval date, or the URL if the DOI is listed.

> Erdfelder, E. (2008). Experimental psychology: Good news. *Experimental
> Psychology, 55*(1), 1–2. doi: 0.1027/1618-3169.55.1.1

APA References List: Online Sources

24. Online publication by a known author

Authorship is sometimes hard to discern for online sources. If you do have an author or creator to cite, follow the rules for periodicals and books.

> Carr, A. (2003. May 22). AAUW applauds senate support of title IX resolution.
> Retrieved from http://www.aauw.org/about/newsroom/press_releases/
> 030522. cfm

25. Online publication by a group or organization

If the only authority you find is a group or organization, list its name as the author.

> Girls Incorporated. (2003). Girls' bill of rights. Retrieved from
> http://www.girlsinc.org/gc/page.php?id=9

26. Article in an online scholarly journal

> Brown, B. (2004). The order of service: the practical management of customer interaction. *Sociological Research Online, 9*(4). Retrieved from http://www.socresonline.org.uk/9/4/brown.html

27. Article in an online newspaper

> Slevin, C. (2005, April 25). Lawmakers want to put limits on private toll roads. *Boulder Daily Camera.* Retrieved from http:// www.dailycamera.com

28. Article in an online magazine

> Pein, C. (2005, April 20). Is Al-Jazeera ready for prime time? *Salon.* Retrieved from http://www.salon.com

APA References List: Other Sources

29. Television program

> Burgess, M., & Green, M. (Writers). (2004). Irregular around the margins. [Television series episode]. In D. Chase (Producer), *The sopranos.* New York: HBO.

30. Film, Video, or DVD

> Kaurismäki, A. (Director). (1999). *Leningrad cowboys go America* [DVD]. United States: MGM.

31. Musical recording

List both the title of the song and the title of the album or CD. In the in-text citation, include side or track numbers.

> Lowe, N. (2001). Lately I've let things slide. On *The convincer* [CD]. Chapel Hill, NC: Yep Roc Records.

A Guide to Avoiding Plagiarism

Plagiarism is using someone else's work—words, ideas, or illustrations, published or unpublished—without giving the creator of that work proper credit. Plagiarism is a serious breach of scholarly ethics and can have severe consequences. Students risk a failing grade or disciplinary action ranging from suspension to expulsion. A record of such action can adversely affect professional opportunities in the future as well as graduate school admission.

This appendix presents an overview of how to avoid plagiarism. Additional and more detailed coverage of all aspects of writing from sources—conducting research, using and evaluating sources, avoiding plagiarism, and documenting sources in MLA and APA styles—can be found in Chapters 16–21.

Documentation: The Key to Avoiding Unintentional Plagiarism

It can be difficult to tell when you have unintentionally plagiarized something. The legal doctrine of **fair use** allows writers to use a limited amount of another's work in their own papers and books. However, to make sure that they are not plagiarizing that work, writers need to take care to credit the source accurately and clearly for *every* use. **Documentation** is the method writers employ to give credit to the creators of material they use. It involves providing essential information about the source of the material, which enables readers to find the material for themselves. It requires two elements: (1) a list of sources used in the paper and (2) citations in the text to items in that list. To use documentation and avoid unintentionally plagiarizing from a source, you need to know how to

- Identify sources and information that need to be documented.
- Document sources in a list of works cited or list of references.
- Use material gathered from sources: in summary, paraphrase, and quotation.

- Create in-text references.
- Use correct grammar and punctuation to blend quotations into a paper.

Identifying Sources and Information That Must be Documented

Whenever you use information from **outside sources,** you need to identify the source of that material. Major outside sources include books, newspapers, magazines, government sources, radio and television programs, material from electronic databases, correspondence, films, plays, interviews, speeches, and information from Web sites. Virtually all the information you find in outside sources requires documentation. The one exception to this guideline is that you do not have to document common knowledge. **Common knowledge** is widely known information about current events, famous people, geographical facts, or familiar history. However, when in doubt, the safest strategy is to provide documentation. For more on what you do and do not have to document, see pages 271–272.

Documenting Sources in a List of Works Cited or List of References

You need to choose the documentation style that is dominant in your field or required by your instructor. Take care to use only one documentation style in any one paper and to follow its documentation formats consistently. The most widely used style manuals are the *MLA Handbook for Writers of Research Papers*, published by the Modern Language Association (MLA) and often used in the fields of English language and literature; the *Publication Manual of the American Psychological Association* (APA), favored in the social sciences; and *The Chicago Manual of Style*, published by the University of Chicago Press (CMS) and preferred in other humanities and sometimes business. Other, more specialized style manuals are used in various fields. Certain information is included in citation formats in all styles:

- Author or other creative individual or entity
- Source of the work
- Relevant identifying numbers or letters
- Title of the work
- Publisher or distributor
- Relevant dates

For detailed coverage of MLA style and sample works-cited entries, see Chapter 20 (pages 280–296). For detailed coverage of APA style, see Chapter 21 (pages 304–312).

Using Material Gathered From Sources: Summary, Paraphrase, and Quotation

You can integrate borrowed material into your paper in three ways—by summarizing, paraphrasing, and quoting. A quotation, paraphrase, or summary must be used in a manner that accurately conveys the meaning of the source. For detailed coverage of these topics, see pages 273–276.

A **summary** is a brief restatement in your own words of the source's main ideas. Summary is used to convey the general meaning of the ideas in a source without giving specific details or examples that may appear in the original. A summary is always much shorter than the work it treats. Take care to give the essential information as clearly and succinctly as possible in your own language.

Rules to Remember
- Write the summary using your own words.
- Indicate clearly where the summary begins and ends.
- Make sure your summary is an accurate restatement of the source's main ideas.
- Check that the summary is clearly separated from your own contribution.
- Use attribution and parenthetical reference to tell the reader where the material came from.

A **paraphrase** is a restatement, in your own words and using your own sentence structure, of specific ideas or information from a source. The chief purpose of a paraphrase is *to maintain your own writing style* throughout your paper. A paraphrase can be about as long as the original passage.

Rules to Remember
- Use your own words and sentence structure. Do not duplicate the source's words, phrases, or sentence structure.
- Use quotation marks within your paraphrase to indicate words and phrases you do quote.
- Make sure your readers know where the paraphrase begins and ends.
- Check that your paraphrase is an accurate and objective restatement of the source's specific ideas.
- Immediately follow your paraphrase with a parenthetical reference indicating the source.

A **quotation** reproduces an actual part of a source, word for word, to support a statement or idea, to provide an example, to advance an argument, or to add interest or color to a discussion. The length of a quotation can range from a word or a phrase to several paragraphs. In general, quote the least amount possible that gets your point across to the reader.

Rules to Remember

- Copy the words from your source to your paper exactly as they appear in the original. Do not alter the spelling, capitalization, or punctuation of the original. If a quotation contains an obvious error, you may insert [sic], which is Latin for "so" or "thus," to show that the error is in the original.
- Enclose short quotations (four or fewer lines of text) in quotation marks, and set off longer quotations as block quotations.
- Immediately follow each quotation with a parenthetical reference that gives the specific source information required.

Creating In-Text Citations

In-text citations need to supply enough information to enable a reader to find the correct source in the works-cited or references list. To cite a source properly in the text of your paper, you generally need to provide some or all of the following information for each use of the source:

- Name of the person or organization that authored the source.
- Title of the source (if there is more than one source by the same author or if no author is given).
- Page, paragraph, or line number, if the source has one.

These items can appear as an attribution in the text ("According to Smith . . .") or in a parenthetical reference placed directly after the summary, paraphrase, or quotation.

For detailed coverage and examples of MLA style, see Chapter 20 (pages 280–296). For detailed coverage of APA style, see Chapter 21 (pages 304–312).

Using Correct Grammar and Punctuation to Blend Quotations into a Paper

Quotations must blend seamlessly into the writer's original sentence, with the proper punctuation, so that the resulting sentence is neither ungrammatical nor awkward.

Using a Full-Sentence Quotation of Fewer Than Four Lines

A quotation of one or more complete sentences can be enclosed in double quotation marks and introduced with a verb, usually in the present tense and followed by a comma. Omit a period at the close of a quoted sentence, but keep any question mark or exclamation mark. Insert the parenthetical reference, then a period.

> One commentator asks, "What accounts for the government's ineptitude in safeguarding our privacy rights?" (Spinello 9).

> "The test had originally been scheduled for 4:00 A.M. on July 16," Jennet Conant writes, "when most of the surrounding population would be sound asleep" (304–05).

Introducing a Quotation with a Full Sentence

Use a colon after a full sentence that introduces a quotation.

> Spinello asks an important question: "What accounts for the government's ineptitude in safeguarding our privacy rights?" (9).

Introducing a Quotation with "That"

A single complete sentence can be introduced with a *that* construction.

> Chernow suggests that "the creation of New York's first bank was a formative moment in the city's rise as a world financial center" (199–200).

Quoting Part of a Sentence

Make sure that quoted material blends grammatically into the new sentence.

> McNichol and Lav assert that during that period, state governments were helped by "an array of fiscal gimmicks" (87).

Using a Quotation That Contains Another Quotation

Replace the internal double quotation marks with single quotation marks.

> Lowell was "famous as a 'confessional' writer, but he scorned the term," according to Bidart (vii).

Adding Information to a Quotation

Any addition for clarity or any change for grammatical reasons should be placed in square brackets.

> Describing how the weather would affect the testing of the first atom bomb, Jennet Conant says, "The test had originally been scheduled for 4:00 A.M. on July 16, [1945,] when most of the surrounding population would be sound asleep" (304–05).

Omitting Information from Source Sentences

Indicate an omission with ellipsis marks (three spaced dots).

> Describing how the weather would affect the testing of the first atom bomb, Jennet Conant says, "The test had originally been scheduled for 4:00 A.M. on July 16, when . . . there would be the least number of witnesses" (304–05).

Using a Quotation of More Than Four Lines

Begin a long quotation on a new line and set off the quotation by indenting it one inch from the left margin and double spacing it throughout. Do not enclose it in quotation marks. Put the parenthetical reference after the period at the end of the quotation.

> Human Rights Watch recently documented the repression of women's rights in Libya:
>
> > The government of Libya is arbitrarily detaining women and girls in "social rehabilitation" facilities, . . . locking them up indefinitely without due process. Portrayed as "protective" homes for wayward women and girls, . . . these facilities are de facto prisons . . . [where] the government routinely violates women's and girls' human rights, including those to due process, liberty, freedom of movement, personal dignity, and privacy. (114)

Is It Plagiarism? Test Yourself On In-Text Citations

Read the excerpt below. Can you spot the plagiarism in the examples that follow it?

Original source

To begin with, language is a system of communication. I make this rather obvious point because to some people nowadays it isn't obvious: they see language as above all a means of "self-expression." Of course, language is one way that we express our personal feelings and thoughts—but so, if it comes to that, are dancing, cooking and making music. Language does much more: it enables us to convey to others what we think, feel and want. Language-as-communication is the prime means of organizing the cooperative activities that enable us to accomplish as groups things we could not possibly do as individuals. Some other species also engage in cooperative activities, but these are either quite simple (as among baboons and wolves) or exceedingly stereo-typed (as among bees, ants and termites). Not surprisingly, the communicative systems used by these animals are also simple or stereotypes. Language, our uniquely flexible and intricate system of communication, makes possible our equally flexible and intricate ways of coping with the world around us: in a very real sense, it is what makes us human.

—Robert Claiborne. *Our Marvelous Native Tongue: The Life and Times of the English Language.* New York: New York Times, 1983.

Works-cited entry

Claiborne, Robert. *Our Marvelous Native Tongue: The Life and Times of the English Language.* New York: New York Times, 1983. Print.

Plagiarism Example 1

One commentator makes a distinction between language used as a **means of self-expression** and **language-as-communication.** It is the latter that distinguishes human interaction from that of other species and allows humans to work cooperatively on complex tasks (8).

What's wrong?

The source's name is not given, and there are no quotation marks around words taken directly from the source (in **boldface** in the example).

Plagiarism Example 2

Claiborne notes that language "is the prime means of organizing the cooperative activities." Without language, we would, consequently, not have civilization.

What's wrong?

The page number of the source is missing. A parenthetical reference should immediately follow the material being quoted, paraphrased, or summarized. You may omit a parenthetical reference only if the information that you have included in your attribution is sufficient to identify the source in your works-cited list and no page number is needed.

Plagiarism Example 3

> Other animals also **engage in cooperative activities.** However, these actions are not very complex. Rather they are either the very **simple** activities of, for example, **baboons and wolves** or the **stereotyped** activities of animals such as **bees, ants and termites** (Claiborne 8).

What's wrong?

A paraphrase should capture a specific idea from a source but must not duplicate the writer's phrases and words (in **boldface** in the example). In the example, the wording and sentence structure follow the source too closely.

Avoiding Plagiarism: Note-Taking Tips

The most effective way to avoid unintentional plagiarism is to follow a systematic method of note taking and writing.

- **Keep copies of your documentation information.** For all sources that you use, keep photocopies of the title and copyright pages and the pages with quotations you need. Highlight the relevant citation information in color. Keep these materials until you've completed your paper.

- **Quotation or paraphrase?** Assume that all the material in your notes is direct quotation unless you indicated otherwise. Double-check any paraphrase for quoted phrases, and insert the necessary quotation marks.

- **Create the list of works cited or references** *first.* Before you start writing your paper, your list is a **working bibliography,** a list of possible sources to which you add source entries as you discover them. As you finalize your list, you can delete the items you decided not to use in your paper.

LINDA STERN
PUBLISHING SCHOOL OF CONTINUING AND PROFESSIONAL STUDIES
NEW YORK UNIVERSITY

Glossary

A

abstract A summary of an article or book

aesthetic criteria Evaluative criteria based on perceptions of beauty and good taste

analogy An extended comparison of one situation or item to another

APA American Psychological Association

APA documentation Documentation style commonly used in social-science and education disciplines

argument A claim supported by at least one reason

assumption An unstated belief or knowledge that connects a claim with evidence

audience Real or assumed individuals or groups to whom a verbal or written communication is directed

B

bandwagon appeal A fallacy of argument based on the assumption that something is true or correct because "everyone" believes it to be so

bar chart Visual depiction of data created by the use of horizontal or vertical bars that comparatively represent rates or frequencies

because clause A statement that begins with the word *because* and provides a supporting reason for a claim

begging the question A fallacy of argument that uses the claim as evidence for its own validity

bias A personal belief that may skew one's perspective or presentation of information

bibliography List of books and articles about a specific subject

blog A Web-based journal or diary featuring regular entries about a particular subject or daily experiences (also known as a Web log)

brainstorming A method of finding ideas by writing a list of questions or statements about a subject

C

causal argument An argument that seeks to identify the reasons behind a certain event or phenomenon

claim A declaration or assertion made about any given topic

claim of comparison A claim that argues something is like or not like something else

common factor method A method used by scientists to identify a recurring factor present in a given cause–effect relationship

consequence The cause–effect result of a given action

context The combination of author, subject, and audience and the broader social, cultural, and economic influences surrounding a text

contextual analysis A type of rhetorical analysis that focuses on the author, the audience, the time, and the circumstances of an argument

counterargument An argument offering an opposing point of view with the goal of demonstrating that it is the stronger of two or more arguments

criteria Standards used to establish a definition or an evaluation

critical reading A process of reading that surpasses an initial understanding or impression of basic content and proceeds with the goal of answering specific questions or examining particular elements

cropping In photography, the process of deleting unwanted parts of an image

cultural assumptions Widely held beliefs that are considered common sense in a particular culture

D

database Large collection of digital information organized for efficient search and retrieval

debate A contest or game in which two or more individuals attempt to use arguments to persuade others to support their opinion

definition argument An argument made by specifying that something does or does not possess certain criteria

diction The choice and use of words in writing and speech

E

either–or A fallacy of argument that presents only two choices in a complex situation

emotional appeal An argumentation strategy that attempts to persuade by stirring the emotions of the audience

empirical research Research that collects data from observation or experiment

ethos An appeal to the audience based on the character and trustworthiness of the speaker or writer

evaluation argument An argument that judges something based on ethical, aesthetic, and/or practical criteria

evaluation of sources The assessment of the relevance and reliability of sources used in supporting claims

evidence Data, examples, or statistics used to support a claim

experimental research Research based on obtaining data under controlled conditions, usually by isolating one variable while holding other variables constant

F

fallacy of argument Failure to provide adequate evidence to support a claim. See *bandwagon appeal, begging the question, false analogy, hasty generalization, name calling, non sequitur, oversimplification, polarization, post hoc fallacy, rationalization, slippery slope, straw man*

false analogy A fallacy of argument that compares two unlike things as if they were similar

feasibility The ability of a proposed solution to be implemented

figurative language The symbolic transference of meaning from one word or phrase to another, such as with the use of metaphor, synecdoche, and metonymy

firsthand evidence Evidence such as interviews, observations, and surveys collected by the writer

font The specific size and weight of a typeface

freewriting A method of finding ideas by writing as fast as possible about a subject for a set length of time

G

generalization A conclusion drawn from knowledge based on past occurrences of the phenomenon in question

good reason A reason that an audience accepts as valid

H

hasty generalization A fallacy of argument resulting from making broad claims based on a few occurrences

HTML (HyperText Markup Language) Display language used for creating Web pages

hypertext Document that allows you to connect to other pages or documents by clicking on links (the Web can be thought of as one huge hypertext)

I

idea map A brainstorming tool that visually depicts connections among different aspects of an issue

image editor Software that allows you to create and manipulate images

intellectual property Any property produced by the intellect, including copyrights for literary, musical, photographic, and cinematic works; patents for inventions and industrial processes; and trademarks

J

JPEG (Joint Photographic Experts Group) The preferred Web format for photographs

journal A general category of publications that includes popular, trade, and scholarly periodicals

K

keyword search A Web-based search that uses a robot and indexer to produce results based on a chosen word or words

L

line graph A visual presentation of data represented by a continuous line or lines plotted at specific intervals

logos An appeal to the audience based on reasoning and evidence

M

metaphor A figure of speech using a word or phrase that commonly designates one thing to represent another, thus making a comparison

metonymy A type of figurative language that uses one object to represent another that embodies its defining quality

MLA Modern Language Association

MLA documentation Documentation style commonly used in humanities and fine-arts disciplines

N

name calling A fallacy of argument resulting from the use of undefined, and therefore meaningless, names

narrative arguments A form of argument based on telling stories that suggest the writer's position rather than explicitly making claims

non sequitur A fallacy of argument resulting from connecting two or more unrelated ideas

O

oversimplification A fallacy in argument caused by neglecting to account for the complexity of a subject

P

pathos An appeal based on the audience's emotions or deeply held values

periodical A journal, magazine, or newspaper published at standard intervals, usually daily, weekly, monthly, or quarterly

periodical index Paper or electronic resource that catalogs the contents of journals, magazines, and newspapers

pie chart A circular chart resembling a pie that illustrates percentages of the whole through the use of delineated wedge shapes

plagiarism The improper use of the unauthorized and unattributed words or ideas of another author

podcast Digital media files available on the Internet for playback on a portable media player, such as an iPod

polarization A fallacy of argument based on exaggerating the characteristics of opposing groups to highlight division and extremism

popular journal A magazine aimed at the general public; usually includes illustrations, short articles, and advertisements

position argument A general kind of argument in which a claim is made for an idea or way of thinking about a subject

post hoc fallacy A fallacy of argument based on the assumption that events that follow each other have a causal relationship

practical criteria Evaluative criteria based on usefulness or likely results

primary research Information collected directly by the writer through observations, interviews, surveys, and experiments

process of elimination method A means of finding a cause by systematically ruling out all other possible causes

proposal argument An argument that either advocates or opposes a specific course of action

R

rationalization A fallacy of argument based on using weak explanations to avoid dealing with the actual causes

reason In an argument, the justification for a claim

rebuttal argument An argument that challenges or rejects the claims of another argument

reference librarian Library staff member who is familiar with information resources and who can show you how to use them (you can find a reference librarian at the reference desk in your library)

refutation A rebuttal argument that points out the flaws in an opposing argument

rhetorical analysis Careful study of a written argument or other types of persuasion aimed at understanding how the components work or fail to work

rhetorical situation Factors present at the time of writing or speaking, including the writer or speaker, the audience, the purpose of communicating, and the context

S

sans serif type A style of type recognized by blunt ends and a consistency in thickness

scholarly journals Journals containing articles written by experts in a particular field; also called peer-reviewed or academic journals

secondary research Information obtained from existing knowledge, such as research in the library

secondhand evidence Evidence from the work of others found in the library, on the Web, and elsewhere

serif type A style of type developed to resemble the strokes of an ink pen and recognized by wedge-shaped ends on letter forms

single difference method A method of finding a cause for differing phenomena in very similar situations by identifying the one element that varies

slippery slope A fallacy of argument based on the assumption that if a first step is taken, additional steps will inevitably follow

straw man A fallacy of argument based on the use of the diversionary tactic of setting up the opposing position in such a manner that it can be easily rejected

sufficiency The adequacy of evidence supporting a claim

synecdoche A type of figurative language in which a part is used to represent the whole

T

textual analysis A type of rhetorical analysis that focuses exclusively on the text itself

thesis One or more sentences that state the main idea of an argument

typeface A style of type, such as serif, sans serif, or decorative

U

URL (Universal Resource Locator) An address on the Web

V

visual argument A type of persuasion using images, graphics, or objects

voice In writing, the distinctive style of a writer that provides a sense of the writer as a person

W

Web directory A subject guide to Web pages grouped by topic and subtopic

Web editors Programs that allow you to compose Web pages

wiki A Web-based application designed to let multiple authors write, edit, and review content, such as Wikipedia

working thesis A preliminary statement of the main claim of an argument, subject to revision

Index